IMAGES of America

WINDSOR

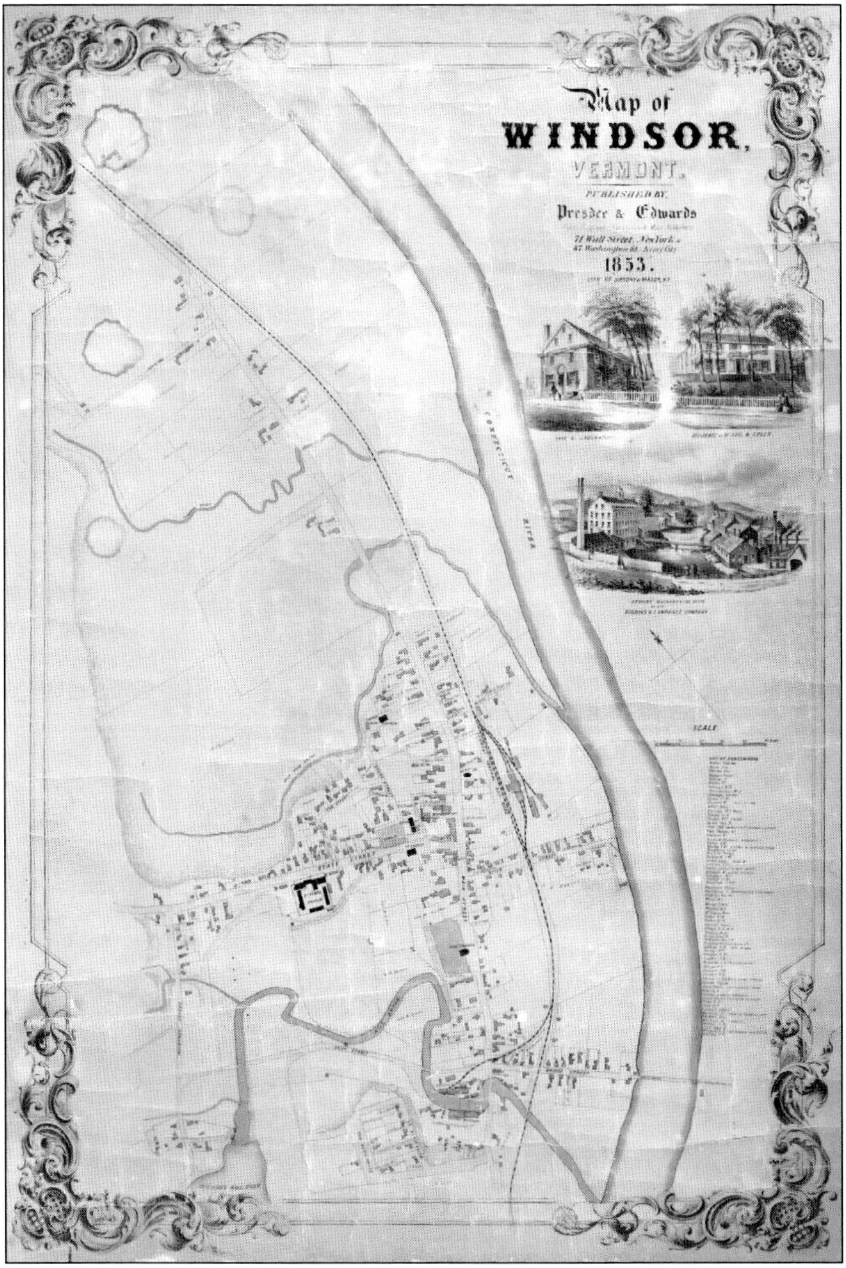

This 1853 view of Windsor shows the contrast between the concentration of buildings in and around the town as opposed to the wide-open landscape of Vermont. A list of subscribers on the right reveals a roster of the names of those citizens who made Windsor great, such as Ayers, Coolidge, Forbes, Green, Hatch, Hubbard, Phelps, Skinner, Stone, Tuxbury, and Wardner, to name a few. (Courtesy Windsor Historical Society.)

On the Cover: The Lamson family spends the day at leisure on the grounds of their estate in this 1890 photograph. Ebenezer Lamson was a partner in numerous Windsor factories. He was responsible for the production of firearms, and later, cotton production in Windsor. The home was on the former Leverett property. (Courtesy Windsor Historical Society.)

IMAGES
of America

WINDSOR

Liz Ross

ARCADIA
PUBLISHING

ISBN 978-0-7385-7648-0

Published by Arcadia Publishing
Charleston, South Carolina

Printed in the United States of America

Library of Congress Control Number: 2011928026

For all general information, please contact Arcadia Publishing:
Telephone 843-853-2070
Fax 843-853-0044
E-mail sales@arcadiapublishing.com
For customer service and orders:
Toll-Free 1-888-313-2665

Visit us on the Internet at www.arcadiapublishing.com

To Windsor, may she thrive and prosper in the coming years; to David for his support and assistance; and to my father, who often said, "Write a book!" and so I did.

Contents

Acknowledgments

This project would not have been possible without the dedication, tenacity, and good humor of Barbara Rhoad, who is the heart of the Windsor Historical Society. For extensive writings on Windsor, Katherine Conlin must be remembered posthumously. Her research and insight has served as a cornerstone of my work. To the many wonderful souls at the Windsor town offices, including Paul Belaski, Marianne Blake, Sandy Micka, and Lynn Grace, who were always happy to share stories, memories, and possibly even a little gossip. Posthumously to Edwin A. Battison for founding the American Precision Museum, and Ann Lawless, Beau Harris, John Alexander, and Nancy Hoggson of the museum; James Haff and Sally for shedding light on Dinah; Judy Hayward of Historic Windsor; Eric Brocklehurst, Robert Dean, and Paul Carnahan of the Vermont Historical Society; Ken Slater and Rick Hunter of Stellafane; and to Nancy Nash Cummings for a kick-start on the project. One more extra thanks goes to Barbara Rhoad.

I also wish to thank my editors at Arcadia Publishing, Lissie Cain and Hilary Zusman.

At times, "the bridge" is referred to as the Cornish-Windsor Bridge, and at other times, as the Windsor-Cornish Covered Bridge. We felt it only fair to continue the friendly parry from both sides of the river.

Unless otherwise noted, all photographs are courtesy of the Windsor Historical Society.

INTRODUCTION

"We are the children of our landscape; it dictates behavior and even thought in the measure to which we are responsive to it."

—Lawrence Durrell

The title of the first chapter, "Landscape and Memory," is a tribute to the author Simon Schama and his book by the same name. So often, it is not only the landscape we have traversed during our lives, but also the landscape that came before that shapes and influences who we are and who we become. When walking down the historic streets of Windsor, or turning the pages of this book and looking through these photographs, one may recall the memories of what was, what is, and what might have been. Stories of fortunes made and lost, inventors and schemers, visionaries and dignitaries, and the footsteps of the many real folks who contributed to the evolution of the Town of Windsor.

The first records of the town date to 1761, when Governor Wentworth of the Province of New Hampshire issued charters to three towns, one of which was Windsor. The first settlement occurred in 1764, and it was a dark and stormy night 13 years later when the Republic of Vermont was born. Vermont was the first state to prohibit slavery within her boundaries, long before it was admitted into the Union.

Like many towns settled in New England's early history, Windsor has experienced good times and better times. The founding years brought enthusiasm for the landscape and the potential of the town's settlers, business people, farmers, and manufacturers. Granite from the mountains built foundations and paved streets, not only of Windsor and its surrounding towns, but also of towns and architecture throughout the Northeast. The landscape and Mt. Ascutney provided new opportunities for industry and exploration. Trails up the mountain were cleared in preparation for the visit of the Marquis de Lafayette. Skiing soon became a popular local sport, and attracted visitors and vacationers from surrounding areas when the arrival of the train made it possible. Bridges and dams were built to tame the landscape, but inevitably, nature won that battle many, many times, challenging, humbling, and reminding everyone of the power of the wind and rain.

Windsor was an incubator of ideas and inventions before and during the Industrial Revolution. Inventors and factories designed and manufactured a broad array of items, including church organs, percolators, pumps, sewing machines, and rifles. During those times, the economy dictated many successes and failures. While wars around the world caused scarcity and hardship, they were also a catalyst, supporting Windsor's growing machine tooling and manufacturing industries. Windsor also has a history of producing shoes. There were several shoe factories in town beginning in the early 1800s, and the arrival of the Goodyear plant in 1936 perpetuated the tradition, making heels, soles, and other rubber goods for both the armed services and the general population.

Windsor's architecture is of note, having benefited from the major talents of the times, including Asher Benjamin, Amni Young, Alexander Parris, and Henry Bacon. Names associated with structures such as the Lincoln Memorial in Washington, DC, came to Windsor to build churches, libraries, and private homes. The famed Cornish-Windsor Bridge crossing the Connecticut River brought artists and writers like Maxfield Parrish and J.D. Salinger to the streets of Windsor to conduct their business. Both used Windsor as a locus for banking, shopping, socializing, and dining. Parrish gave a painting to the local bank's tellers in appreciation for their help, which still graces their wall today.

The beauty of the landscape and the thriving town enticed visitors, many of whom became either seasonal or year-round residents. Politicians and dignitaries came to visit the esteemed and well-connected people of the town's businesses and industries. Presidents visited as well, including Teddy Roosevelt. He was entertained and hosted by members of the well-known Evarts family, significant landowners and philanthropists of Windsor. Descendants of the Evarts family include renowned Scribner's editor Maxwell Perkins and special prosecutor Archibald Cox.

Downtown merchants of the past boasted the best of everything. Purveyors of fine coffees and teas advertised their wares in the new large, glass-fronted stores. Markets delivered fresh meats and produce, and furniture and fashion were advertised in the local journals and newspapers. Despite this, not everything was pretty. Windsor had also built the Vermont State Prison in 1808. While many of its inmates were incarcerated due to offenses like public drunkenness and adultery, several more noteworthy prisoners passed through its halls. When it closed in 1975, it had been the oldest continuously operating prison in the country. The brick prison complexes, along with several of the historic mansions in town, are now home to Windsor's senior citizens.

Excerpts from speeches, personal accounts, newspaper articles, and scribbled postcard messages have provided some of the text in this book to illustrate the voices of the times, their observations, and their concerns.

During this writing, Hurricane Irene came through and left her mark on the state of Vermont and on the town of Windsor. Though Windsor remained relatively unscathed, Vermont has lost many roads, homes, and several historic covered bridges. Always at the mercy of the whims of nature, the people of Windsor remain determined to enhance and preserve the town for the past, for the present, and for the future.

One

Landscape and Memory

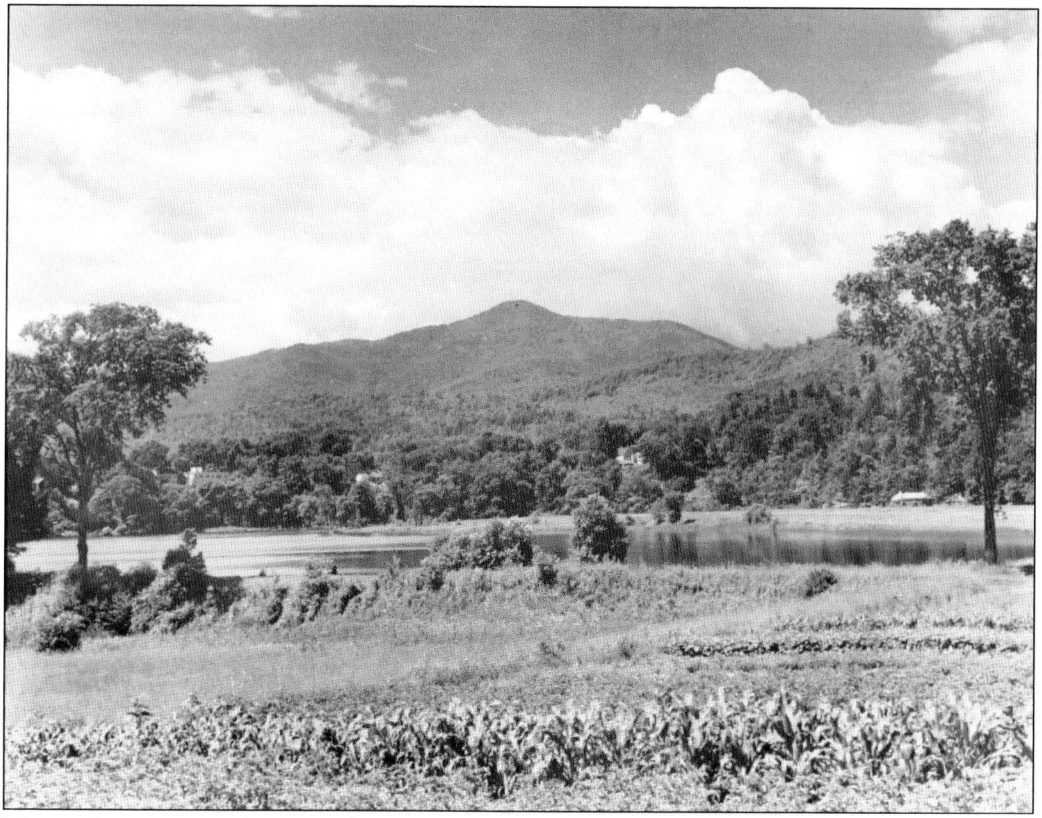

Mount Ascutney watches over the town of Windsor, having served as a beacon and as a source of industry, entertainment, and inspiration. While it is agreed that the name is derived from an Algonquin word, exactly which word is somewhat disputed. One is said to mean "meeting of the rivers," while the other is translated as, "bald or peaked with steep sides." Either meaning would be appropriate. The mountain, along with the historic covered bridge, are the icons of Windsor.

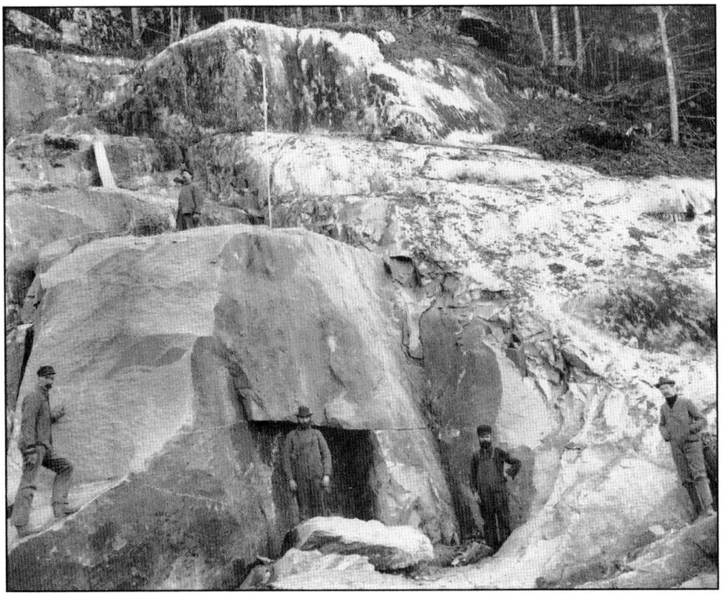

Ascutney granite made its way from Vermont to such states as Ohio and New York. It was transformed into the polished columns of the Columbia University Library in New York City and was used in building the Bank of Montreal in Canada. One of the four quarries, the Tyler, later known as the Reardon, produced gristmill stones and paving stones as far back as 1770, and also supplied blocks of granite for the railroad bridge near Claremont, New Hampshire.

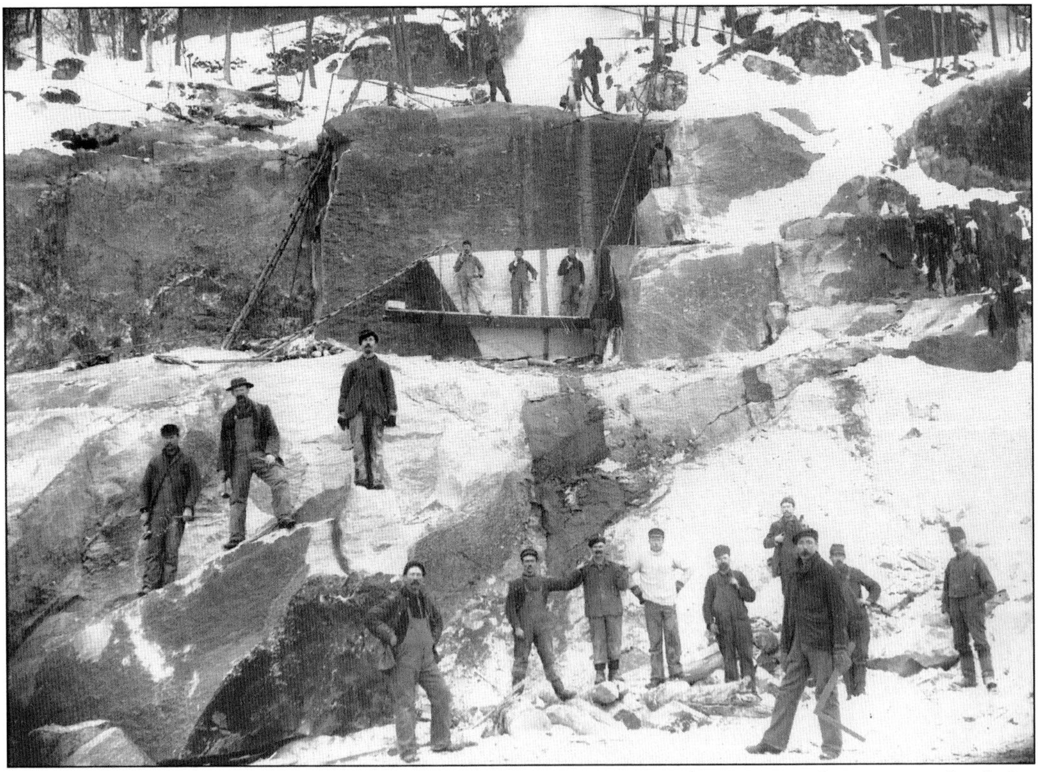

There were at least four granite quarries on the mountain. The Mower Quarry supplied the granite for the sarcophagi in the President McKinley Mausoleum in Canton, Ohio. The Enright Granite Works furnished building stone. The Norcross Quarry was the most extensive, and the Reardon supplied the granite for the railroad bridge across the Connecticut River. Despite the prominence of Norcross, there remains little information and few records, but it is known that it supplied the stone for the columns in front of the Columbia University Library.

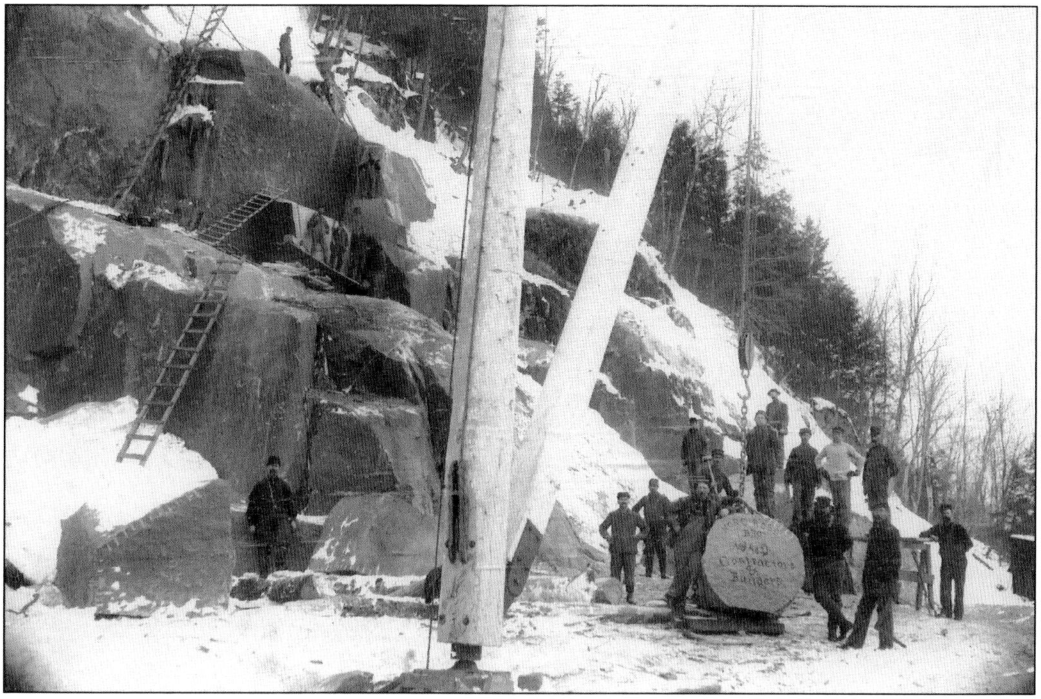

At a height of 1,500 feet—like the others—Norcross operated until roughly 1923 and was located on what is today the Brownsville Trail. What is known is that the promoter of this venture, Windsor attorney Joseph Enright, met a sad fate. Having used all the shareholders' invested capital in a futile search for iron-free granite, and compounded by his additional financial troubles, he took his own life in 1907.

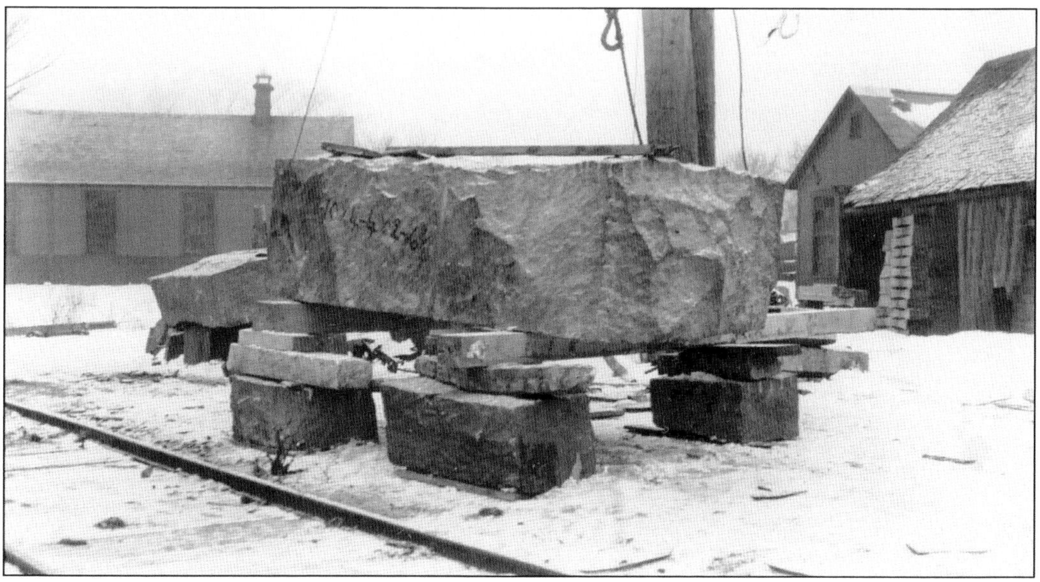

This huge block of granite cut from the Norcross Quarry weighed 20 tons and took a 20-horse hitch to draw it out of the rock bed and down the mountain. Typically, the blocks were then hauled to long sheds in what is now the south section of the St. Francis Cemetery on Enright Avenue. Poised at the Windsor Depot, the block awaits transportation to places unknown.

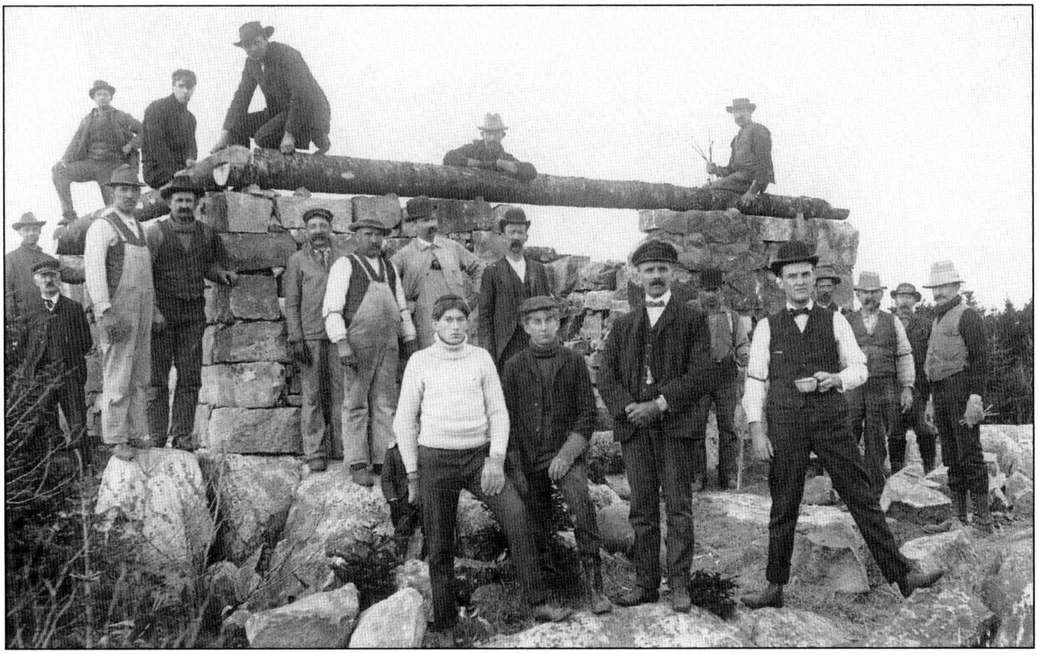

The Enright Granite Works began working the mountain in 1904, later incorporating with the Ascutney Mountain Granite Company. In addition to construction stone, it supplied Ascutney Green granite, which lines the interior of the Daniel Cady Memorial in Brownsville. Cady had established a law practice in New York in 1864, and later penned *Rhymes of Vermont Rural Life*. He was awarded two honorary Doctor of Letters degrees.

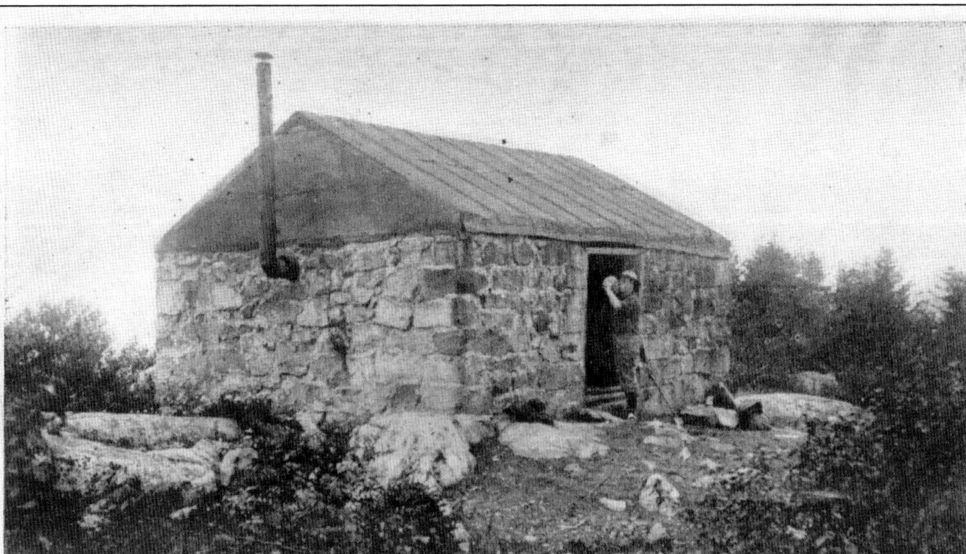

Stone House on Mt. Ascutney, Windsor, Vt.

Mt. Ascutney's hiking trails date back to 1824. That year, General Lafayette visited the United States on a grand tour of the 24 states that composed the country at the time. This stone house at the top was first built in 1858, and has long been a destination for the many hikers venturing up to the peak.

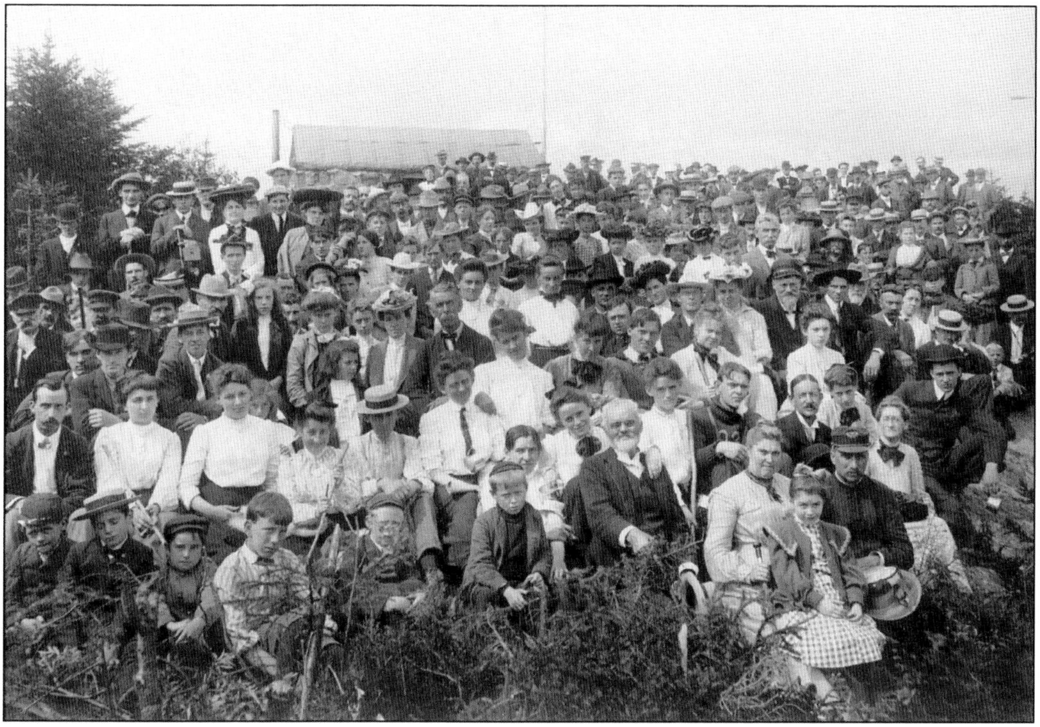

Mt. Ascutney is purported to be the first American mountain with a "certified" hiking trail. On several occasions, entire marching bands scaled the summit to participate in the festivities at the small stone hut. On Labor Day 1905, hundreds of people climbed the mountain accompanied by the band to dedicate the rebuilt stone house at the summit. Vandals had destroyed the original one. The additional trails that have been created over the centuries still provide year-round opportunities for hikers and other adventurers. The annual community hike up the mountain continues today, with a picnic lunch waiting for those who make it to the top.

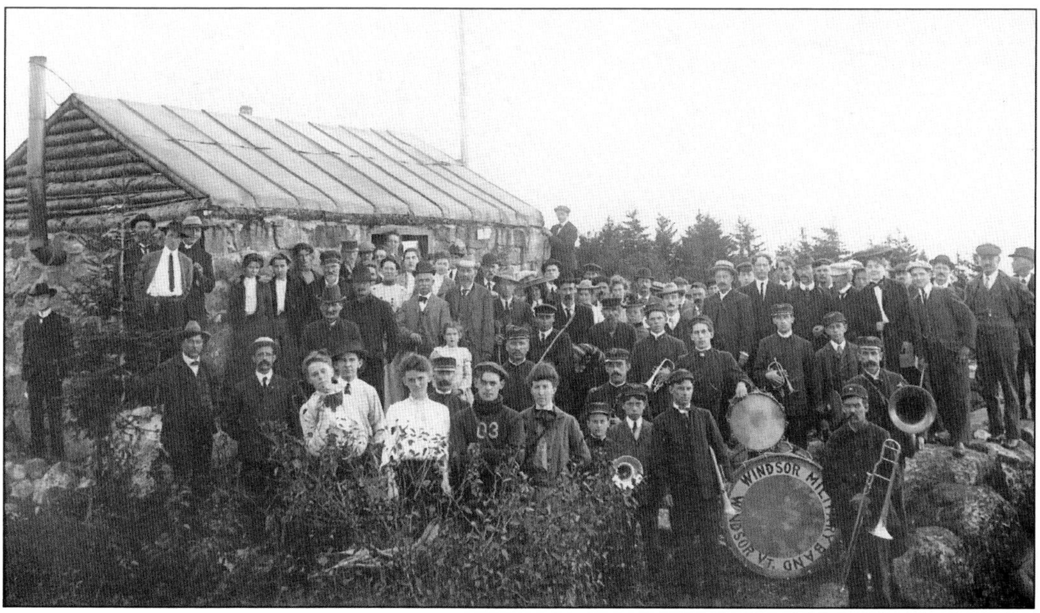

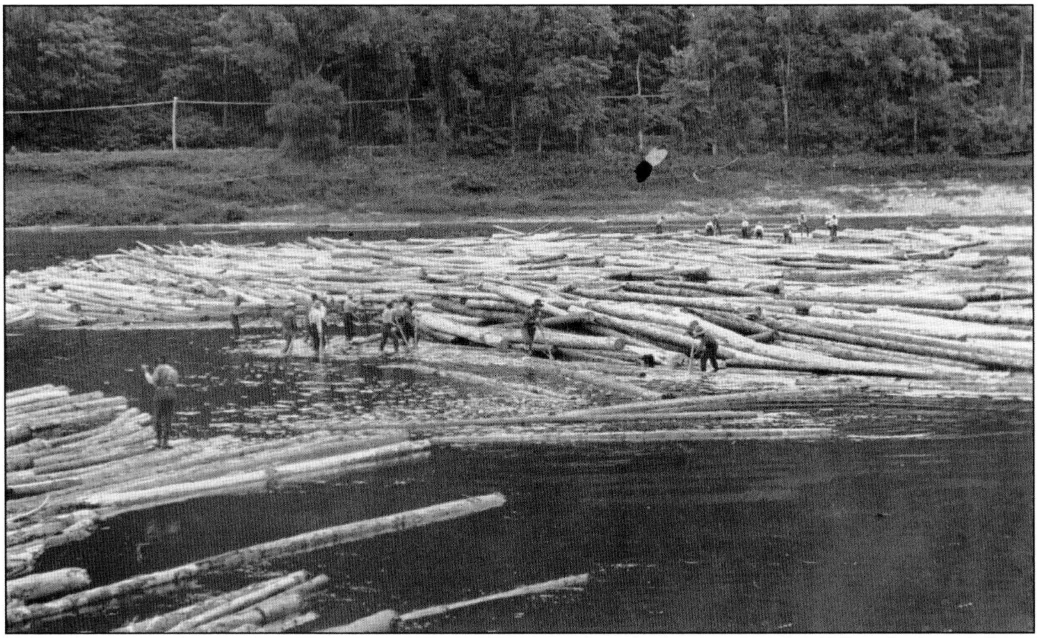

In the 1880s, it was not unusual to see the Connecticut River filled with logs from bank to bank. Families often gathered on the riverbank to watch the log drives, which would sometimes carry as much as 65 million feet of lumber down the river. Rafts were used to carry men, supplies, and also the horses needed to pull logs back into the river when they became wedged on rocks or stuck in sandbars. The occasional logjam resulted in some disastrous flooding along the banks of the river. One such jam took out two sections of the railroad bridge just moments after the one o'clock train heading north had crossed over it.

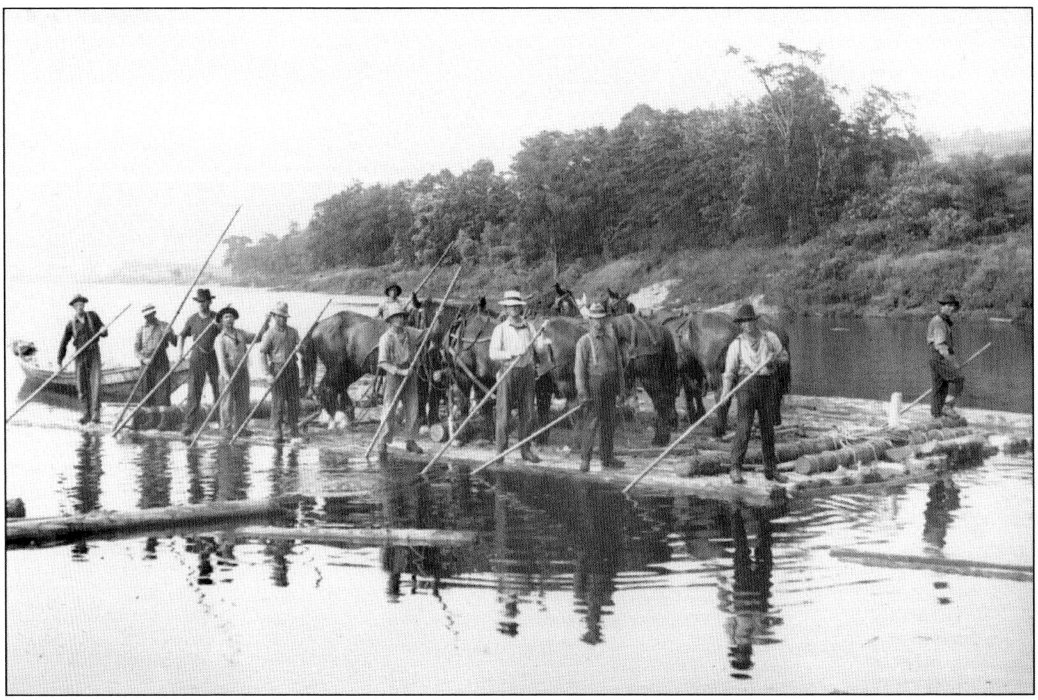

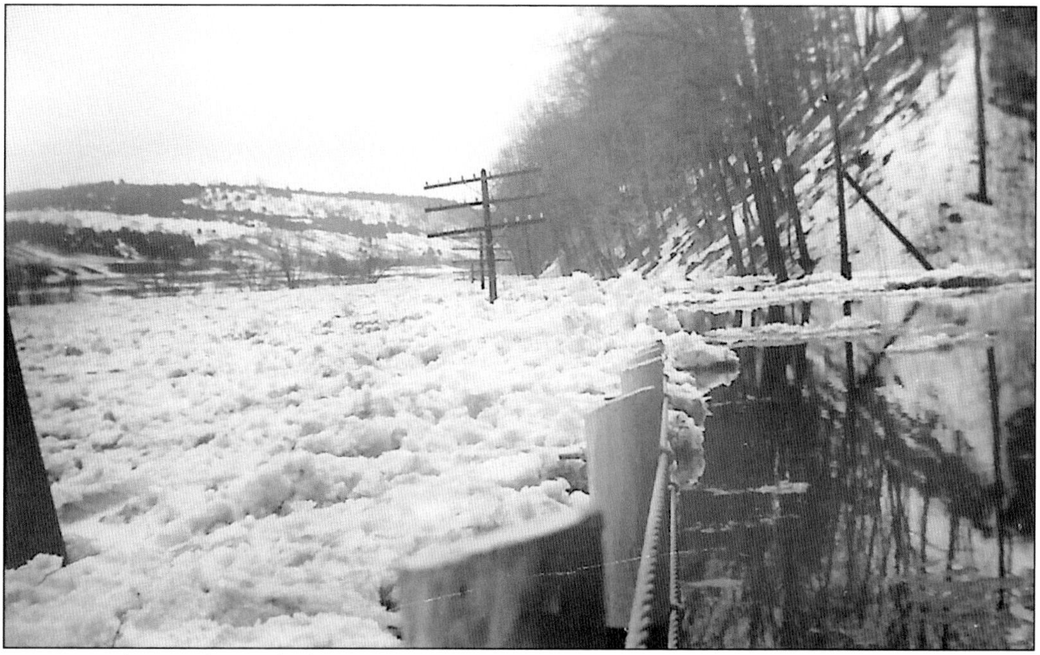

Nature is often said to "take her course," and the course she took in this photograph was to block the Connecticut River with huge wedges of ice. The ice eventually broke apart and created an ice jam, which caused major flooding in the streets of downtown Windsor. Ice also covered the main highway. The building of several dams over the years has ensured that floods no longer plague the town. The most well-known dam is the Mill Pond Dam, built in 1834. Its construction helped to form Mill Pond, which was, and continues to be, a favorite town swimming and recreation area. This tract later became part of the Frank Kennedy Estate.

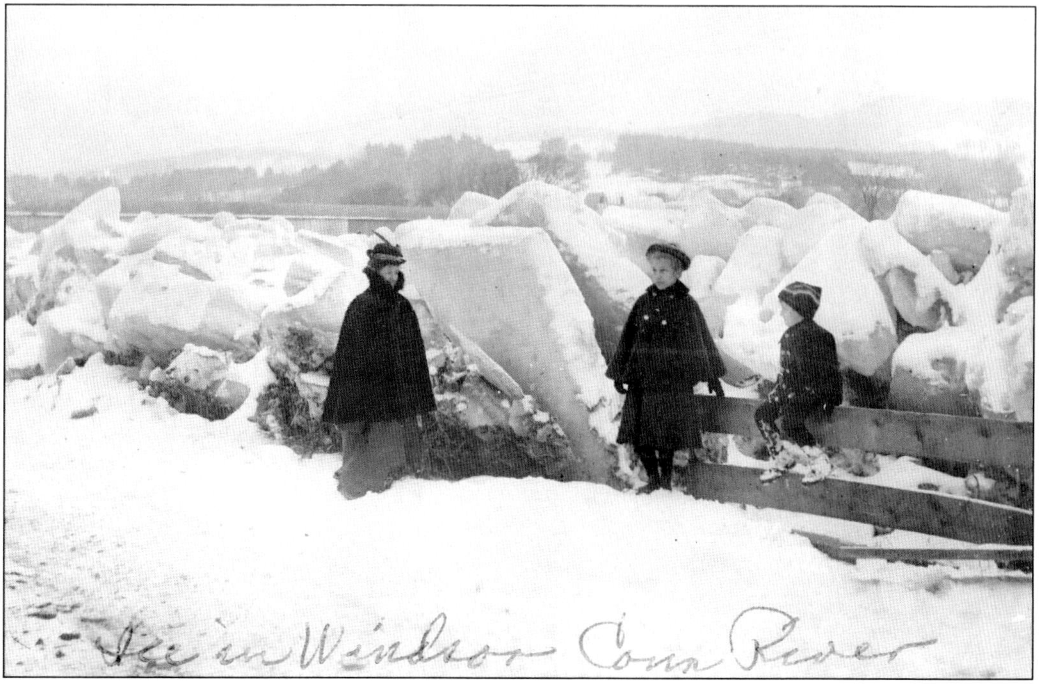

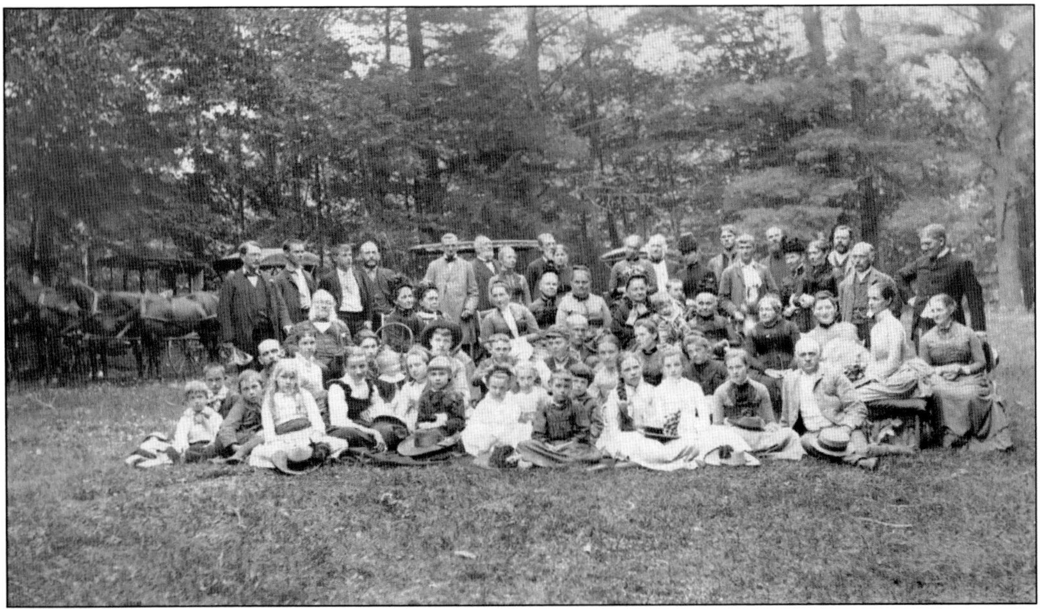

The Evarts family enjoyed the park created by William Evarts as part of his significant land holdings in Windsor. Named Paradise Park, the construction of paths and a dike created his version of paradise. The park is now part of the Windsor Parks and Open Spaces properties that rents some tracts of land for farming and maintains several trails for hikers.

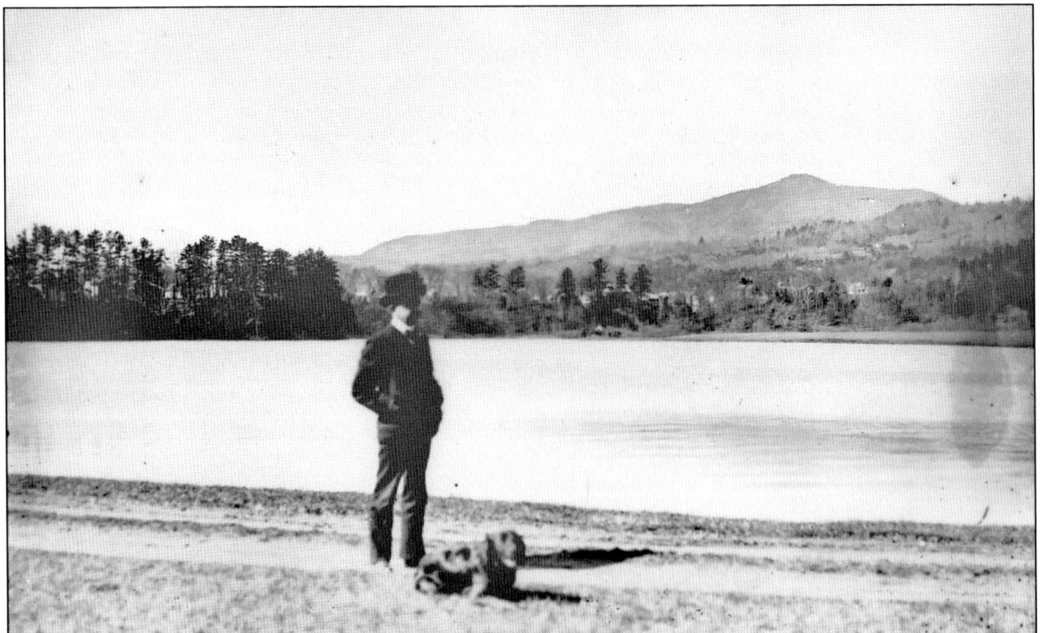

In 1884, as part of his vision of paradise, William Evarts created Lake Runnemede. Runnemede, England, was the location of the signing of the Magna Carta, and naming it for this historical site was his way of paying tribute to Windsor's renown as the site of the signing of the Vermont Constitution. Both documents were based on concepts of freedom and liberty for their citizens. On a lighter note, fishing and strolling along the banks are enjoyed now as they were then.

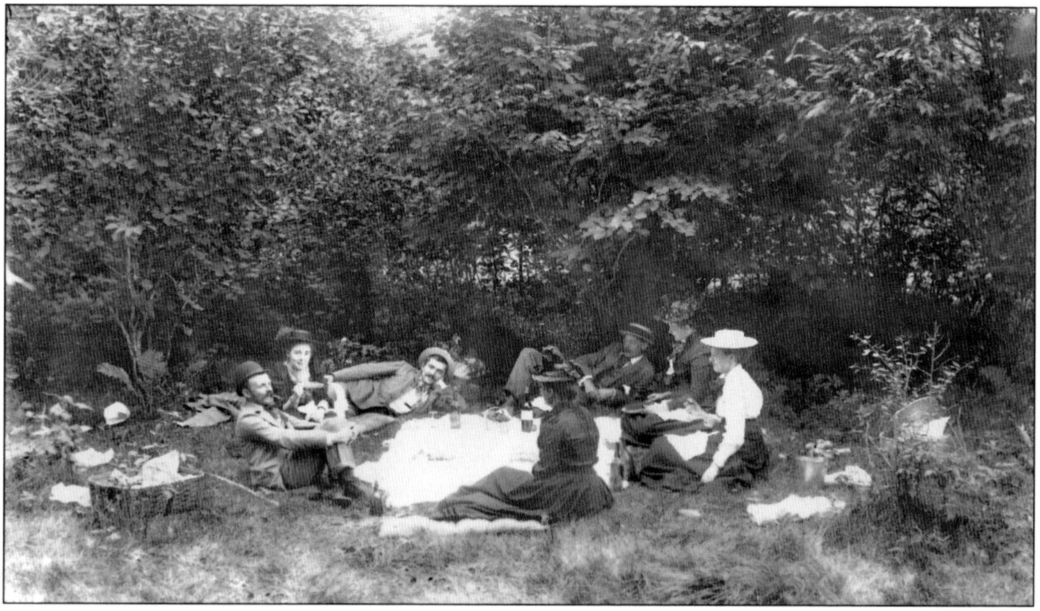

Reminiscent of a 19th century painting by Manet titled *Le Déjeuner sur l'Herbe*, the Tuxbury family enjoys a picture-perfect afternoon in the style of the times. Never without proper attire and appropriate accoutrements, everyone wore their summer straws with wine and wicker basket set nearby. The Tuxburys were merchants in town and also quite active in creating and maintaining high standards of education in Windsor's schools. Below, roasting marshmallows or feasting on recently hunted game? The picnic preparations turn interactive with even the ladies in their country attire participating in the cooking.

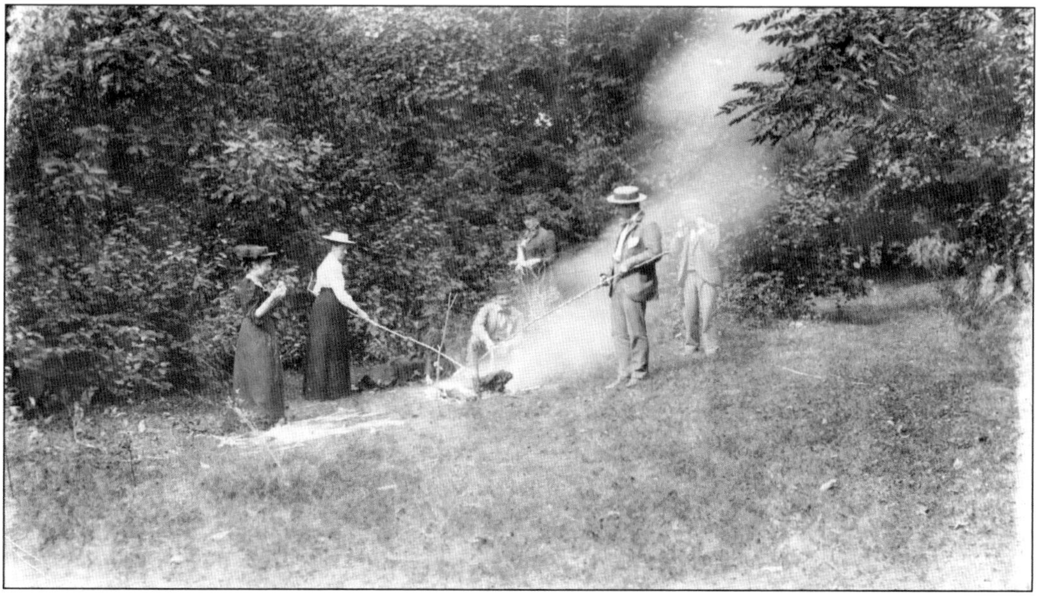

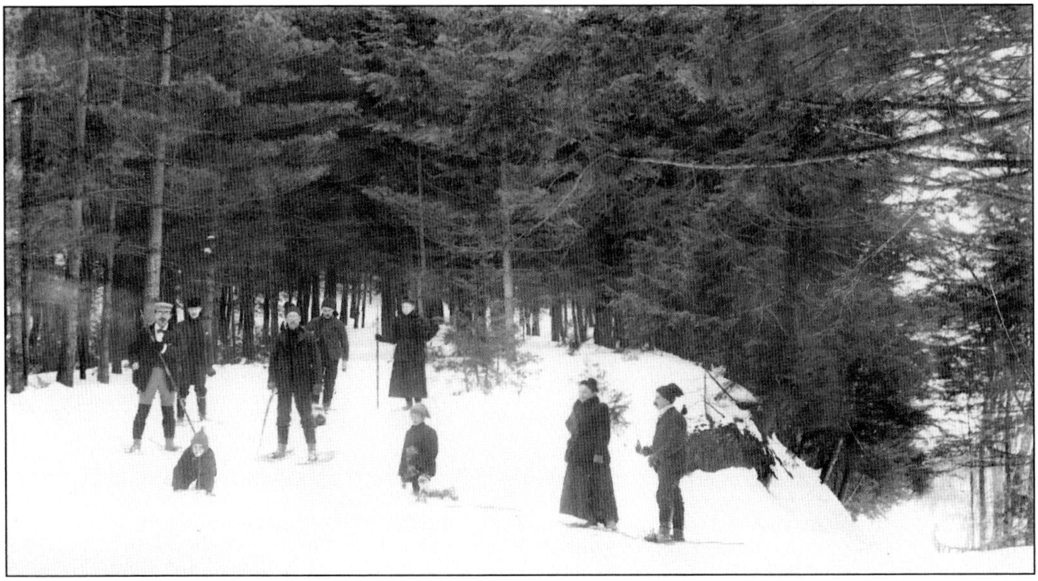

Each of Vermont's seasons provided unique opportunities for sport and fun. Here, the Tuxbury family revels in winter during a family snowshoe outing in Paradise Park. Not far from this location—several miles down Main Street—there were ski slopes for locals. After the train came to town, visitors from Boston and Worcester, Massachusetts, came up to ski as well. Called the "Snow Train," it stopped at the base of the Burrington Ski Area, which had two rope tows and room for toboggans and sleds. Frank H. Harris, writing in *The Vermonter* in 1938, stated, "there is absolutely no reason why every farm in Vermont should not possess several pairs of skis nor why every boy on the farm should not become an expert in the use of them."

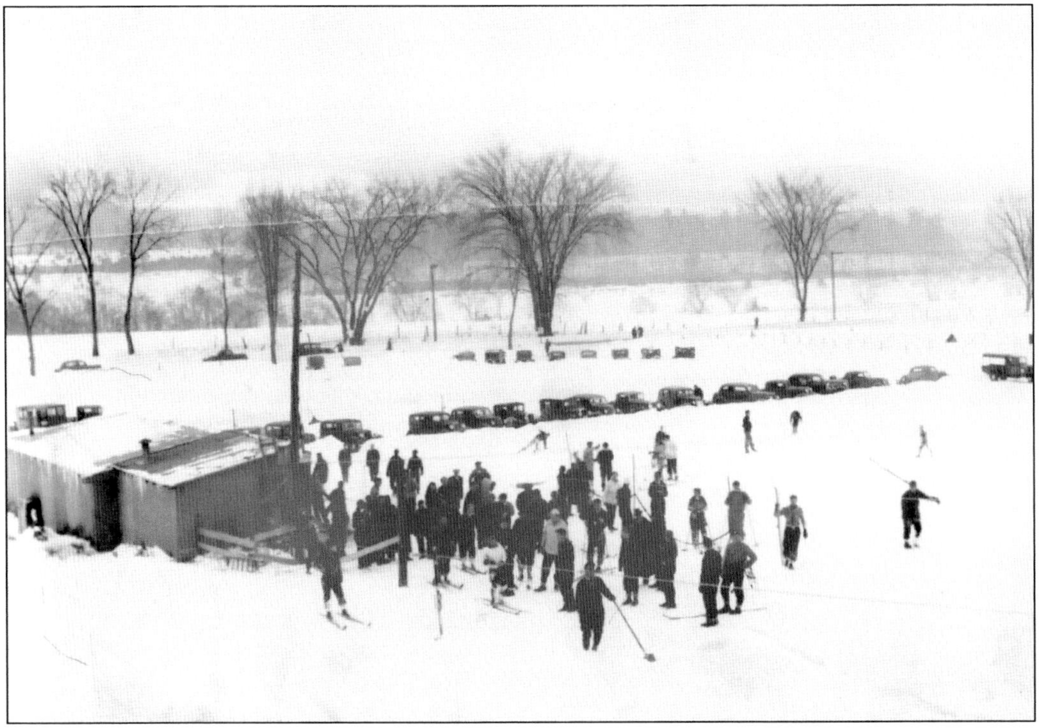

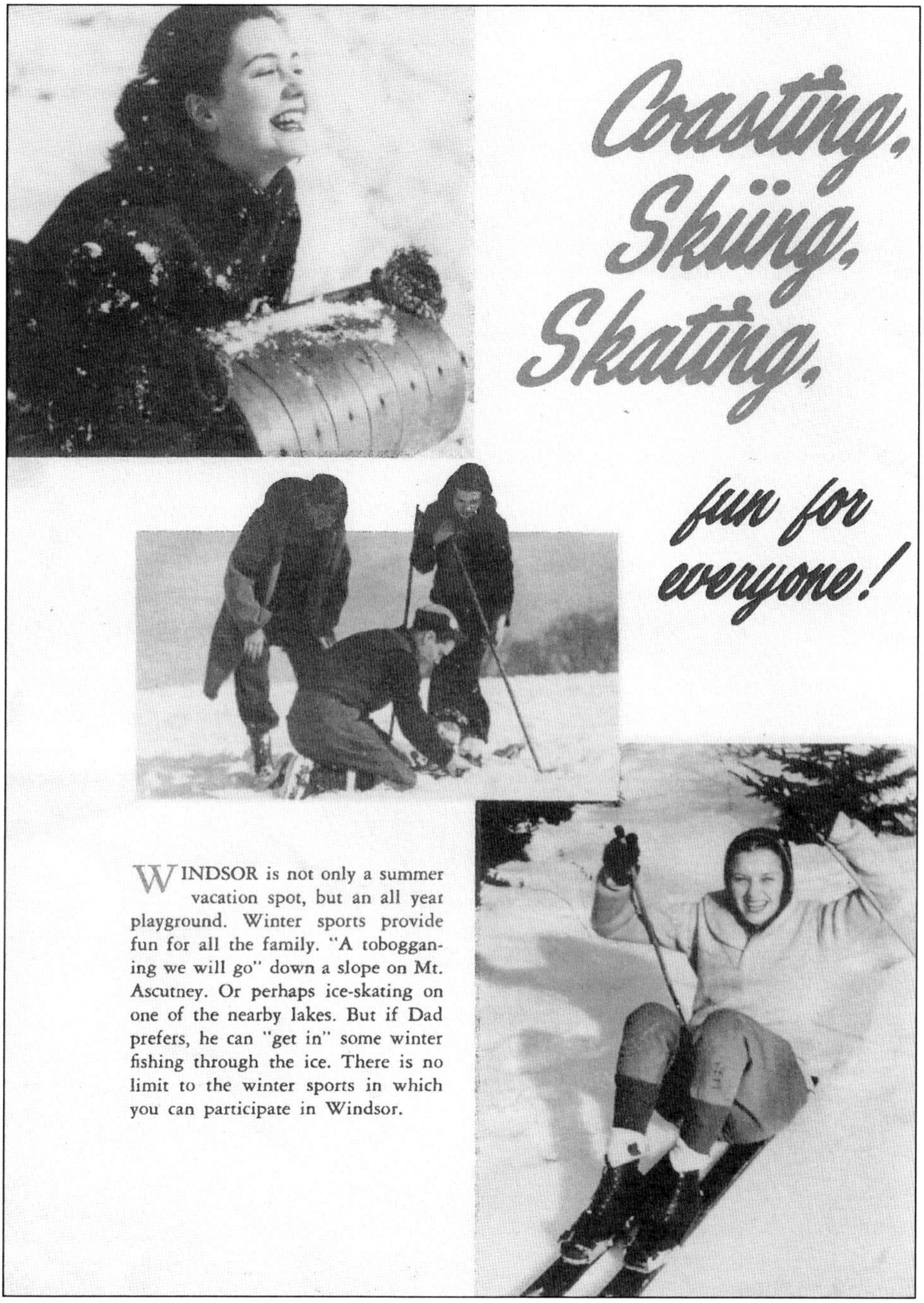

Frank H. Harris continued with some dating advice when he wrote, "Suppose you want to go to a dance in a neighboring town some moonlit night. Think how easily you could slip on your skis. Some afternoon when you want to see that girl badly, how convenient it would be to combine a good afternoon's sport with the pleasure of her company. She might ask you to stay to supper, you can't tell! The next step would be to get her a pair of skis and have her go out with you." The Windsor Chamber of Commerce published this brochure in the mid-20th century, extending a warm welcome to visitors and an invitation to settle down in "this picturesque Connecticut River town . . . where men wrought farms, where Indians once trod, where the great glacier once coursed."

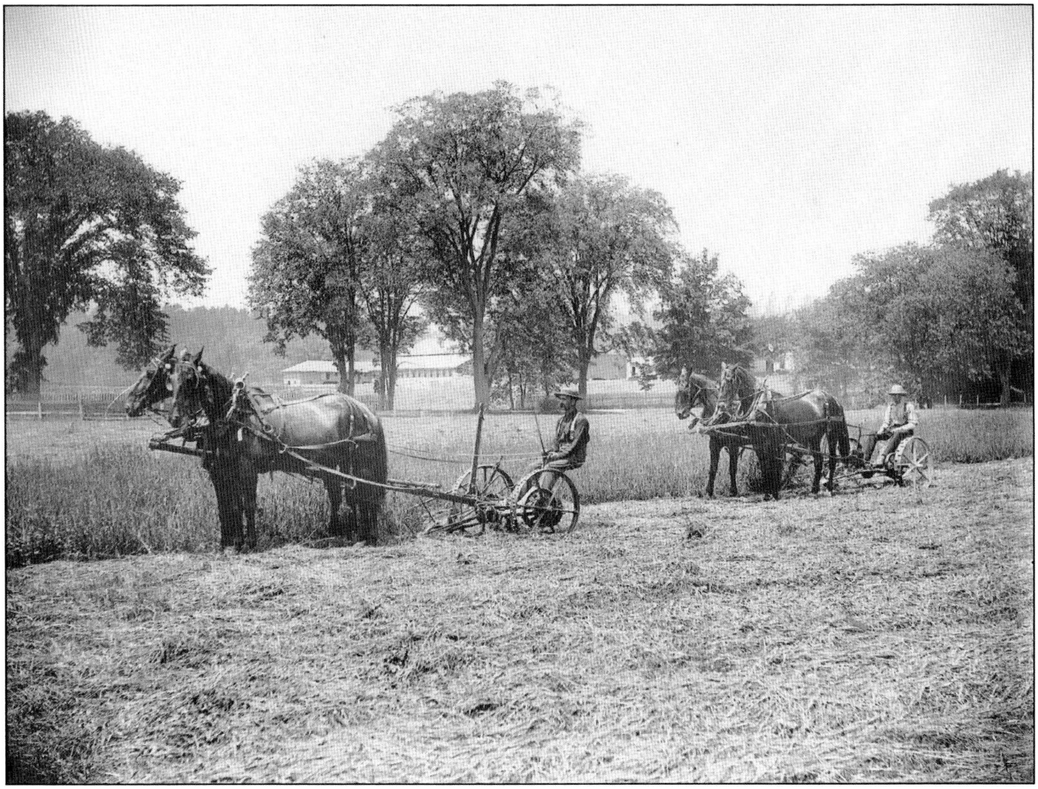

Paradise Park was not only for picnics. With Main Street pictured in the background, haying is taking place on the Evarts farm. Stables on the property housed his horses. William Evarts also used the land to graze cattle, sheep, and other livestock. The property was maintained with the help of a significant staff. The gazebo pictured in the background below was one of several resting spots scattered across the Evarts property. One remains today on the far edge of Lake Runnemede and is a picturesque reward after a stroll around the lake.

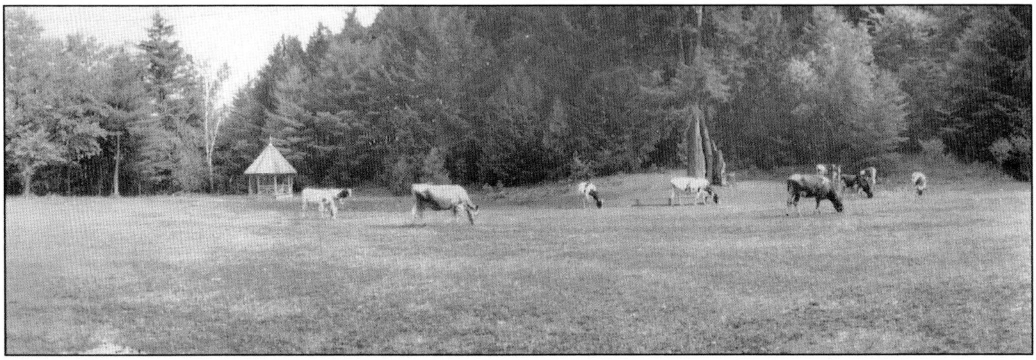

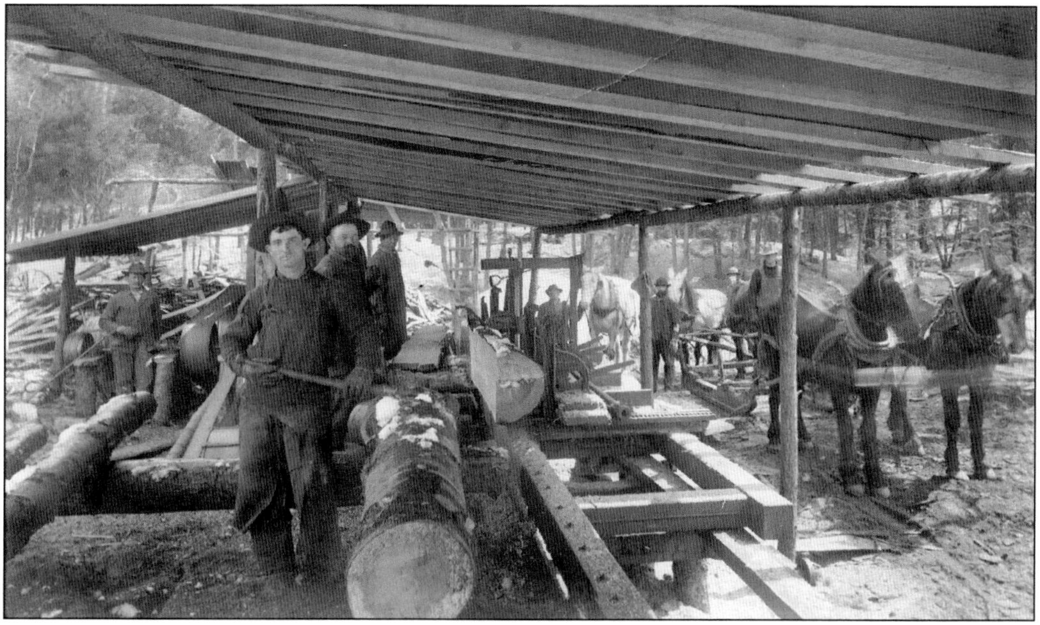

The Stacey Company owned and operated this portable sawmill, which was built and rebuilt repeatedly on sites where logging was needed. The family owned the Stacey Fuel and Logging Company, later known as Stacey Fuel and Lumber, for four generations. Thinning and harvesting of the woods was needed to properly maintain the forest, then as much as now, and lumber was needed for building the growing town.

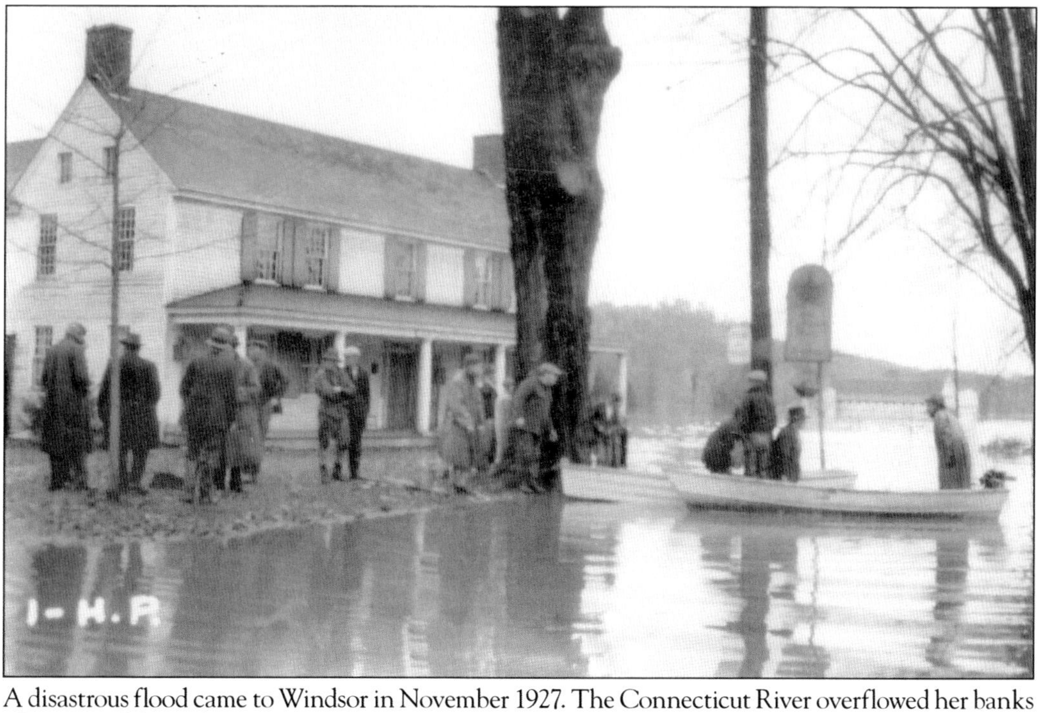

A disastrous flood came to Windsor in November 1927. The Connecticut River overflowed her banks after several days of rain and caused dams to give way and water to rise above the first floor in many homes and businesses. Fortunately, there was not extensive damage to the Constitution House.

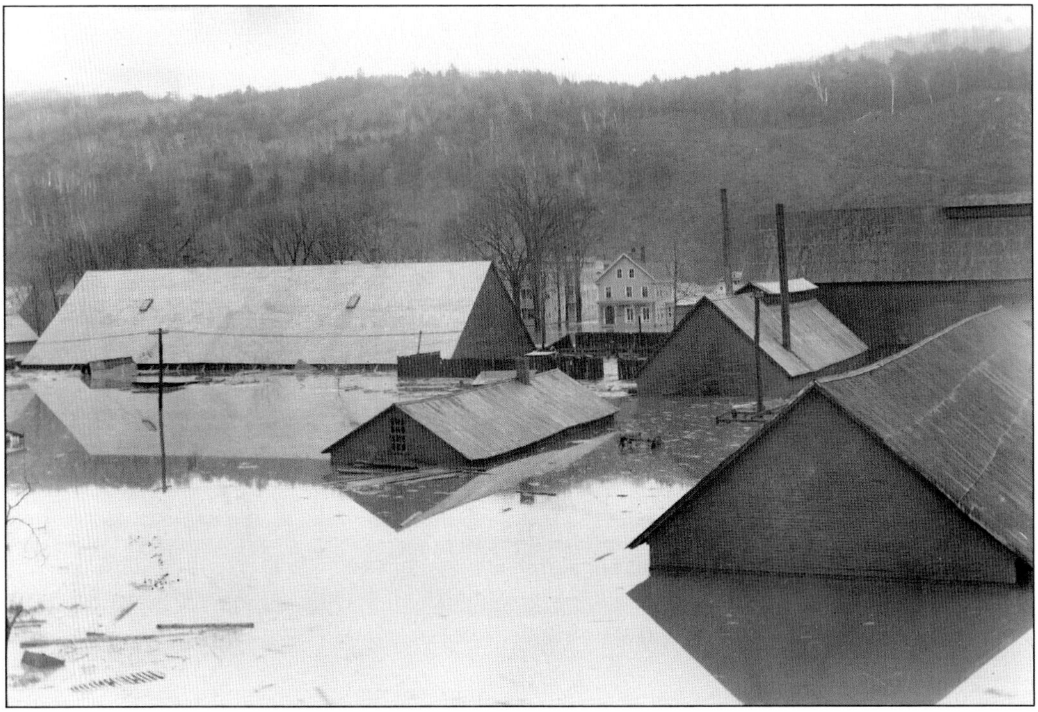

In 1927, the Windsor Machine Company was inundated by floodwaters. The Windsor Bridge, visible in the background, was rendered useless, and the waters went on to consume Bridge Street. The aftermath of the flood of 1927 catalyzed another rebuilding of the famed bridge. The Windsor Machine Company eventually became NAMCO and later the site of the Goodyear plant.

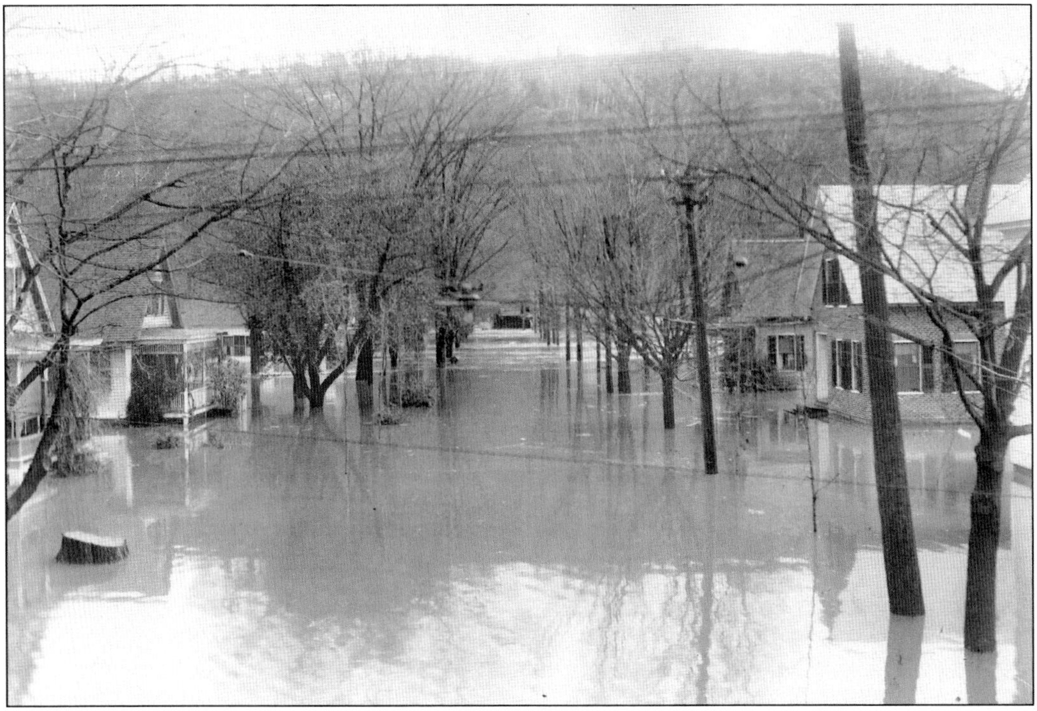

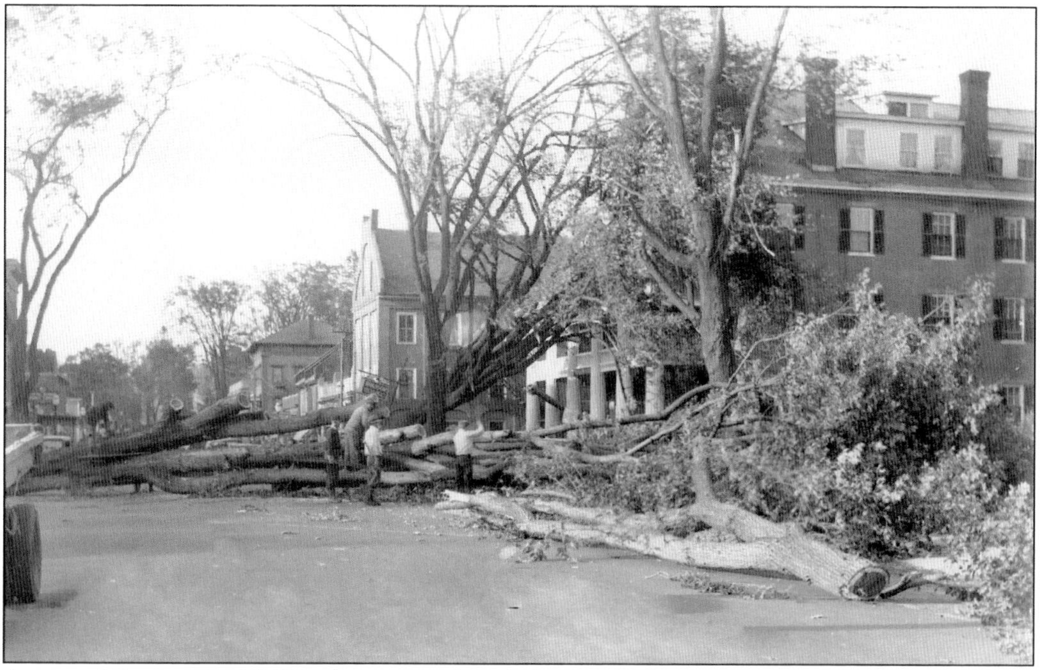

A second disaster befell Windsor just a decade later. The hurricane of 1938 swept into town on September 21, bringing with it fierce winds and rains. The quiet of the following morning revealed the extent of the destruction, as seen in front of the Windsor House. Despite this, schools remained open, and children climbed over logs and other obstacles the next morning on their way to class.

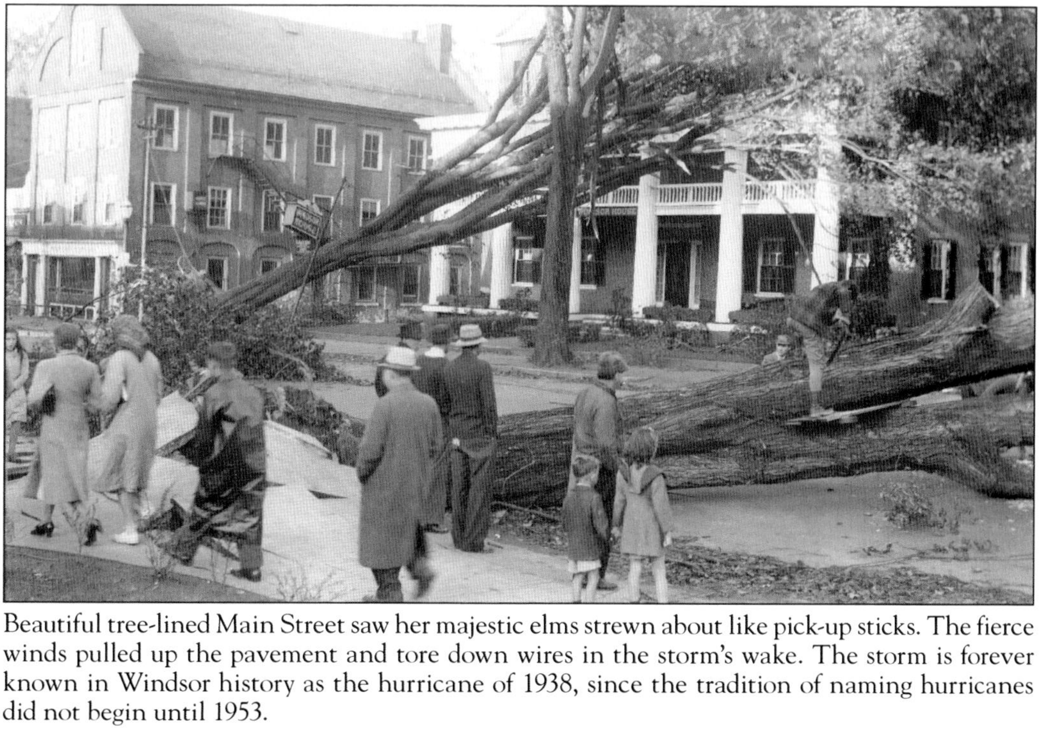

Beautiful tree-lined Main Street saw her majestic elms strewn about like pick-up sticks. The fierce winds pulled up the pavement and tore down wires in the storm's wake. The storm is forever known in Windsor history as the hurricane of 1938, since the tradition of naming hurricanes did not begin until 1953.

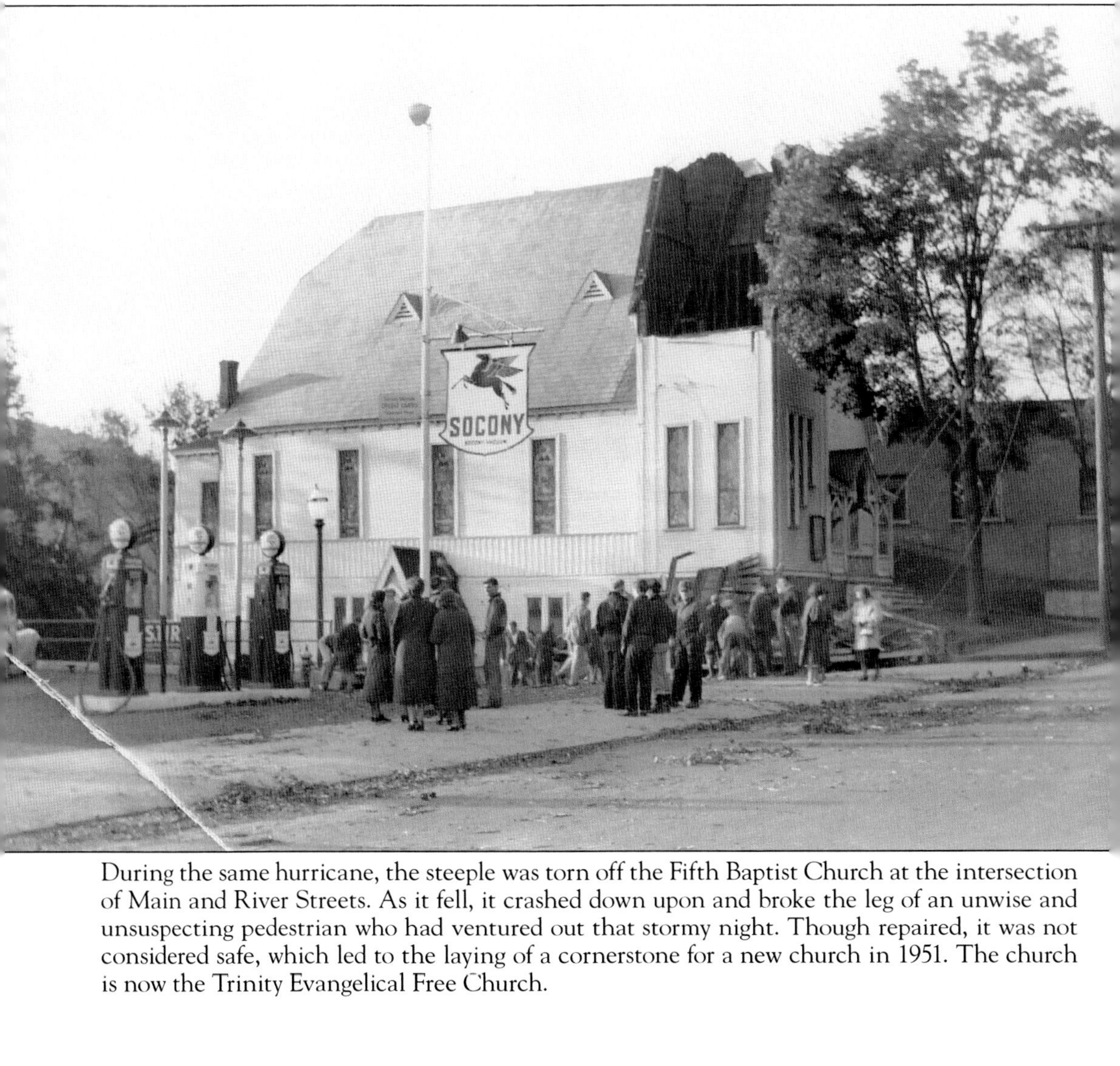

During the same hurricane, the steeple was torn off the Fifth Baptist Church at the intersection of Main and River Streets. As it fell, it crashed down upon and broke the leg of an unwise and unsuspecting pedestrian who had ventured out that stormy night. Though repaired, it was not considered safe, which led to the laying of a cornerstone for a new church in 1951. The church is now the Trinity Evangelical Free Church.

Two

GETTING AROUND

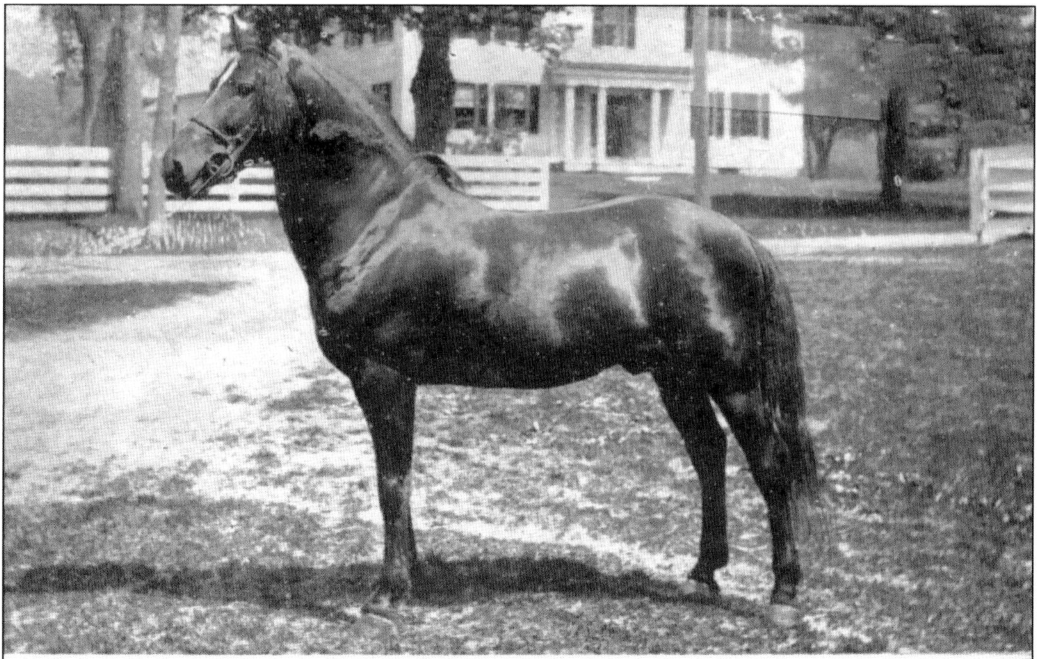

"Welcome," Windsor, Vt.

The Morgan horse can be traced back to its original sire, a stallion named Figure, born in Massachusetts in 1789. His owner, Justin Morgan, eventually settled in Vermont and gave his name to the breed. The horse became popular for its temperament and athleticism. The house in the background was part of the Morgan horse farm and is still standing at the north end of town.

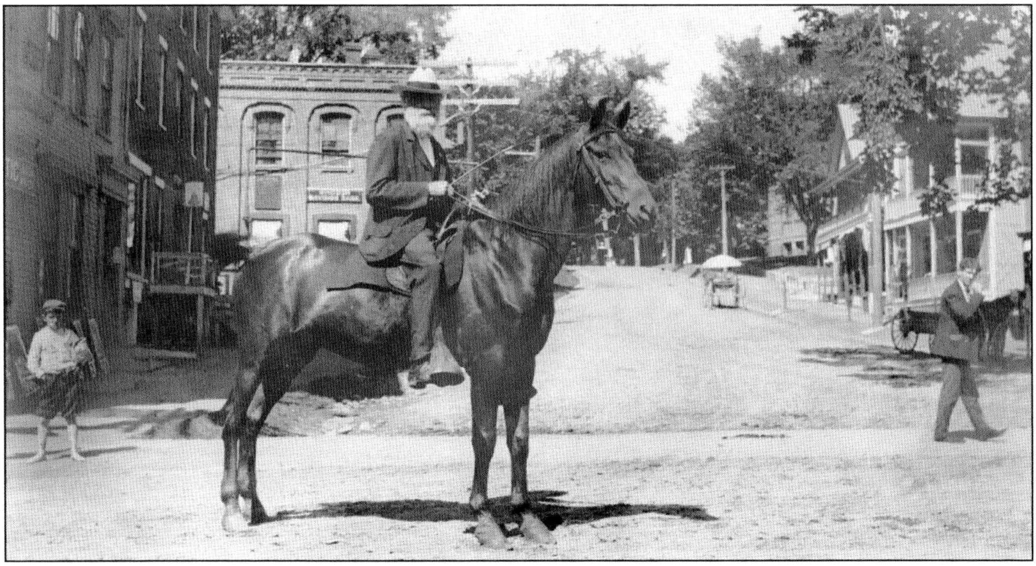

Windsor was the site of several large Morgan horse breeding farms. Windcrest Farm, now known as Time Will Tell Farm, and The Bailey Place were two of the largest. Bailey was superintendent of the prison and his barns are on the same property that actress Marie Dressler once owned north of town. Dressler was one of America's first screen actresses. In 1961, the Morgan Horse was named the official state animal of Vermont.

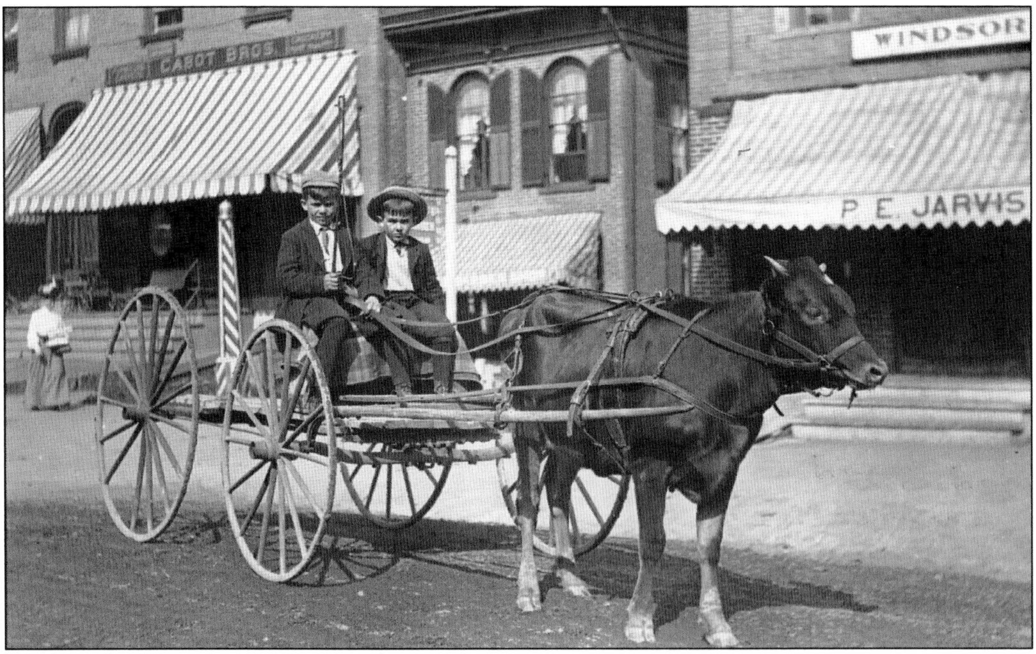

William and Beaman Ayers are pictured in 1908 driving their steer-pulled cart through downtown Windsor. Beaman became the first vice president of the Windsor Machine Company, which later became the National Acme Company. William had a construction company that worked on building the Goodyear factory. The Cabot Company, visible in the background, promoted itself as "the largest display of furniture in this section of New England." It also happened to be the local supplier of caskets.

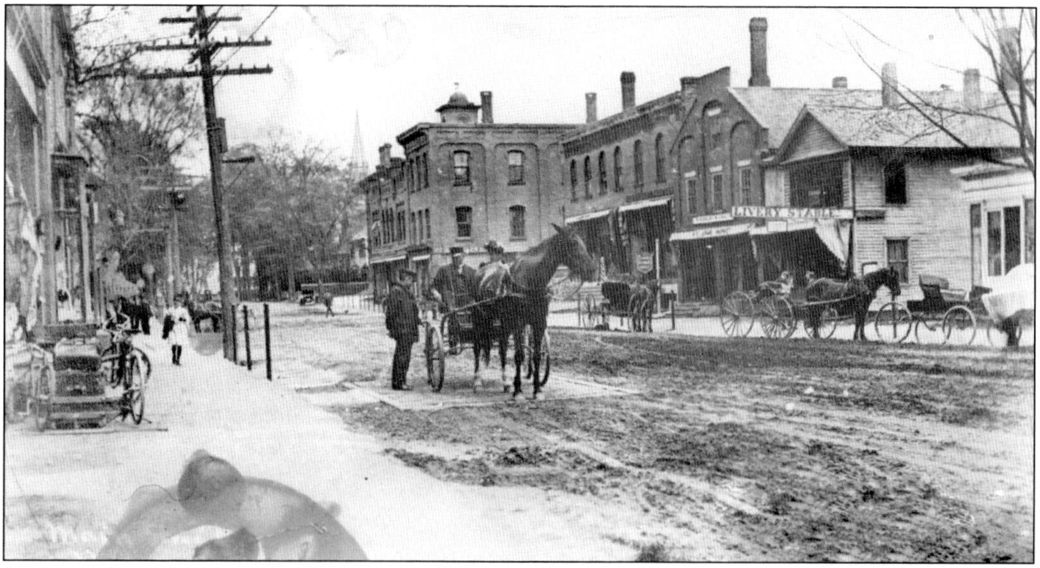

Stopping for a chat on Main Street are John Marcott (standing) and James and Minnie Kiniry (in carriage). Marcott was a partner in the Farmer and Marcott Grocery Store on Main Street. Known for their selection of coffee, their ads claimed, "The fact that our Coffee Sales show a continual increase is pretty good evidence that Windsor people have 'got wise' on buying coffee." A good blend was 20¢ per pound, a fancy blend 25¢ per pound, and their SEAL brand was 35¢ per pound.

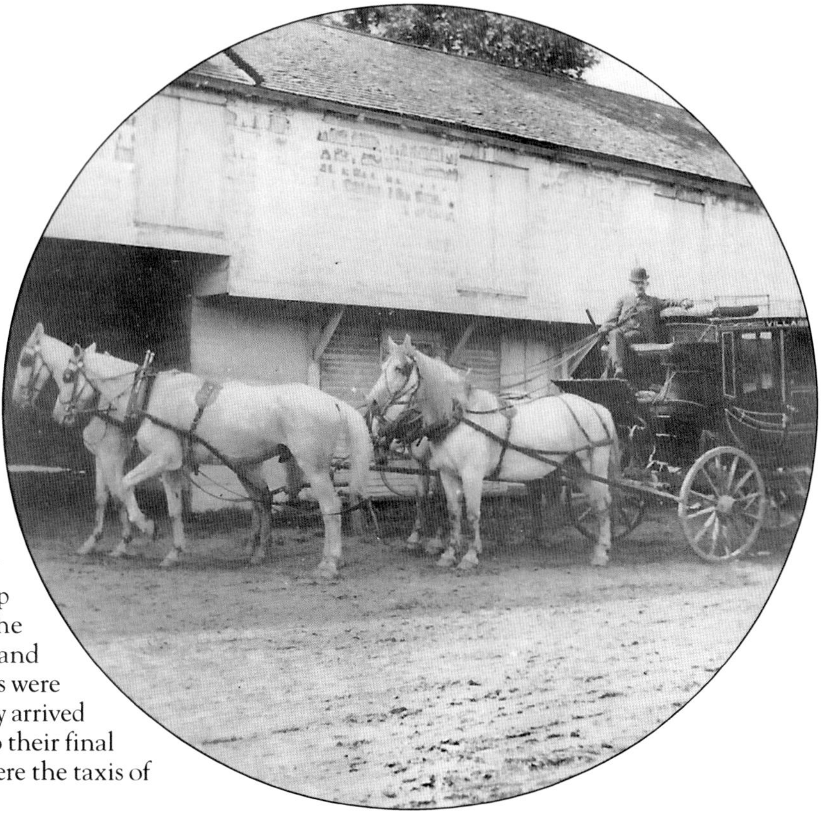

The stable near the depot provided convenient transportation for train passengers as well as for the large quantities of produce and dry goods that came up to Windsor on the rails. Both horses and horses with carriages were available to the newly arrived for transportation to their final destinations; they were the taxis of the 19th century.

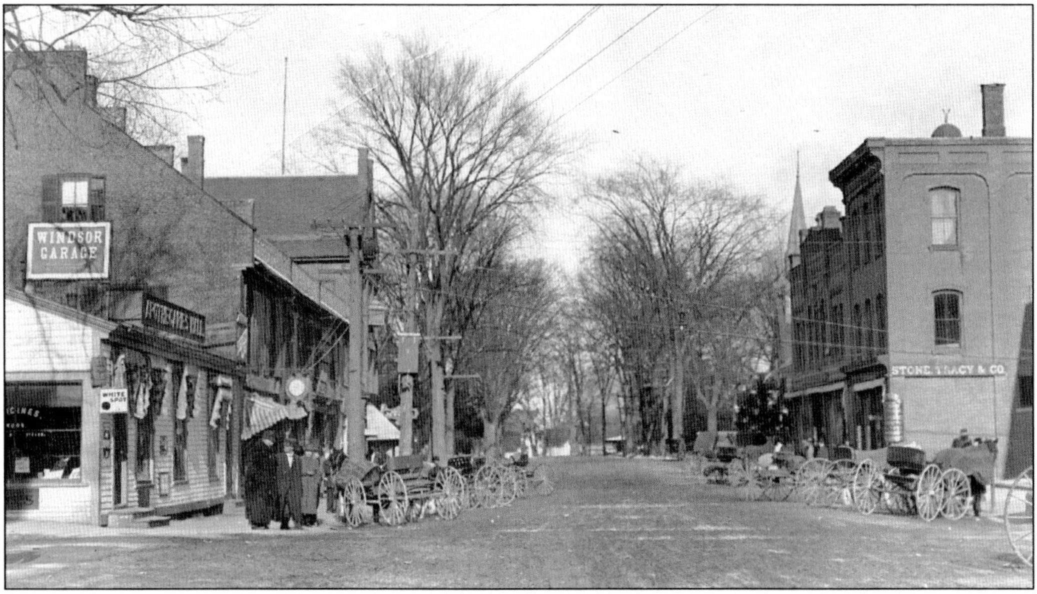

While carriages lined up along Main Street, it seems that occasionally a horse might have strayed. In July 1814, the *Windsor Journal* published a notice announcing, "Strayed or Stolen. From the enclosure of Elizur Hubbard Esq., on the night of the 22nd instant, a dark brown MARE, 13 or 14 years old, with a white face, three white feet, square trotter. Whoever will take up and return to the subscriber either the Thief, Mare, or both, shall be handsomely rewarded and all necessary charges paid."

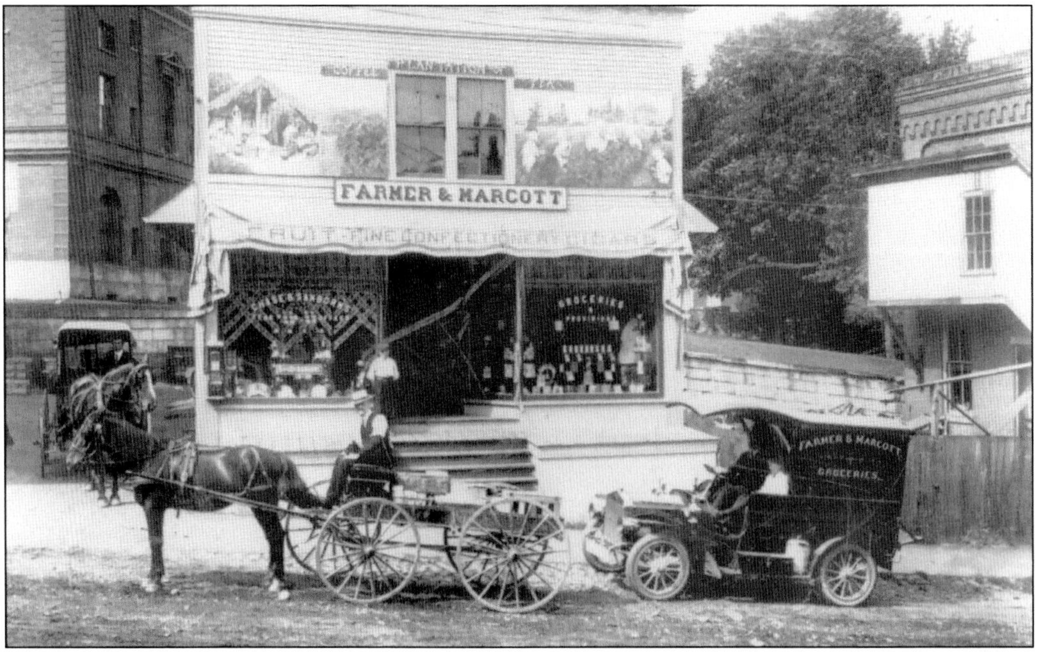

Old meets new in a transition from horse drawn to horseless carriage in front of Farmer and Marcotts Grocery Store on Depot Street. Notice the murals above illustrating the harvesting of tea and coffee, as well as the Chase and Sandborne logo on the window. In addition to their fine coffees, the grocers were very proud of their offerings of the finest teas available at the time.

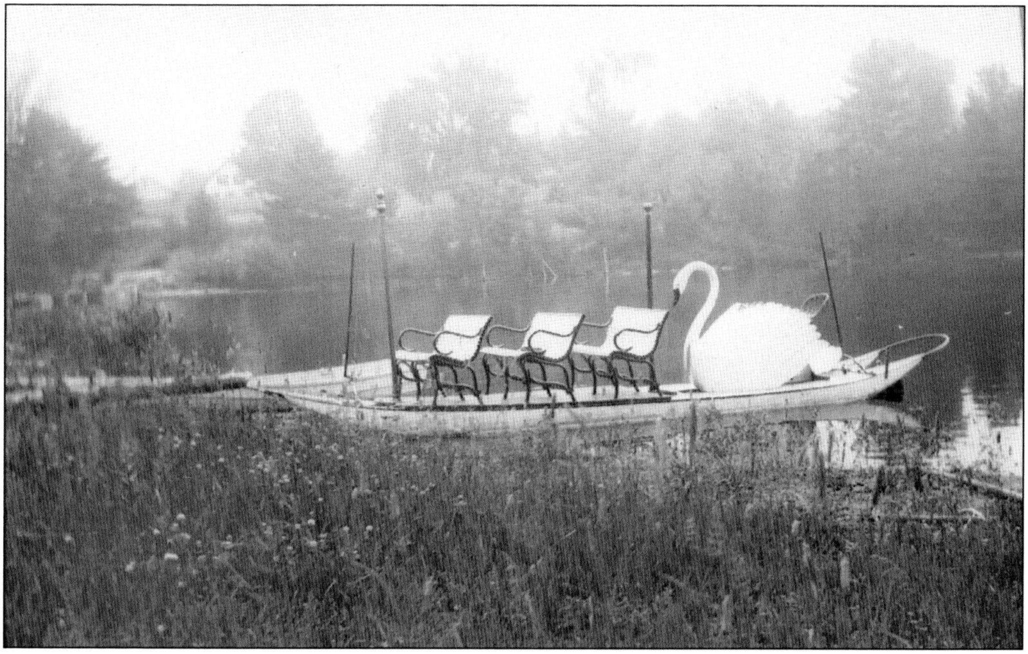

By no means a common method of transport, businessman Frank Kennedy had a copy of the classic Boston swan boat created for use on Kennedy Pond. The boat now rests in storage awaiting restoration; the pond is, and always has been, open to the public. The historic Mill Dam is visible on the left.

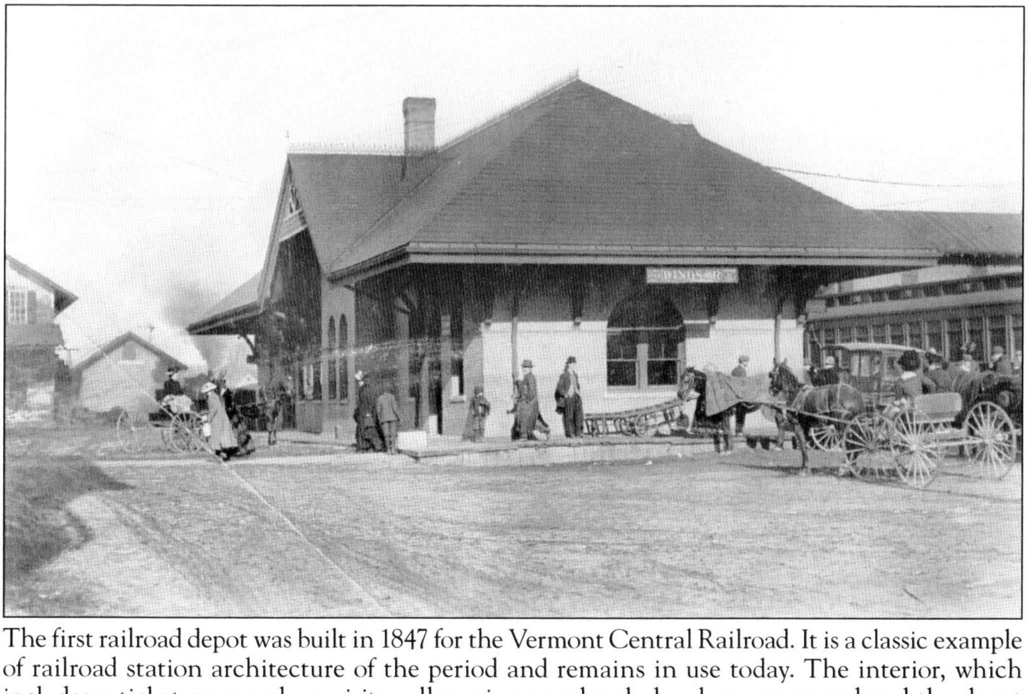

The first railroad depot was built in 1847 for the Vermont Central Railroad. It is a classic example of railroad station architecture of the period and remains in use today. The interior, which includes a ticket cage and exquisite yellow pine woodwork, has been preserved and the depot itself transformed into a restaurant. At 11:30 am and 6:20 pm, the Vermonter line still stops to deposit and pick up passengers.

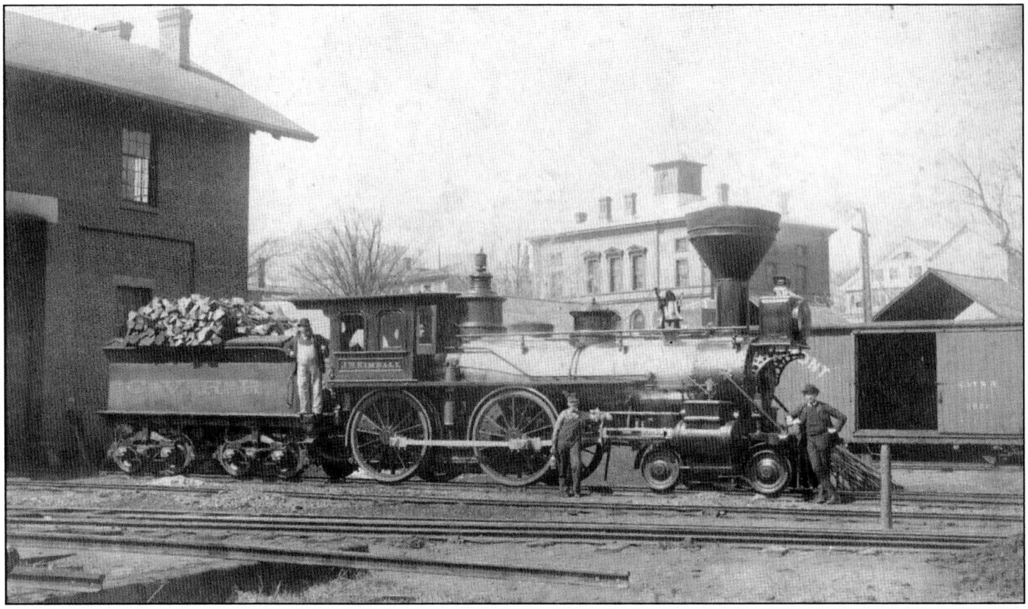

The railroad first came through Windsor in 1849. Carrying goods and passengers up and down the east coast, favorite stops were the Burrington farm on Route 5 north of town, and the Cornish Artist's Colony across the river in New Hampshire. Shown below is the train heading south towards New York, possibly taking visiting artists and writers back home.

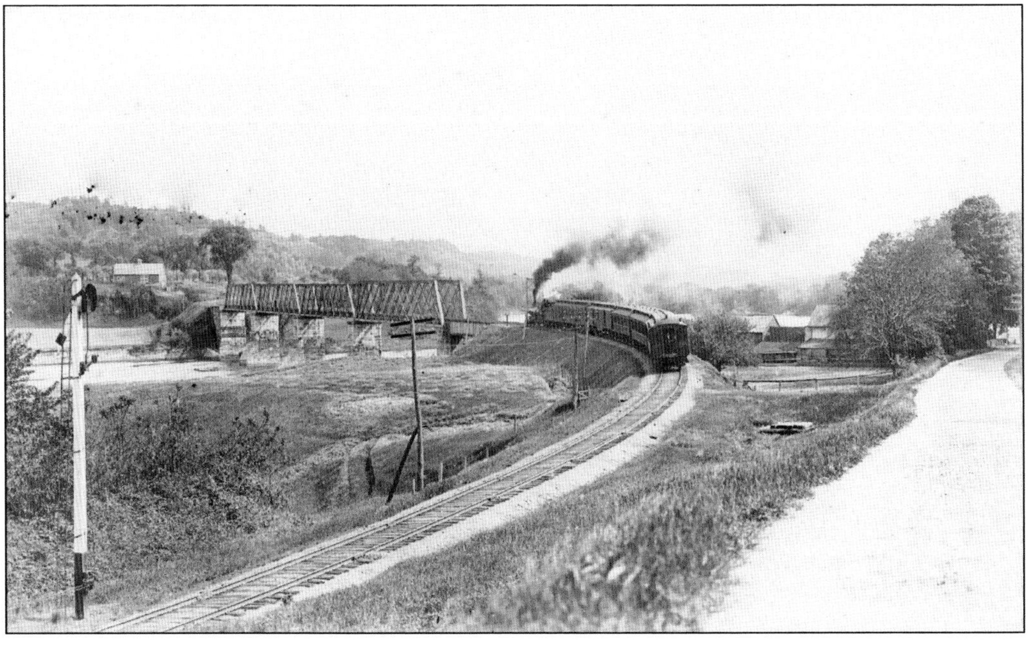

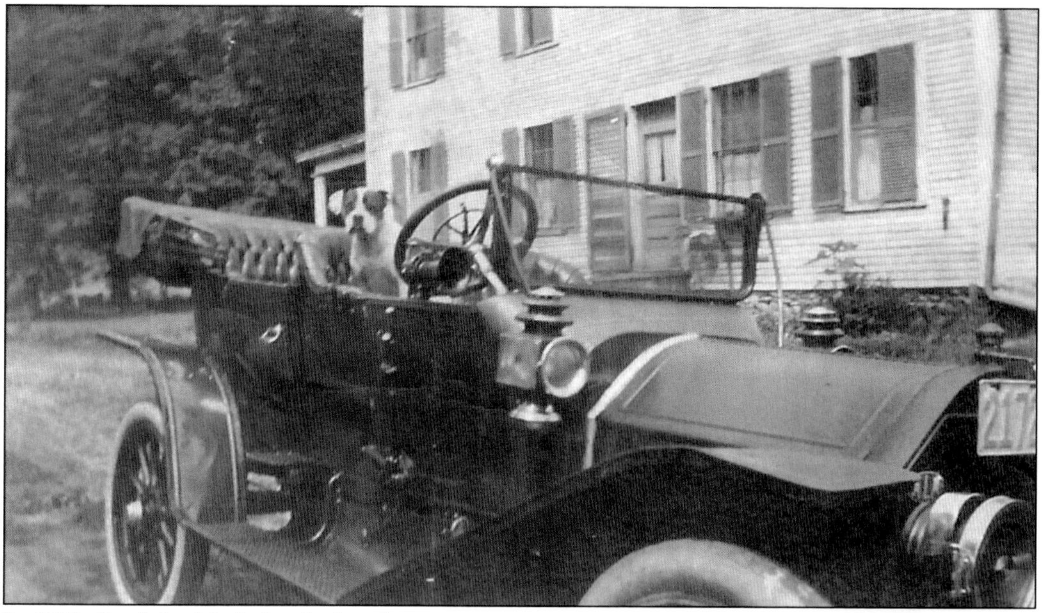

In 1912, Dr. John Nichols, the local veterinarian, brought the horseless carriage to the streets of Windsor. Hitching posts remained in town through 1915, and gradually, livery stables were transformed into garages. The power of the horse was set aside in favor of the horsepower of the automobile, even resulting in one of Windsor's Main Street mansions being converted into an automobile showroom. Automobile garages, service stations, and accessories began to appear on the streets and were advertised in the papers. The advertisement at right shows the Windsor covered bridge in the background.

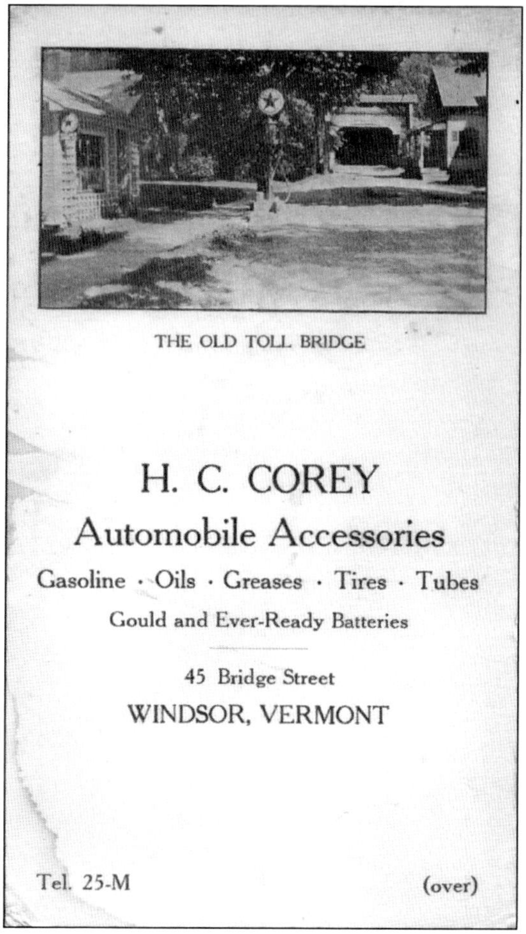

THE OLD TOLL BRIDGE

H. C. COREY

Automobile Accessories

Gasoline · Oils · Greases · Tires · Tubes

Gould and Ever-Ready Batteries

45 Bridge Street

WINDSOR, VERMONT

Tel. 25-M (over)

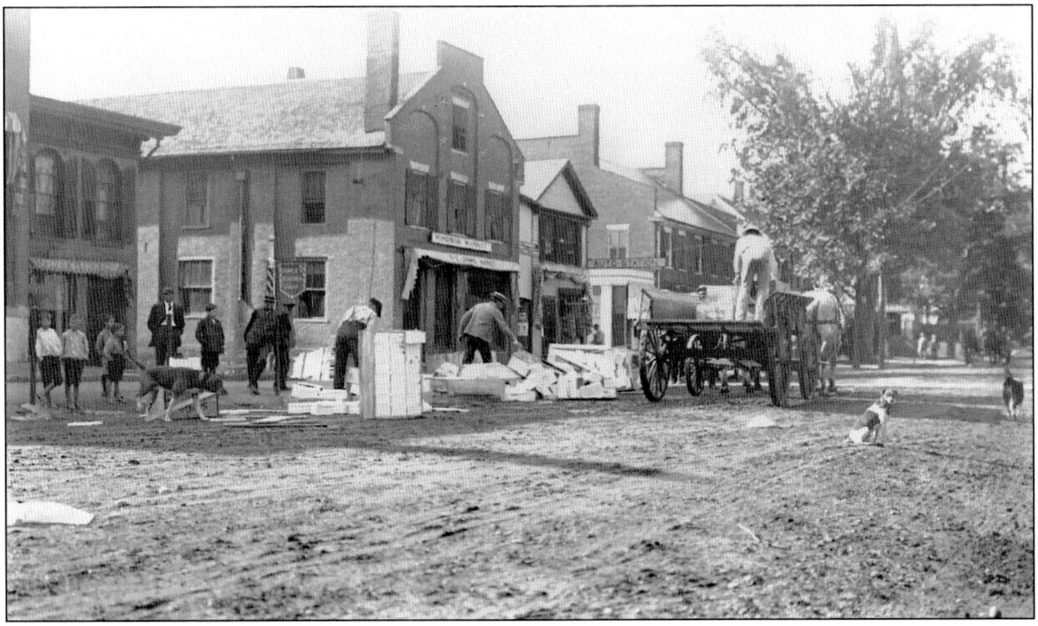

New cars and hardy pedestrians made up the streets of turn of the century Windsor. New sidewalks and curbs were created on Windsor's Main Street using granite from the nearby Mt. Ascutney quarries. Stone from Ascutney quarries also paved the sidewalks of dozens of towns in the surrounding area. On the left above are Jones Barber Shop and the Windsor Market. Below, the wealth and success of the town was apparent by the number of cars parked along the street.

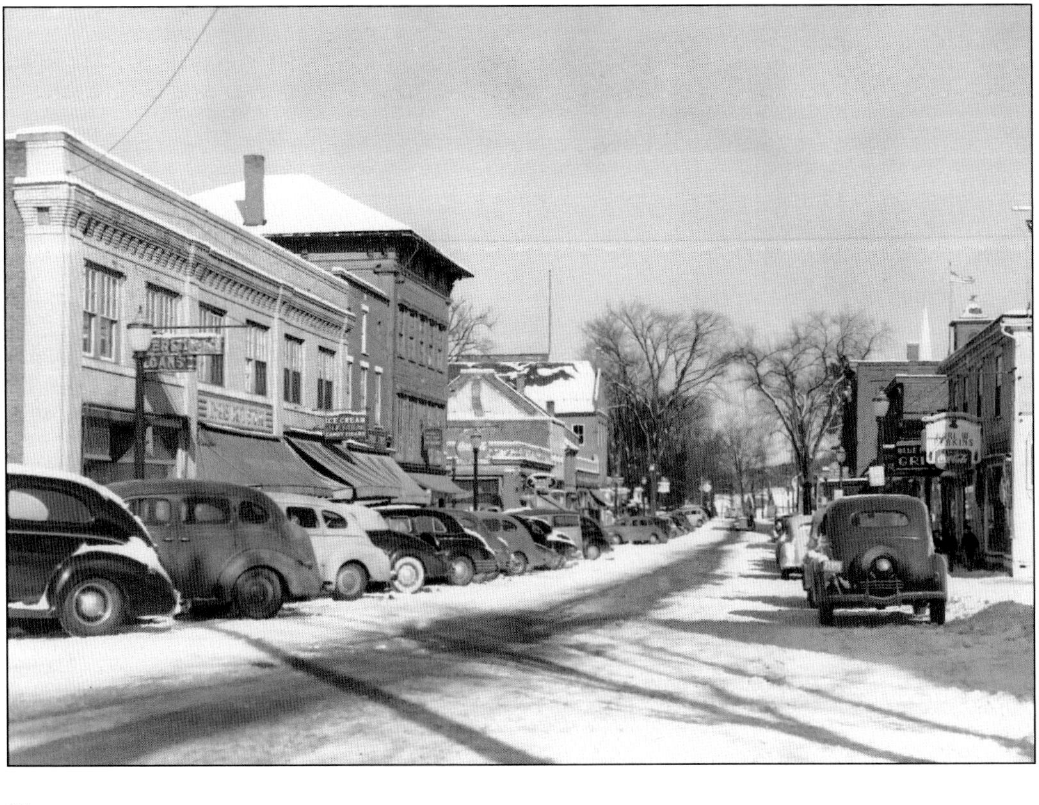

Three

Of Politics and Politicians

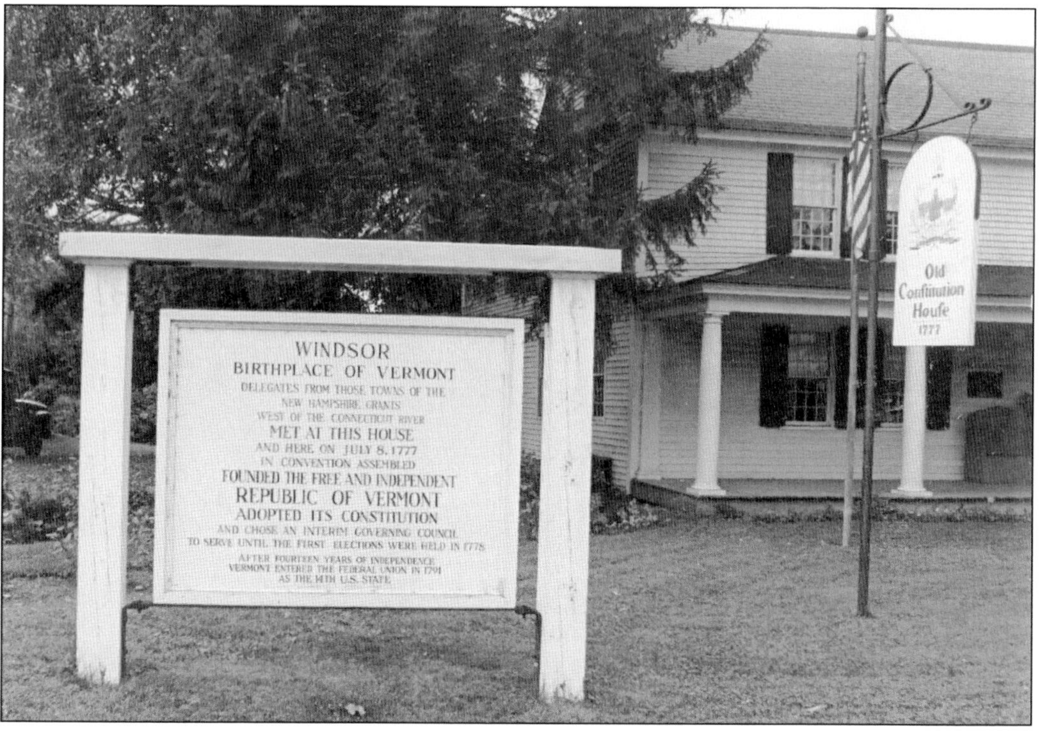

On July 8, 1777, the free and independent Republic of Vermont was founded. The constitution was adopted and signed in Elijah West's tavern on the corner of Depot and Main Streets during a violent thunderstorm and under the threat of invasion. In 1791, after 14 years of independence, Vermont became the 14th state in the Union.

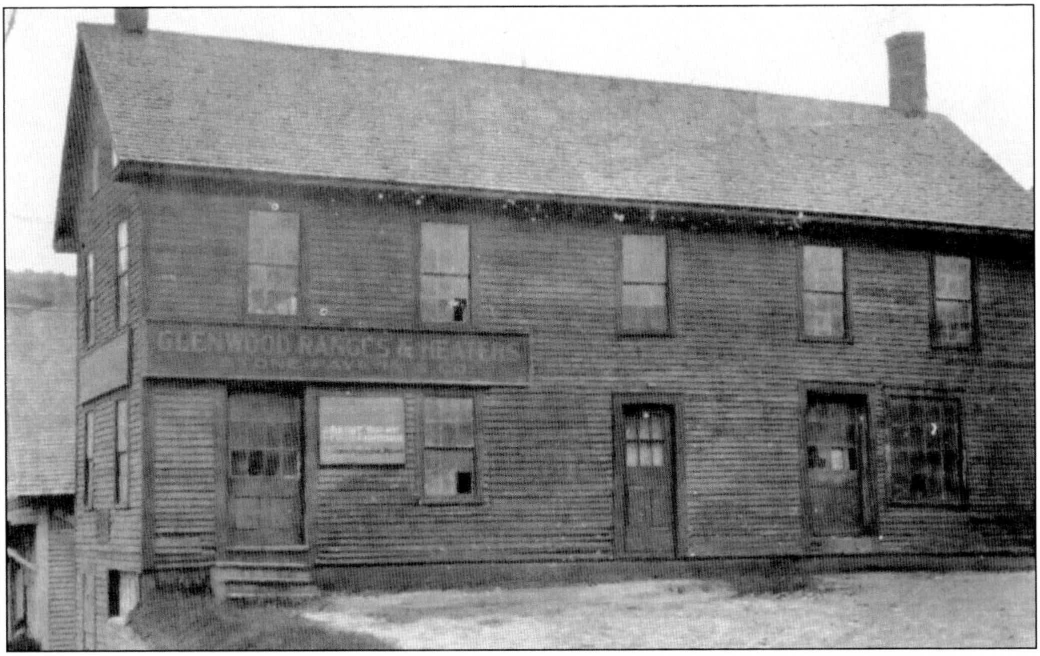

West's tavern was first identified as the "Constitution House" in an 1847 land transfer document. Suffering hard times in the following decades, the building was used as a warehouse and a tenement house. Destined for demolition in the early 1900s, The Old Constitution House Association was formed under the watchful eye of Sherman Evarts.

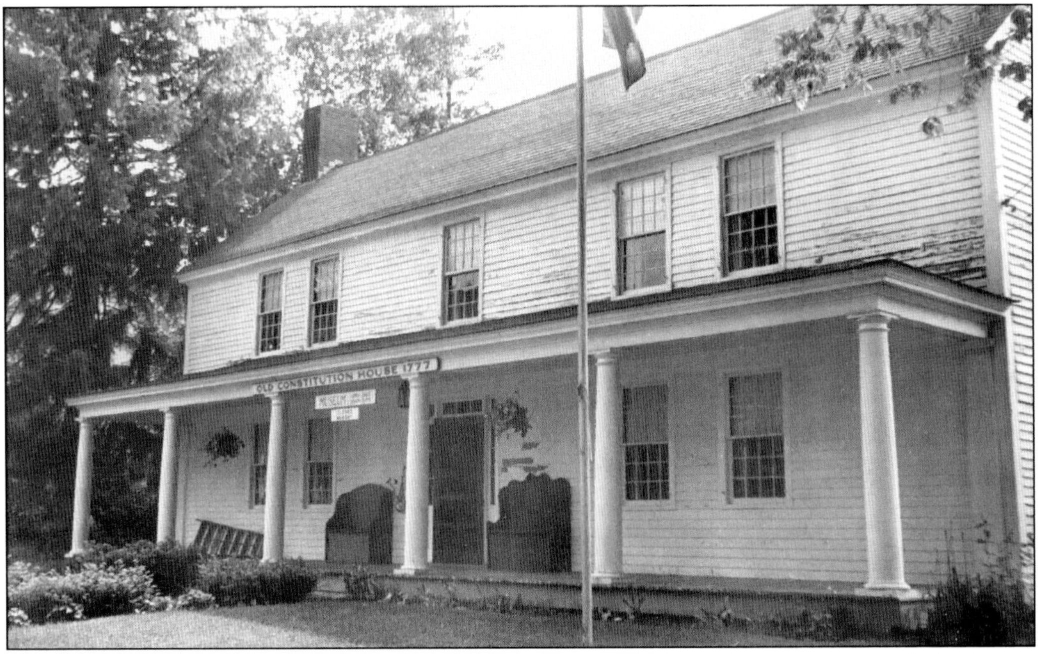

The Fay family gave the Constitution House to the newly formed association and the Evarts family donated the site. Many contributed to having the house moved to its present location, and it was restored in 1914. It functioned as a teahouse and later a restaurant before being designated a museum and historic site and turned over to the state of Vermont.

The original Vermont seal was designed in 1778 by Ira Allen and executed by Rueben Dean of Windsor. Allen was the youngest brother of Ethan Allen. Like his older brother, Ira was a Green Mountain Boy as well as a soldier, statesman, political leader, and the founding father of the University of Vermont. The seal was accepted by resolution of the Vermont General Assembly on February 20, 1779. It has since undergone several revisions, but has retained basically the same iconic images. (Courtesy state of Vermont.)

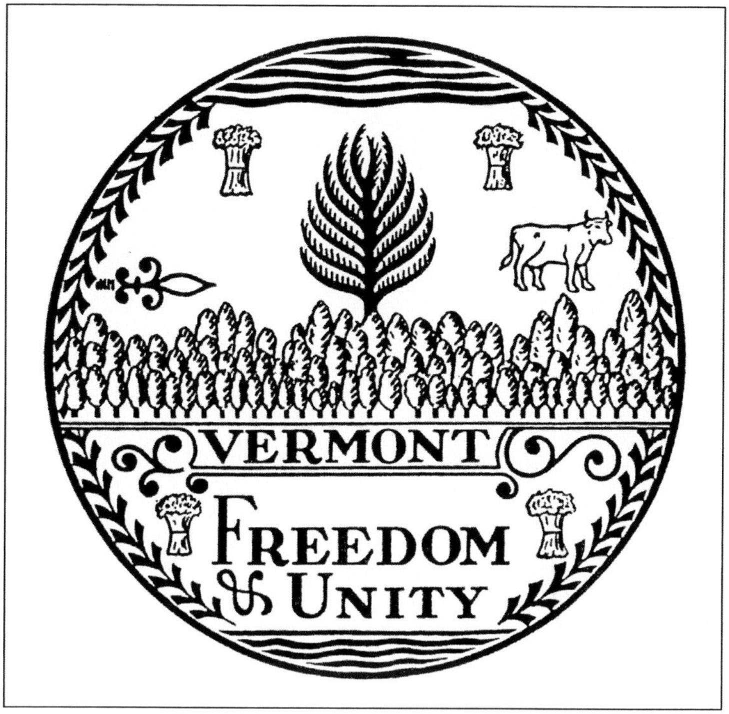

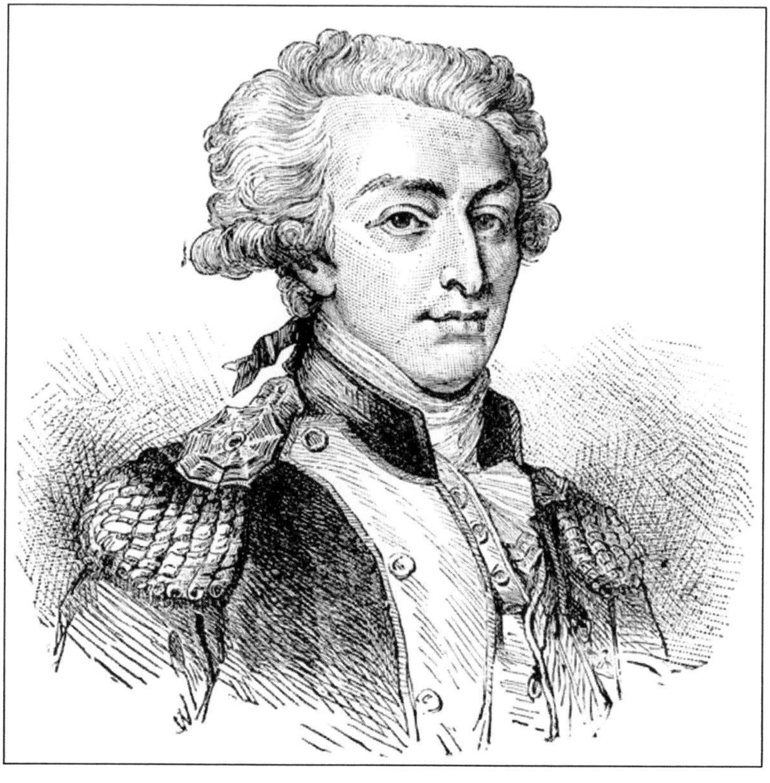

The Marquis de Lafayette was welcomed to Windsor in June 1825 by a committee waiting at the Windsor Bridge. His welcome was followed by a procession down Main Street to Pettes's Coffee House. Veterans from the Revolutionary War came from miles around to pay their respects to the man who had risked so much to aid the beleaguered American army.

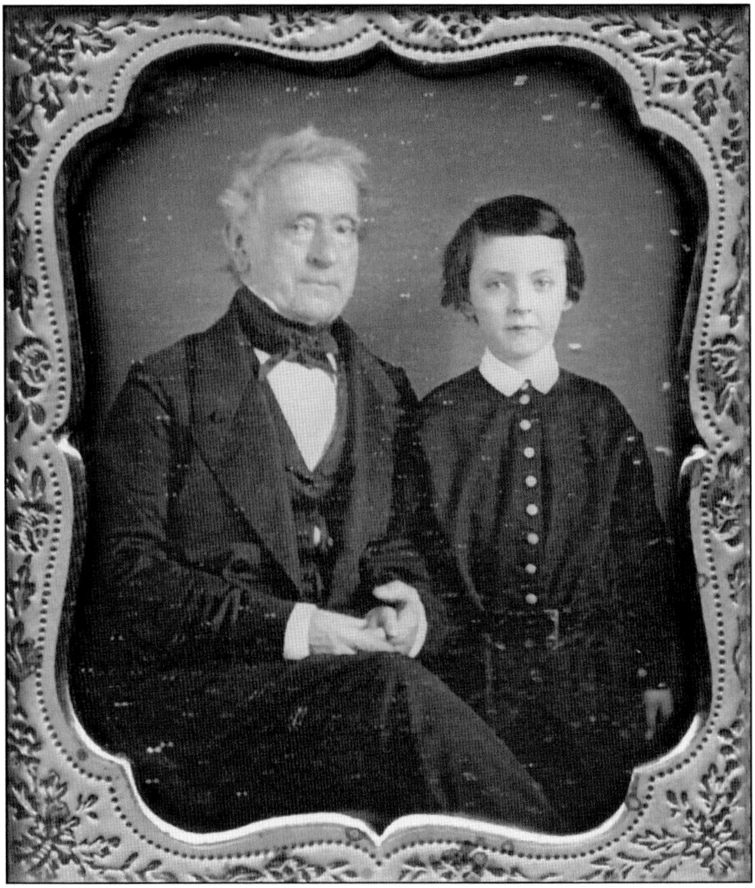

A daguerreotype shows Gov. Carlos Coolidge and his grandson. Carlos Coolidge, a distant relative of Pres. Calvin Coolidge, had a law practice in Windsor in 1814. He enjoyed a long political career as a representative of Windsor, and was governor of Vermont from 1848 to 1849. He was present at many town meetings, and his name is frequently found in the recorded minutes of town books. He later became a senator. Coolidge died in August 1866, and is buried in the Old South Cemetery on Main Street. (Courtesy of Vermont Historical Society, Barre.)

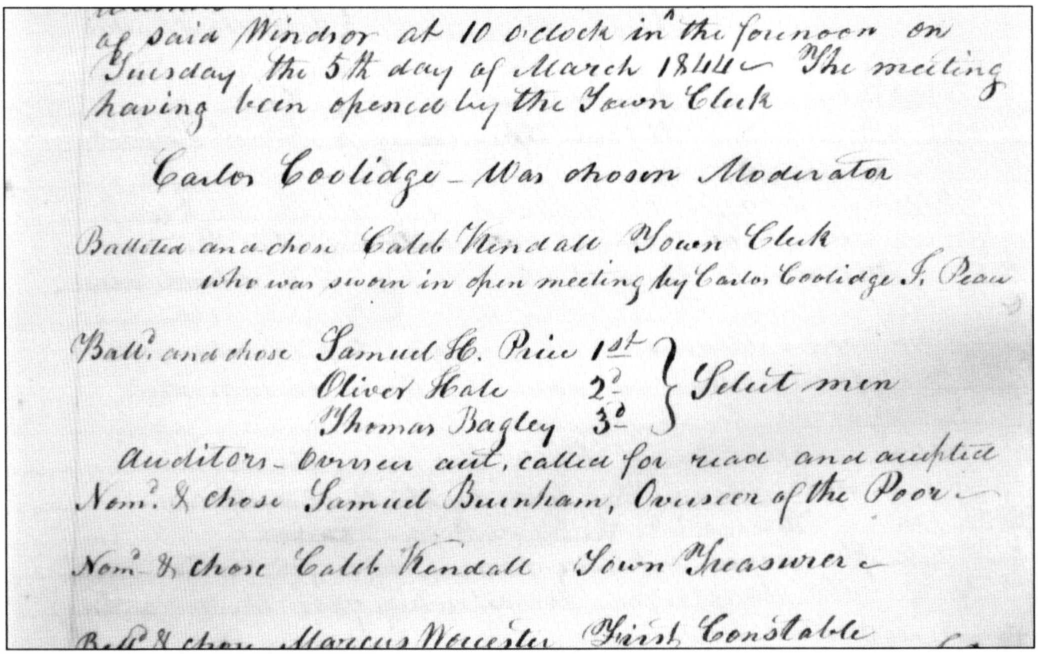

of said Windsor at 10 o'clock in the forenoon on
Tuesday the 5th day of March 1844 — The meeting
having been opened by the Town Clerk

Carlos Coolidge — Was chosen Moderator

Balloted and chose Caleb Kendall Town Clerk
who was sworn in open meeting by Carlos Coolidge J. Peace

Ball. and chose Samuel H. Price 1st, Oliver Hale 2d, Thomas Bagley 3d } Select men
Auditors — Owners acct. called for read and accepted
Nom. & chose Samuel Burnham, Overseer of the Poor —

Nom. & chose Caleb Kendall Town Treasurer —

Ball. & chose Marcus Worcester First Constable

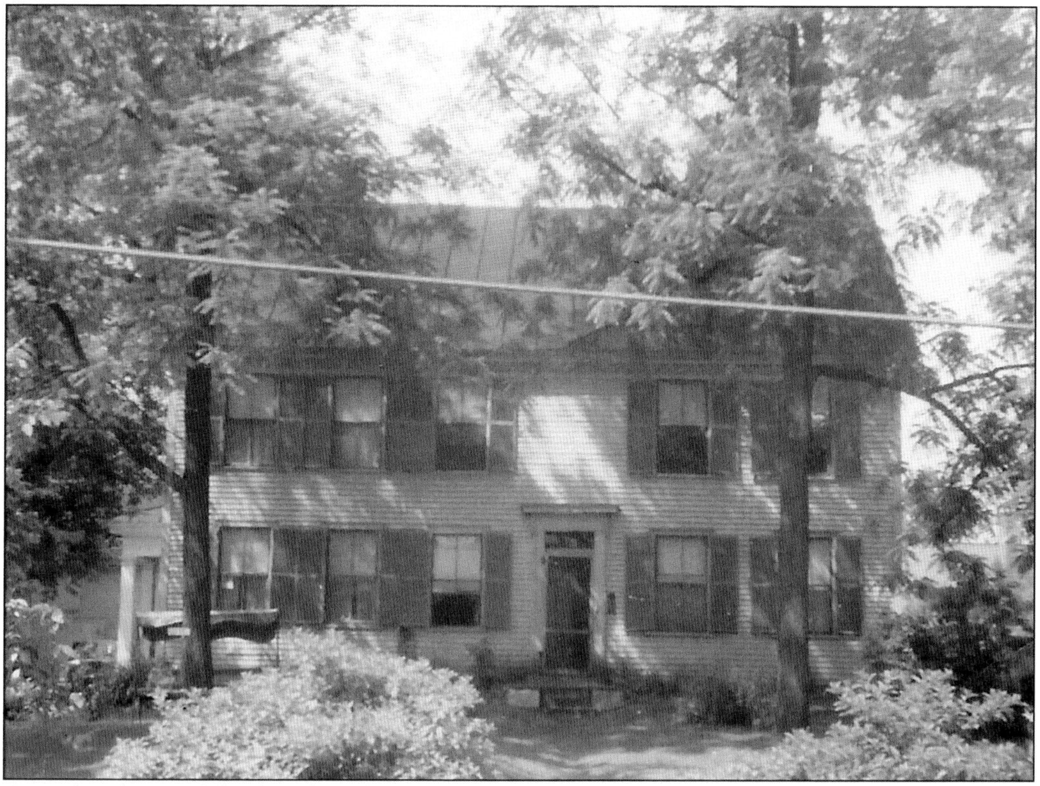

Considered one of the founding fathers of Vermont and instrumental in creating the Vermont Constitution, Judge Stephen Jacob created quite a stir in town at the turn of the 19th century. Clearly opposed to slavery from before it was even granted statehood, Vermont became the first state in the Union to have this edict included in its constitution. Curiously, Judge Jacob had within his home Dinah Mason, described as a woman of color, for whom he had a sales receipt showing his proof of ownership. In 1802, Windsor became the center of a court case that involved Judge Jacob and his responsibilities in regards to Mason. The state upheld the abolition of slavery in what was possibly the first such case in the United States.

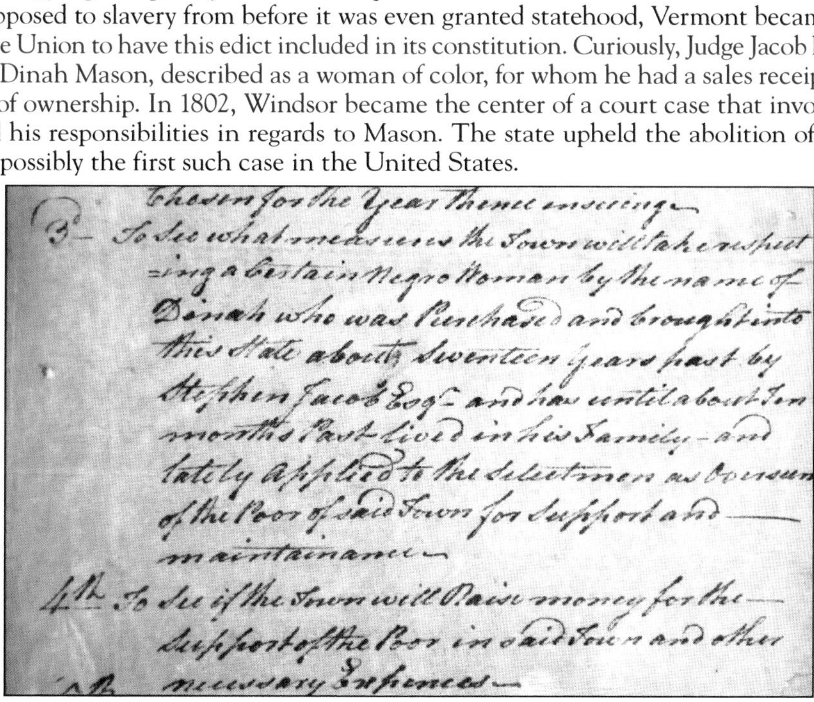

Chosen for the Year Thence ensuing—
3d— To See what measures the Town will take respect
=ing a Certain Negro Woman by the name of
Dinah who was Purchased and brought into
this State about Seventeen years past by
Stephen Jacob Esqr— and has until about Ten
months Past lived in his Family—and
lately Applied to the Selectmen as Overseers
of the Poor of said Town for Support and—
maintainance—
4th To See if the Town will Raise money for the—
Support of the Poor in said Town and other
necessary Expences—

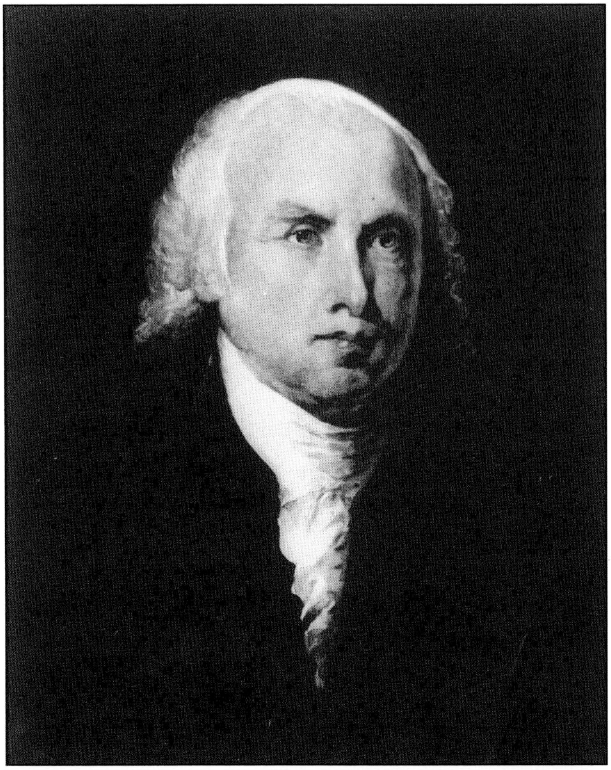

In 1817, Windsor was honored by a visit from Pres. James Monroe. He was feted with a deafening salute from the Jefferson Heavy Artillery as well as the pealing of bells from every church steeple in town. Met and welcomed on the Vermont side of the Windsor-Cornish Covered Bridge, the procession continued up Main Street, stopping in front of what was then the Female Academy and is now the Masonic Hall. (Courtesy Vermont Historical Society, Barre.)

The Hon. William Evarts and his wife, Helen, pose for a portrait in their "Windsor White House." Evarts defended Pres. Andrew Johnson in his senate impeachment trial in 1868. He was later appointed secretary of state in 1877 under Pres. Rutherford B. Hayes, who was the 19th president of the United States.

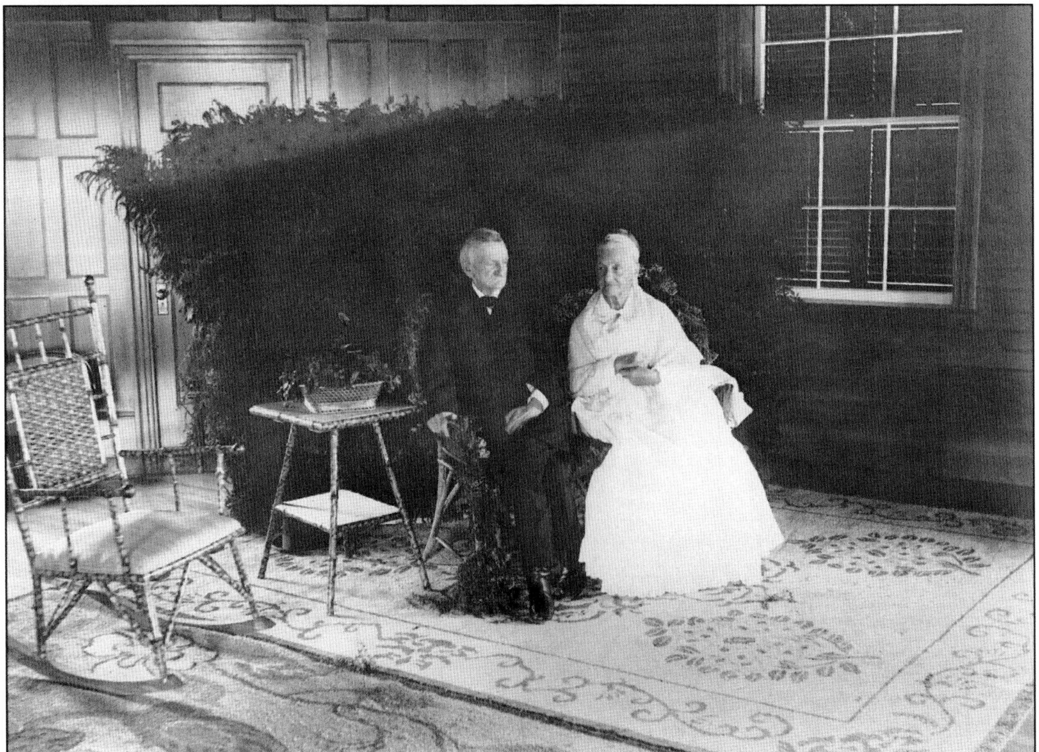

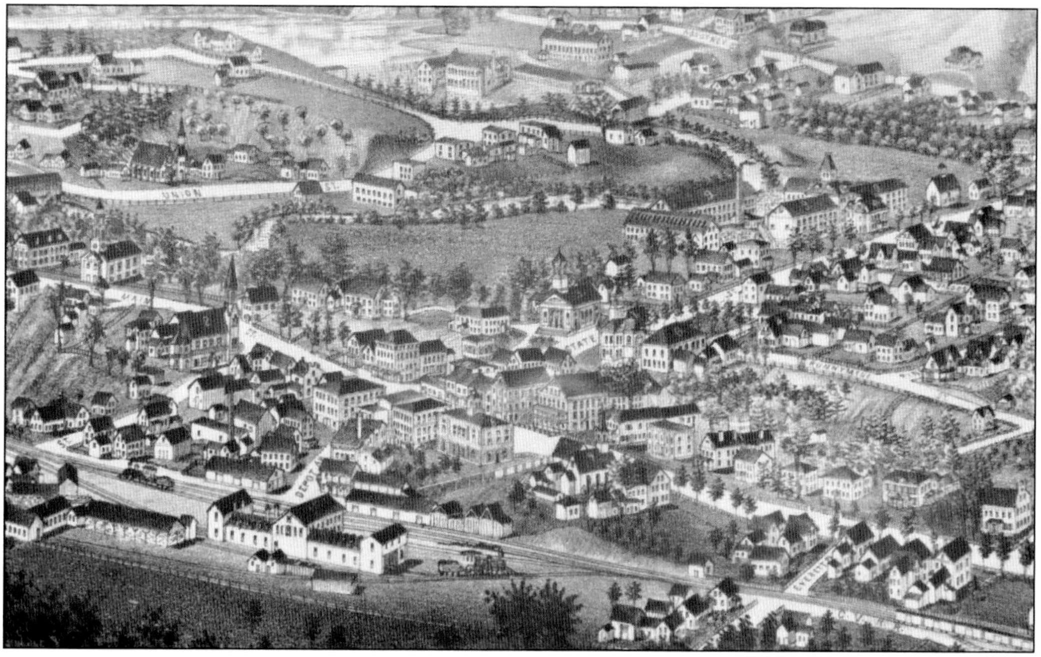

President Hayes and members of his cabinet visited Windsor in August 1877. They were entertained at the home of Secretary of State William Evarts. The year 1891 saw Pres. Benjamin Harrison welcomed in the Evarts home as well, during which Harrison praised Evarts for introducing a model system of farming to Vermont. This 19th century etching shows the town as it looked then.

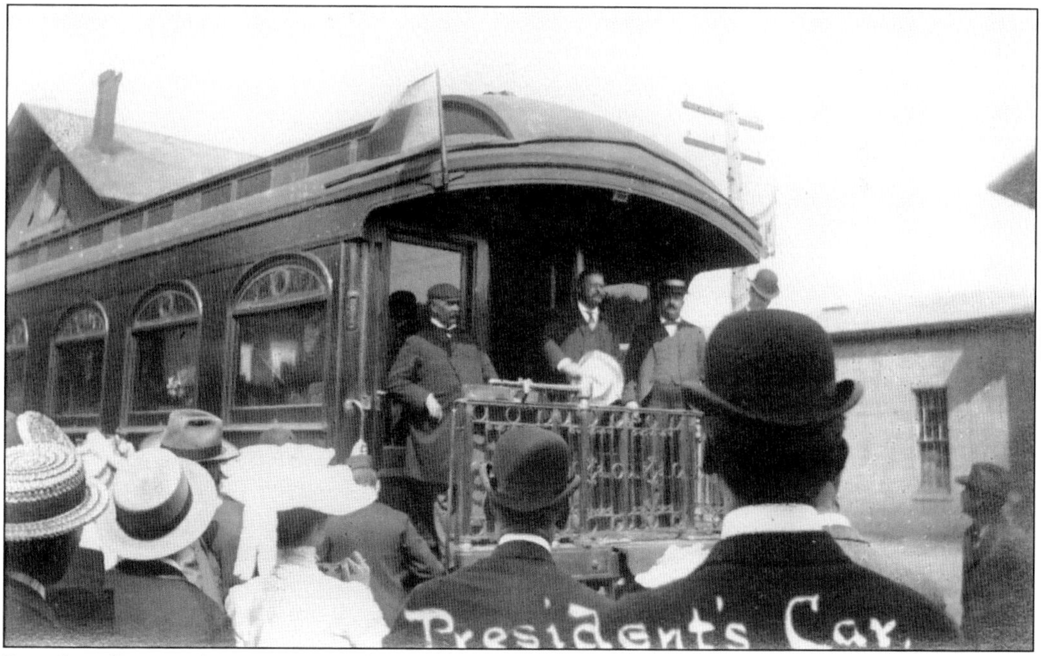

President Roosevelt's 1902 arrival in Windsor was accompanied by celebrations and elaborate preparations. In the days prior to his visit, he was feted in Cornish, New Hampshire. He went wild boar hunting and was later driven across the Cornish-Windsor Covered Bridge by his New Hampshire host, Winston Churchill (not the British prime minister), to the home of William Evarts.

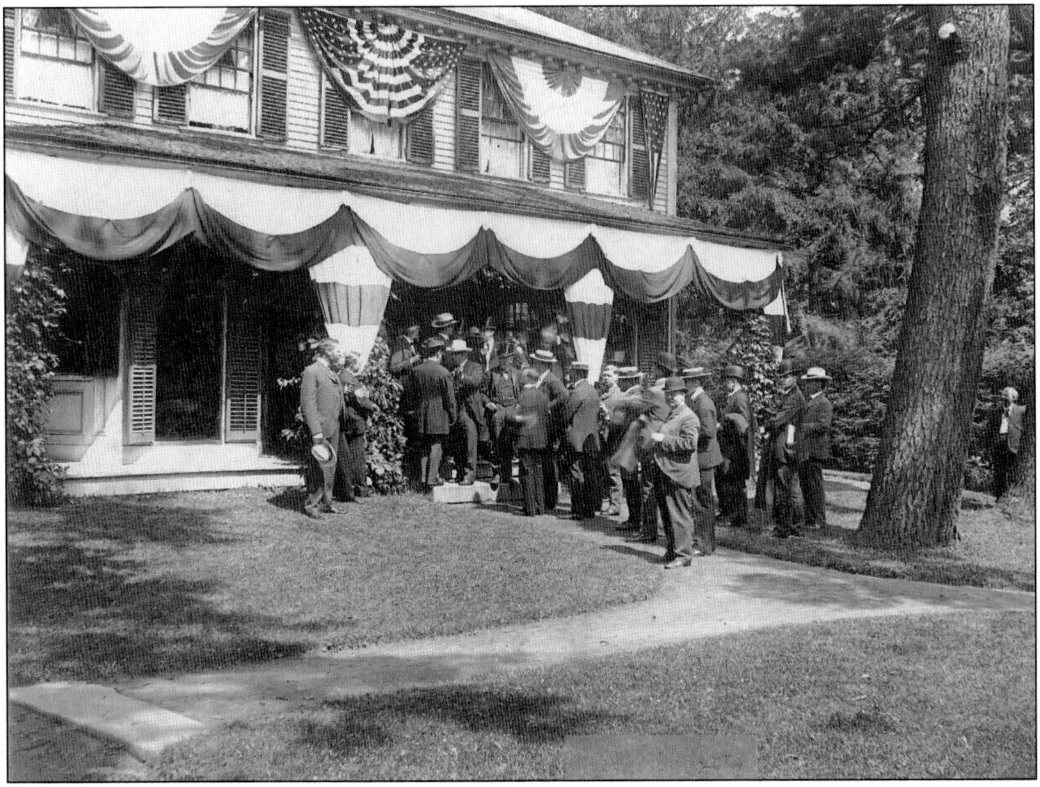

Apparently, that day in 1902 was also the Evarts' 59th anniversary, so President Roosevelt shared some of the original cake that had been preserved from their wedding day. The entourage was welcomed at the coach entrance to the Evarts house. Their mansion was one of the grand homes in Windsor, and is now part of the Historic Homes of Runnemede.

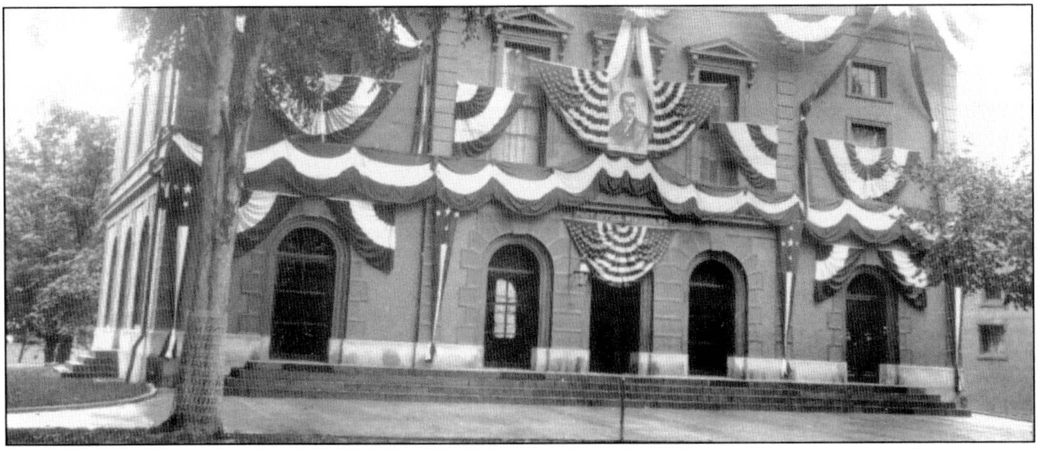

Pres. Woodrow Wilson established his summer executive offices on the second floor of the Windsor Post Office on Main Street. His staff stayed across the street at the Windsor Hotel, now called the Windsor House. Wilson summered regularly across the river in Plainfield at the home of writer Winston Churchill, who was not related to the British prime minister. Churchill was heard to have complained about having to relocate for the summers to accommodate the president and his family.

Four

MANUFACTURING AND INDUSTRY

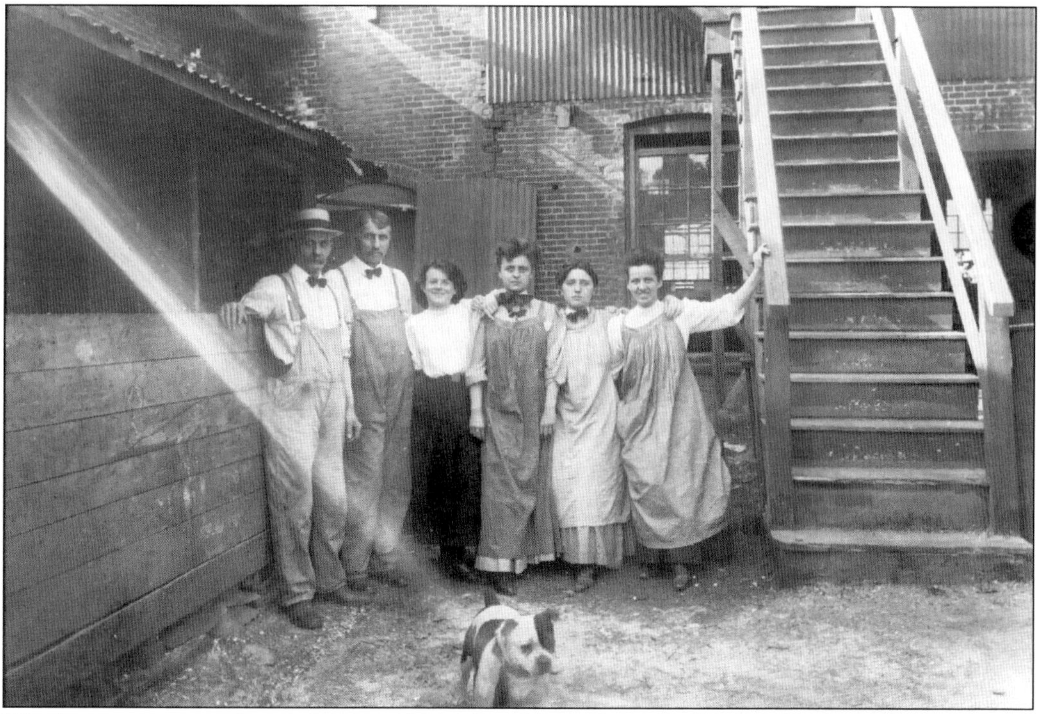

Windsor was a manufacturing town from the late 18th century through the mid-20th century. Manufacturing not only took place in factories, but also in small workshops and even within prison walls. Here, the workers at the Hubbard McClary factory take a break from manufacturing glazier points. The majority of the workers in this particular factory were women.

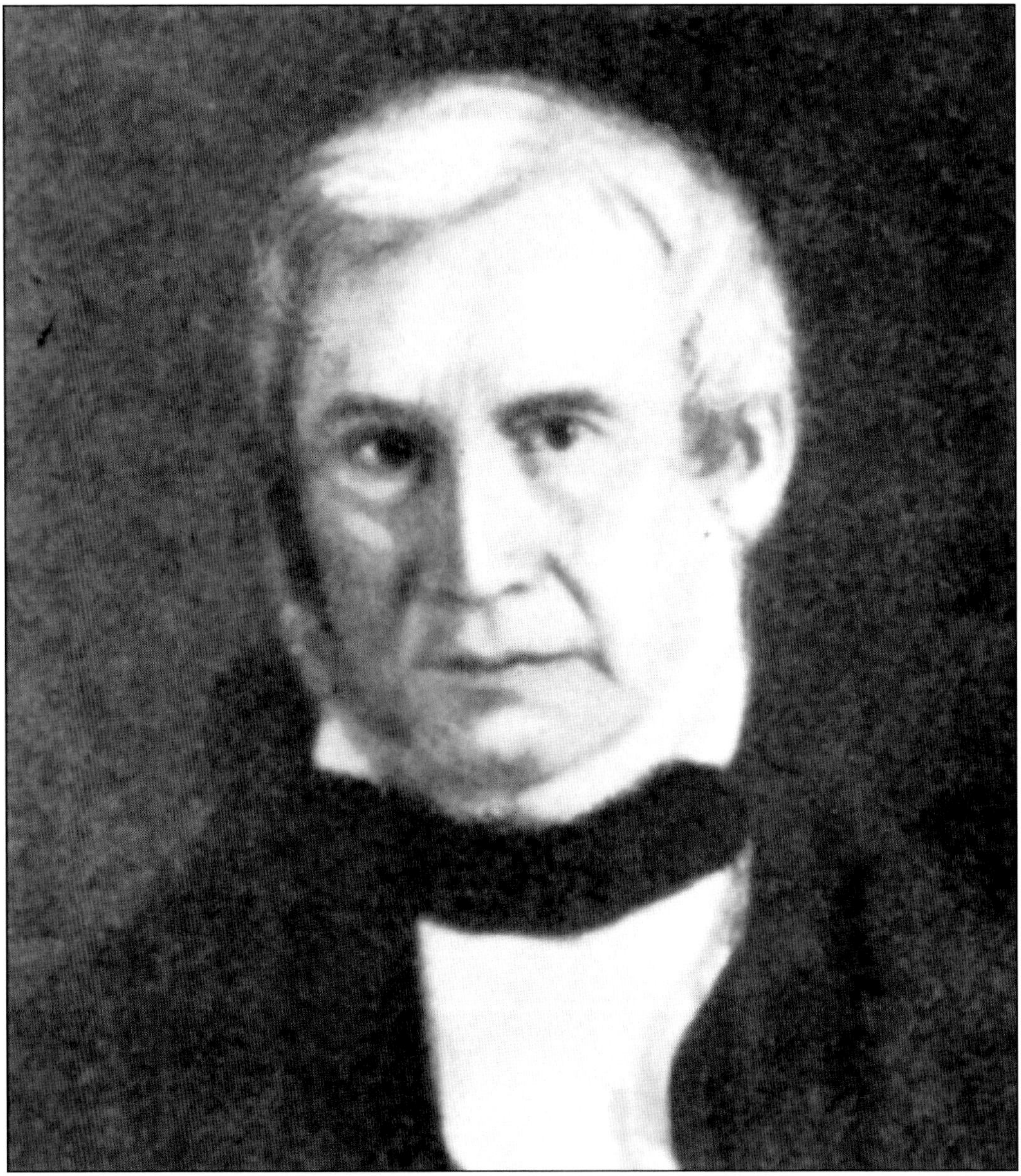

Lemuel Hedge was one of Windsor's celebrated inventors and had numerous patents to his name. He patented a process for ruling paper called the spring pen ruler, and later devised the revolving ruling machine, which was capable of ruling a ream of paper in 12 minutes on both sides. Hedge also built organs for three churches in town. In 1811, he ran this notice in *Spooner's Journal*: "Hedge, Lemuel (Windsor). Respectfully informs the Ladies and Gentlemen of Windsor that he has taken the room under the Vermont Journal Office, where he purposes to make Mahogany & Cherry Furniture, of almost every description . . . Mr. Hedge flatters himself as he has lately labored in different approved shops in Boston, that he shall be able to give complete satisfaction to any who may wish for furniture made and finished in the taste of the Metropolis. He is determined to sell his work on as good terms to the purchaser, as can be had at any good shop in New England . . . Wanted, as an Apprentice to the above business, a likely Lad, about sixteen years of age, to whom good encouragement will be given."

In 1828, Windsor resident and prison superintendent Asahel Hubbard invented and received a patent for the revolving hydraulic engine. By encasing two meshed gears in a watertight compartment, water was taken in at the bottom and forced out in a steady stream at the top. A pump very similar to this one is still in use today in automobiles and oil burners. The pump pictured here was produced at the Vermont State Prison in Windsor. (Courtesy American Precision Museum.)

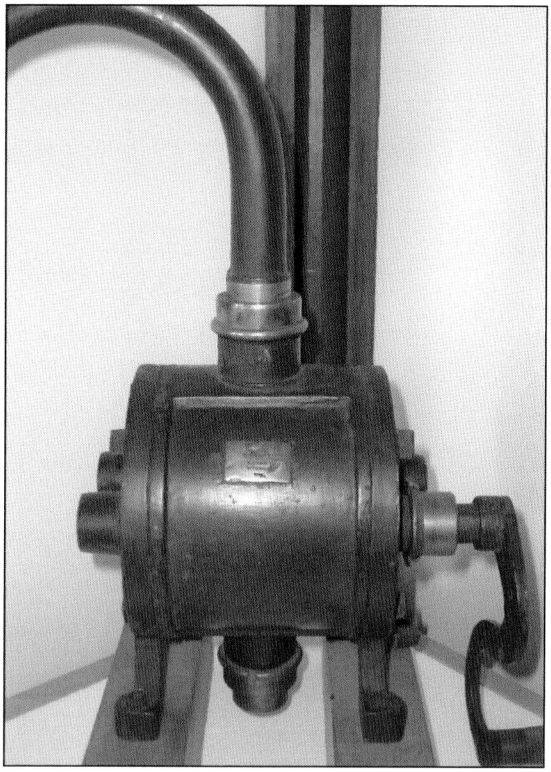

Nicanor Kendall is credited with the invention of the underhammer rifle. The coinciding events of the Mexican War and the California Gold Rush increased the need for guns. This resulted in a boom in the Kendall and Lawrence Company. As Kendall, Robbins, and Lawrence in 1844, they received a government contract for 10,000 rifles, which were constructed at the new armory along Mill Brook. (Courtesy American Precision Museum.)

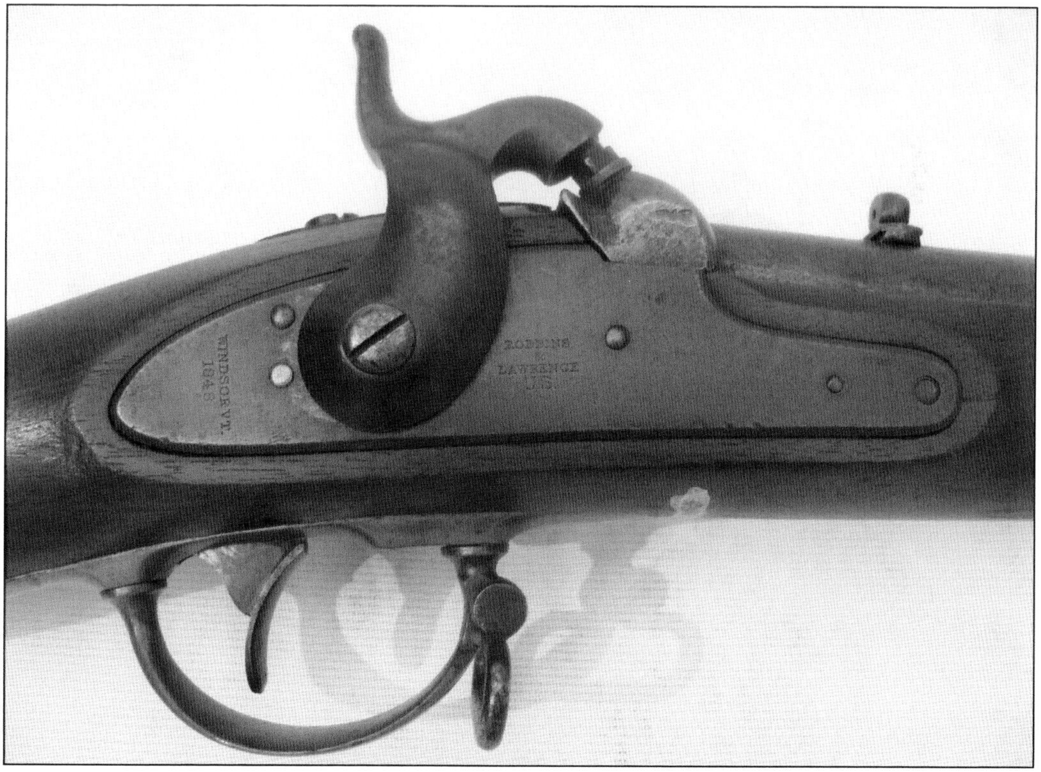

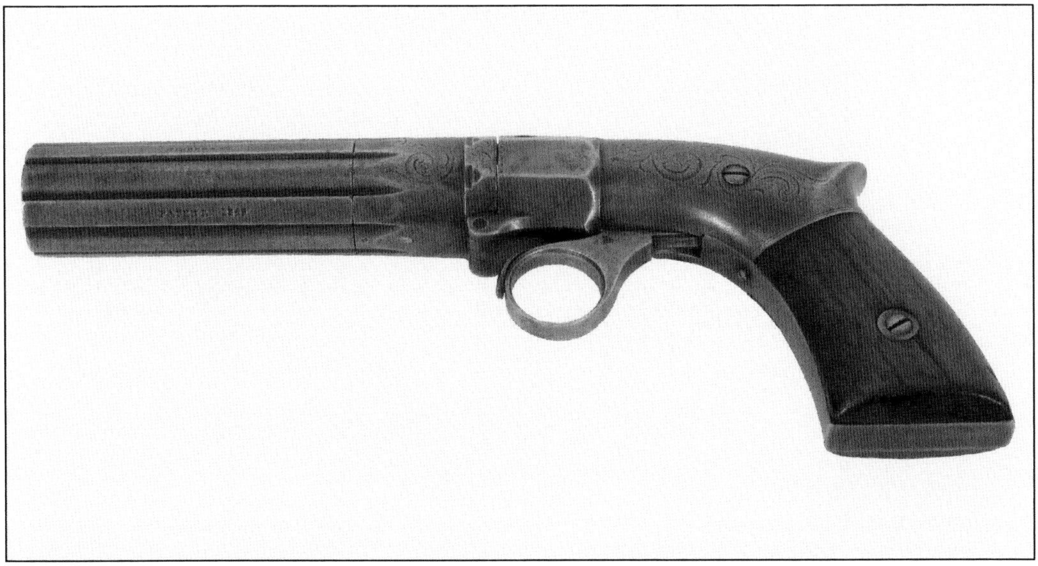

Robbins and Lawrence were the originators of the interchangeable US Army rifle. The genius behind this invention was the mass production of its parts. Prior to this, they were made individually, which significantly reduced efficiency. A later collaboration in the 1850s between Daniel Baird Wesson and Richard Lawrence resulted in the revolving pistol, also called the "pepper pot." (Courtesy American Precision Museum.)

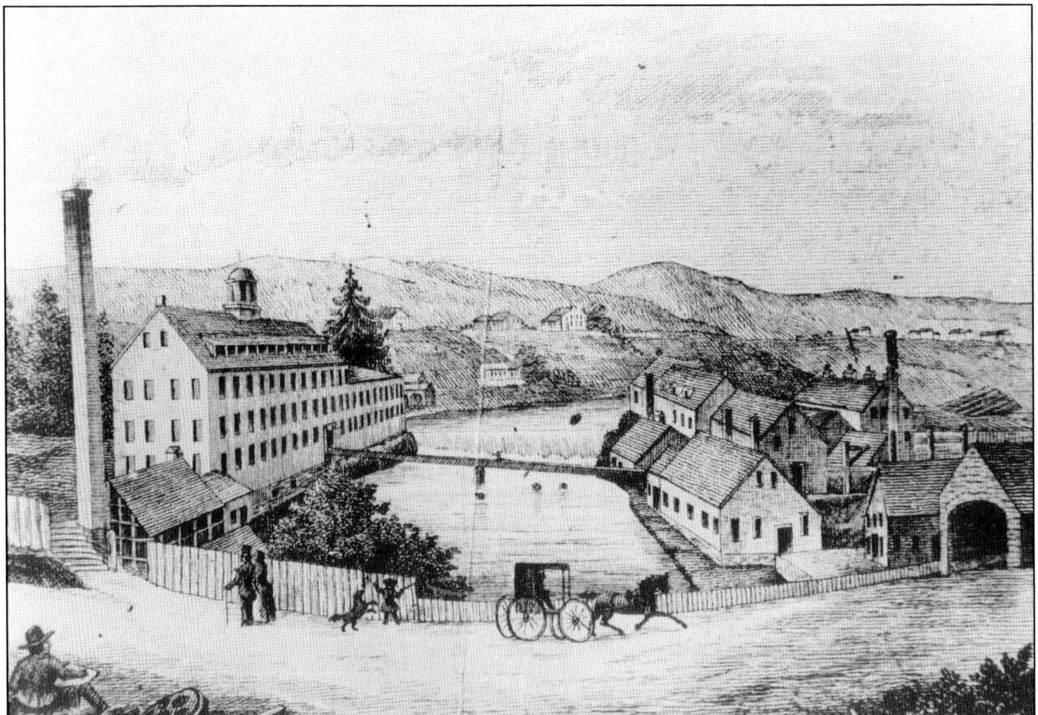

The Robbins and Lawrence factory added steam power by 1850. Seen here in an 1855 etching by Hosea Doton, the steam engine house and stack are in the foreground with the two-story manufacturing addition at the rear. (Courtesy Special Collections, University of Vermont.)

Jones and Lamson were responsible for the turret lathe, which was made in Windsor between 1880 and 1888. It was fondly called the "silent salesman," as it was used to promote the Jones and Lamson Machine Company. The lathe was able to hold several tools at once, which enabled the workers to execute a variety of tasks without having to stop to change tools. (Courtesy of Donald Dill.)

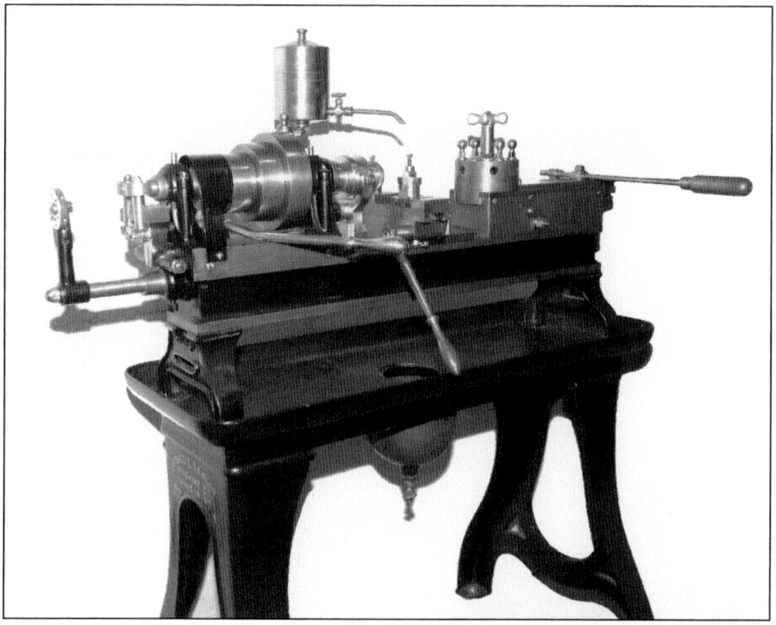

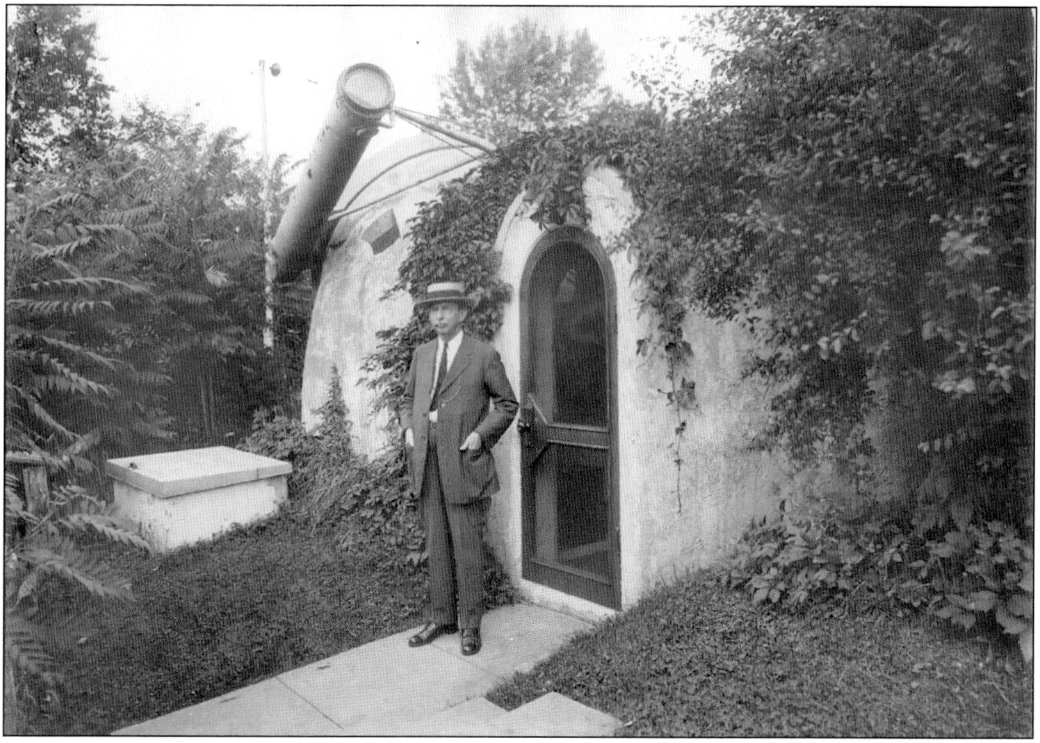

In the late 1880s, James Hartness invented the Hartness Flat Turret Lathe and joined the Jones and Lamson Company. A museum dedicated to his work exists in rooms he constructed underground in Springfield, Vermont. The apartment consisted of a library, workshop, lavatory, study, and lounge room that were connected end to end. All of the rooms were underground and were supplied with electric, heat, and fresh air. Hartness later served as governor of Vermont. (Courtesy Hartness House Inn.)

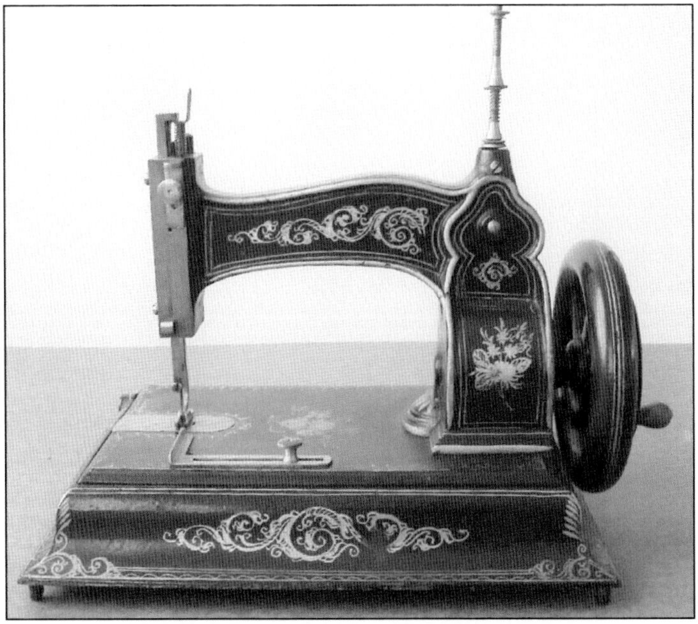

Among the numerous incarnations of the original Robbins and Lawrence armory was also Lamson, Goodnow and Company, which manufactured the Clarke's Revolving Double Threading Sewing Machine. The 1870s saw Jones and Lamson processing cotton in a new addition to the building. To protect and separate the cotton works from the original building, fire doors were added between the old and the new sections. (Courtesy American Precision Museum.)

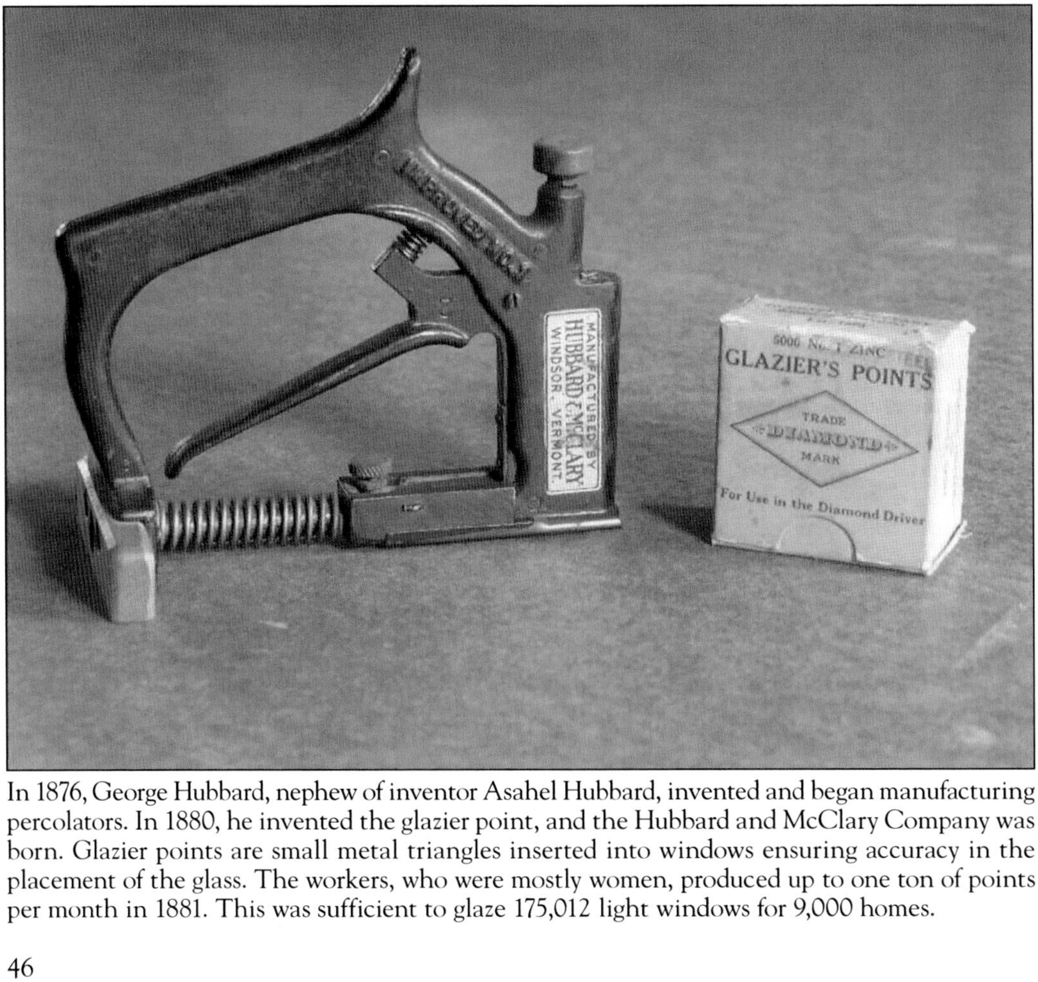

In 1876, George Hubbard, nephew of inventor Asahel Hubbard, invented and began manufacturing percolators. In 1880, he invented the glazier point, and the Hubbard and McClary Company was born. Glazier points are small metal triangles inserted into windows ensuring accuracy in the placement of the glass. The workers, who were mostly women, produced up to one ton of points per month in 1881. This was sufficient to glaze 175,012 light windows for 9,000 homes.

—THE—

Windsor Family Scale!

Weighing 15 lbs. by Ounces!

COMBINES DURABILITY, CONVENIENCE & ECONOMY!

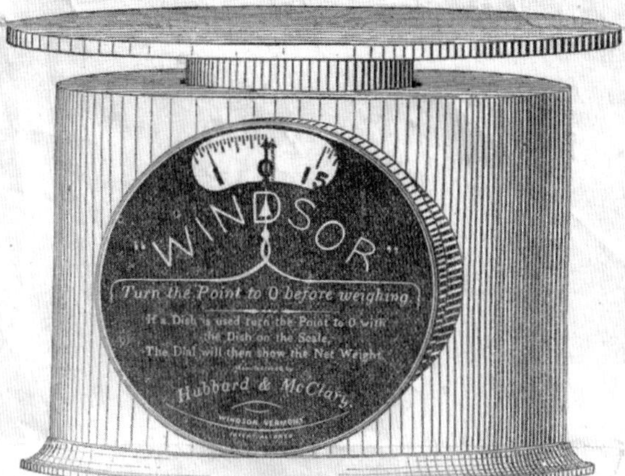

PRICE, $3.00.

WE use in each Scale FIVE thoroughly tested springs, made from the finest steel, which we fully guarantee never to weaken by use. We believe this to be the only scale made in which more than a single spring is employed, and, consequently, that it is the ONLY RELIABLE SPRING SCALE IN MARKET.

Our method of getting NET WEIGHTS is more convenient than any other. By its use a dish may be placed upon the Scale and any number of ingredients mixed in it,—the Scale giving the net weight of each without removing the dish or making any mathematical calculations; thus rendering it a paragon of simplicity and convenience for kitchen use.

THE PRICE is such that any family of moderate means can well afford one. This Scale is carefully constructed of the best material, and will, with proper usage, last a century, hence the real expense amounts to only a few cents each year.

A GOOD SCALE is always a great convenience, and, at times, an actual necessity, in every household. It is used in ordinary cooking; it is used in pie making; it is used in preserving; it is used to prove the honest weights given by grocery and market men, thus often removing unfounded suspicion; it is used to check dishonest weights; it is used for innumerable purposes which will suggest themselves to the mind of every good housekeeper.

MANUFACTURED BY

HUBBARD & MCCLARY, Windsor, Vt.

In addition to percolators, Hubbard and McClary also invented and manufactured the Windsor Family Scale, as seen on this page taken from an 1883 edition of the *Windsor Business Gazetteer*: "The scale, with proper usage will last a century, hence the real expense amounts to only a few cents each year." Another selling feature was that it could be used to check both honest weights and dishonest weights. The ad claimed that it was "A must for every housekeeper."

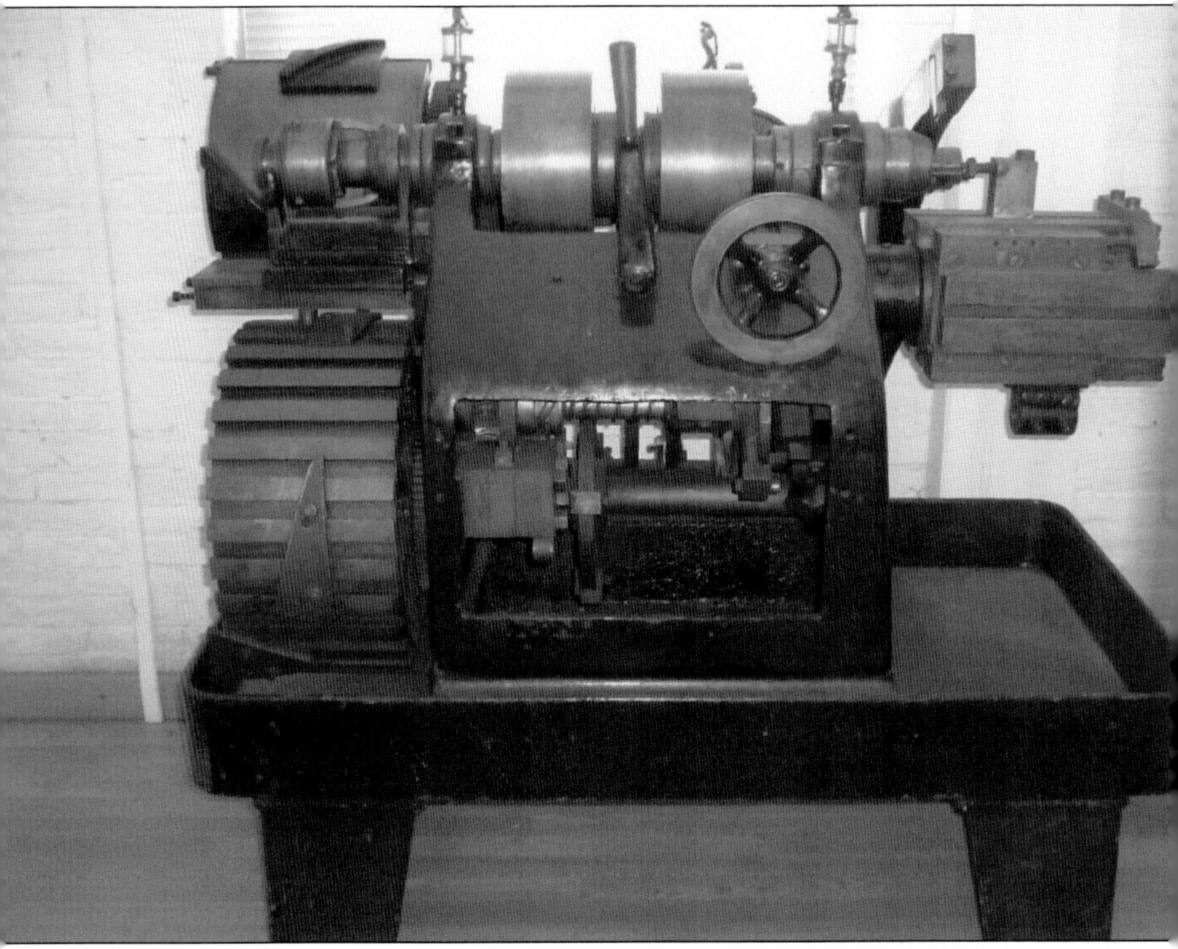

In 1888, in what had been the Robbins and Lawrence factory, George Hubbard founded the Windsor Machine Company. Growing and thriving thanks to an influx of funds from Windsor lawyer Gilbert Davis, the company prospered until it was forced to shut down during the Panic of 1893. Several years later, George O. Gridley arrived on the scene with a focus of creating an automatic lathe. By 1898, he had designed and perfected this concept with the help of Frank L. Cone. In 1904, the Gridley Single Spindle Automatic Lathe was finalized and closely resembles what is still in use today. At that time, Maxwell Evarts invested in the company and became its president, which allowed the Windsor Machine Company to thrive once again.

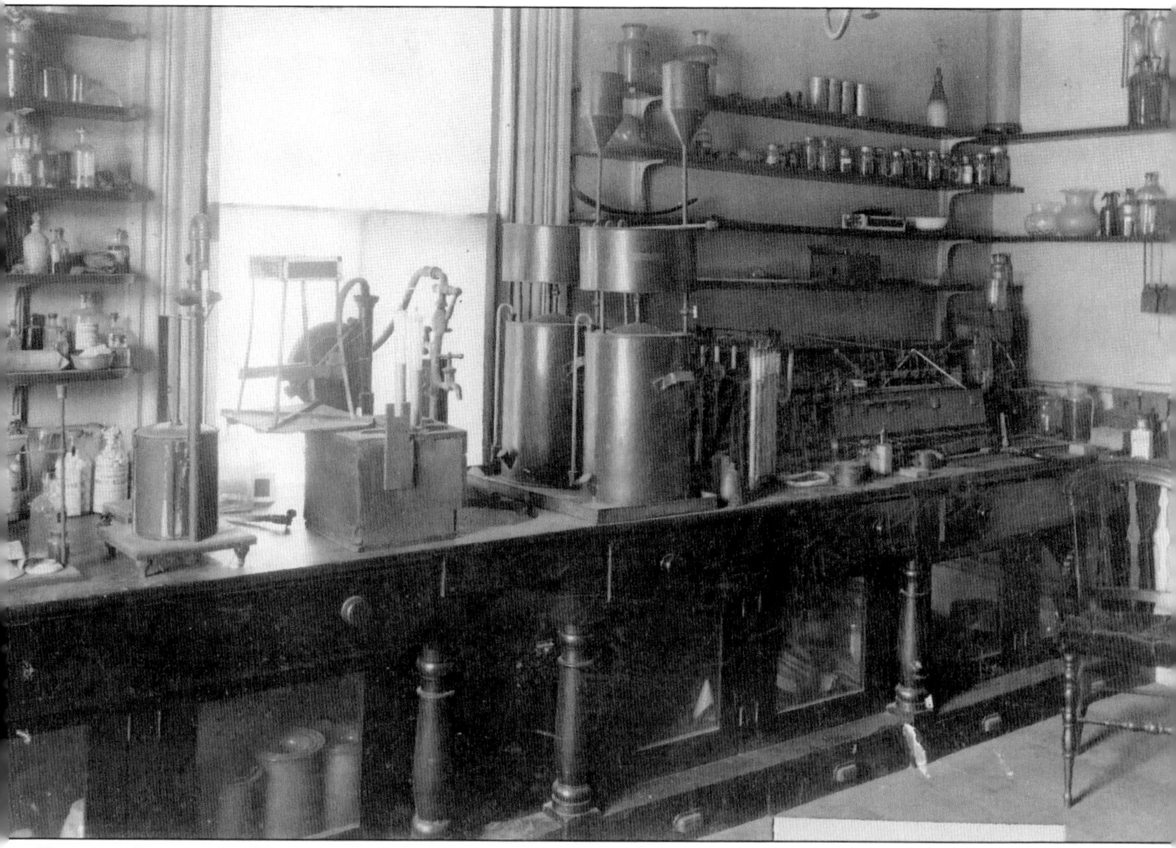

During this time of heavy manufacturing, other interesting things were taking place up the street. In 1849, Col. M.K. Paine founded a drug company in his laboratory on State Street. He collaborated with Dr. Edward Phelps and created the famed celery compound. The best known of his many remedies, he guaranteed it to aid "nervous disease, neuralgia, rheumatism, nervous debility, paralysis, biliousness, dyspepsia, piles, liver complaint, all kidney troubles, female complaints and all diseases arising from an impure state of the blood."

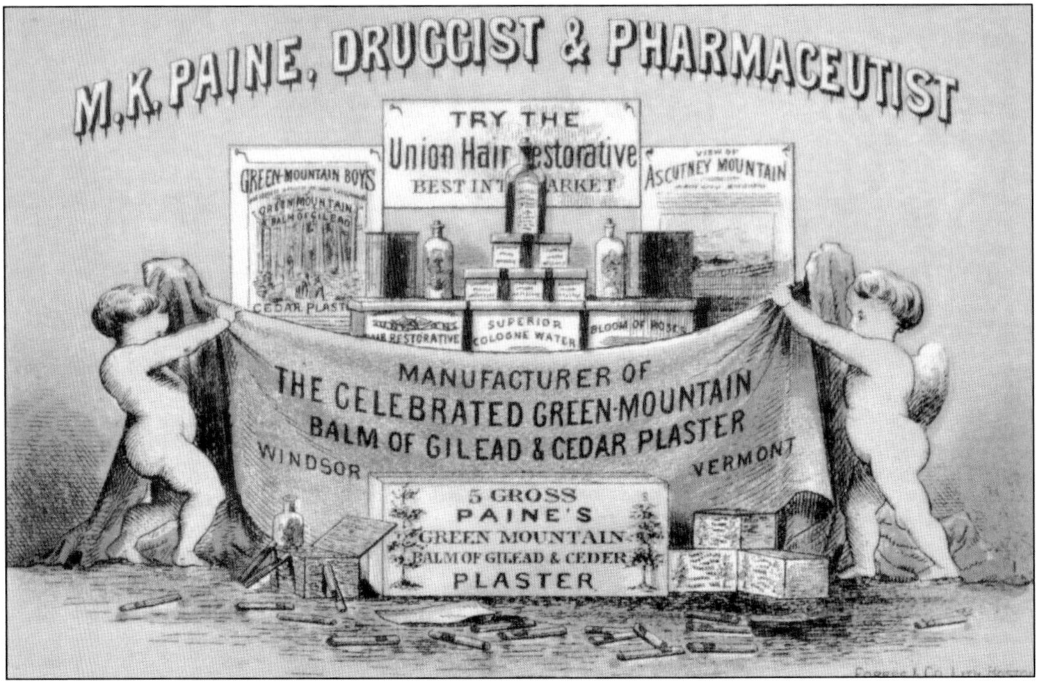

A significant number of Windsor residents swore by Paine's celery compound, the ingredients of which were listed as lupulin, buchu, dandelion, sarsaparilla, pipsissewa, mandrake, rhubarb, gentian, coca, ginger, chamomile, canella, columbo, prickly ash, yellow dock, and, of course, celery seed. In truth, it was 20 percent grain alcohol, but it made Colonel Paine one of the richest men in Vermont.

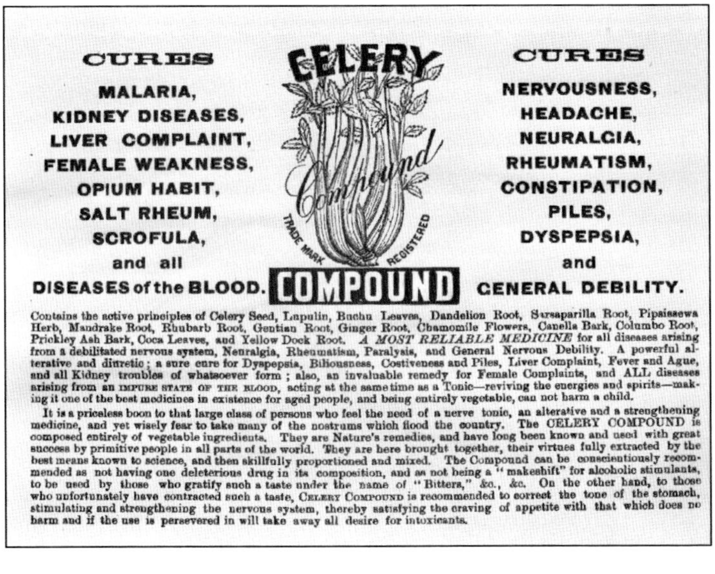

William Wells manufactured Paine's celery compound in Burlington, Vermont. Wells's daughter Bertha married Dr. Horatio Nelson Jackson in 1899. It is assumed it was her money that funded what is known as America's first road trip. Jackson crossed the country in a 1903 Winton automobile named *Vermont* accompanied by a co-driver, Sewall Crocker, a mechanic, and a wonderful pug named Bud.

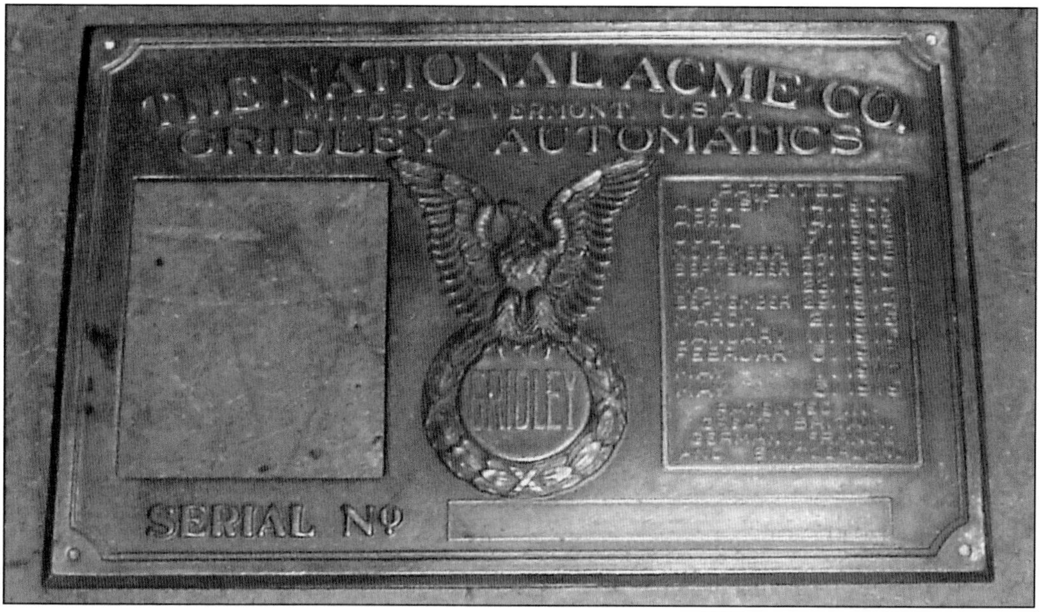

Looking ahead at manufacturing in the early 20th century brings one back to the brick buildings on Main Street. The Windsor Machine Company, located on Union Street, is where Frank Cone began his career. In 1902, when Maxwell Evarts became one of the company's primary investors, the value of its stock increased tenfold. The National Acme Corporation, or NAMCO, then purchased it. It was NAMCO that propelled Windsor to the forefront of the precision tool and manufacturing industries.

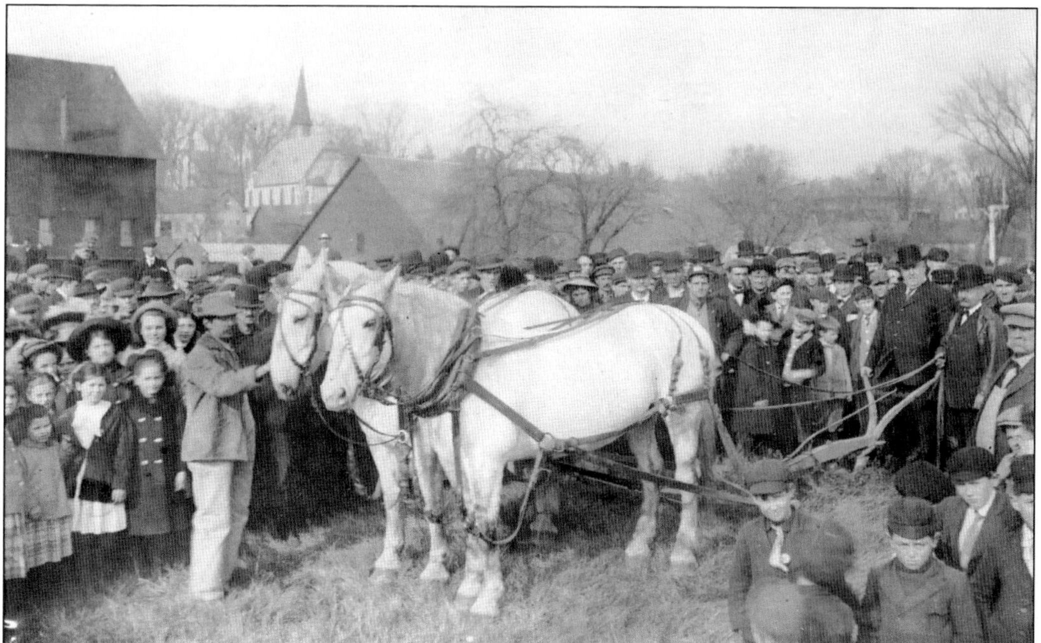

Breaking ground for the new building to house the Windsor Machine Company are Maxwell Evarts holding the reigns, Charles Moore at the plow, and Frank Cone looking on. On November 15, 1909, it was still warm enough to break ground.

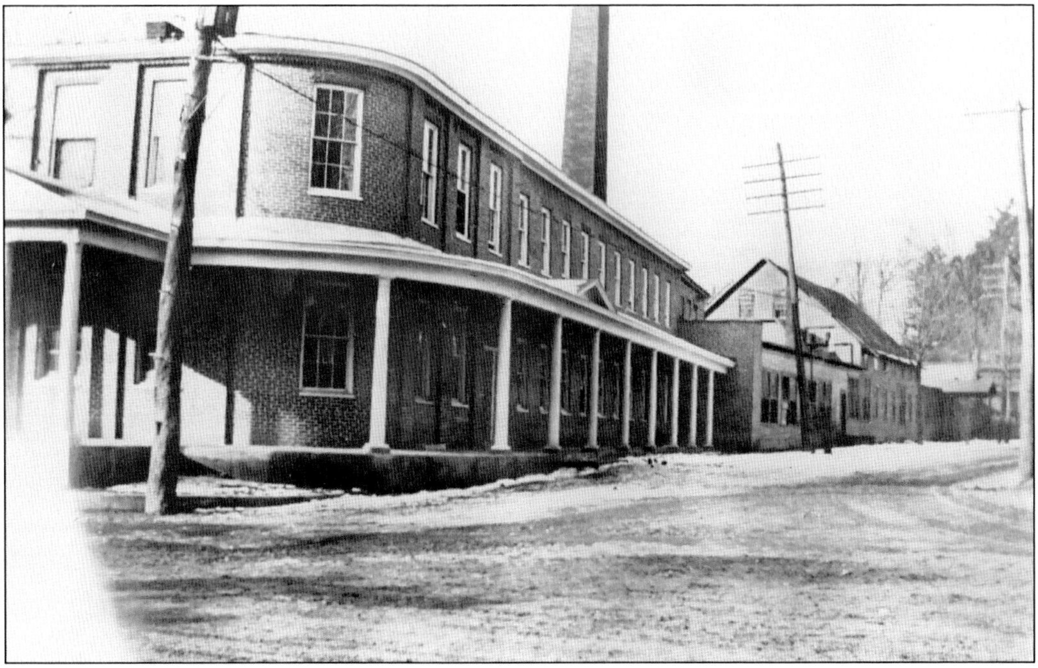

As the National Acme Corporation outgrew its location, the building became the Windsor Club. Founded in 1914, it offered amenities such as a bowling alley, a pool hall, and an elegant dining room for its workers. Dinner was served on white tablecloths every evening.

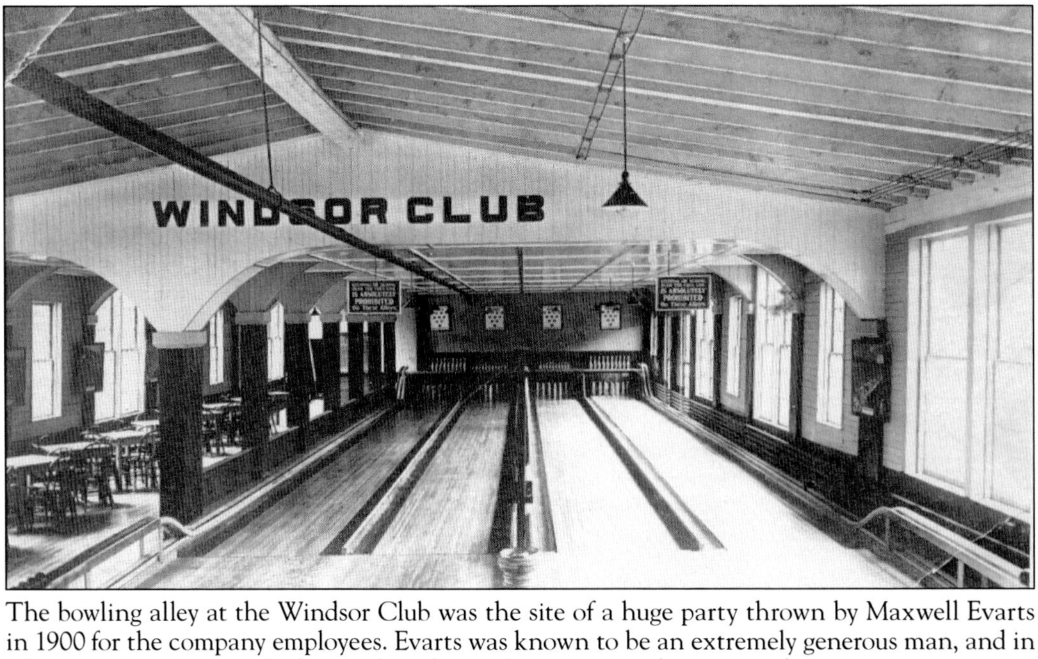

The bowling alley at the Windsor Club was the site of a huge party thrown by Maxwell Evarts in 1900 for the company employees. Evarts was known to be an extremely generous man, and in addition to his concern for his workers, he made great contributions to the community.

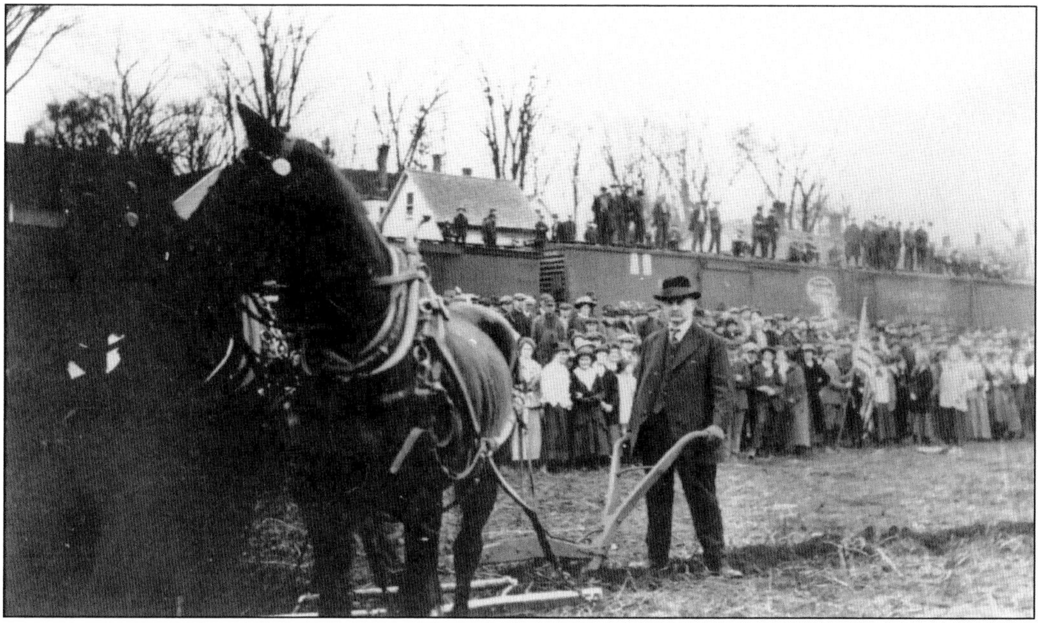

Having begun his career in the back rooms of the Windsor Machine Company, Frank L. Cone grew and prospered both as an innovator and a businessman. Above, he is pictured breaking ground for the Cone Automatic Machine Company in April 1916. The company was formally incorporated in August of that year, later being known as Cone-Blanchard. The Cone factory is pictured below as it looked the 1940s.

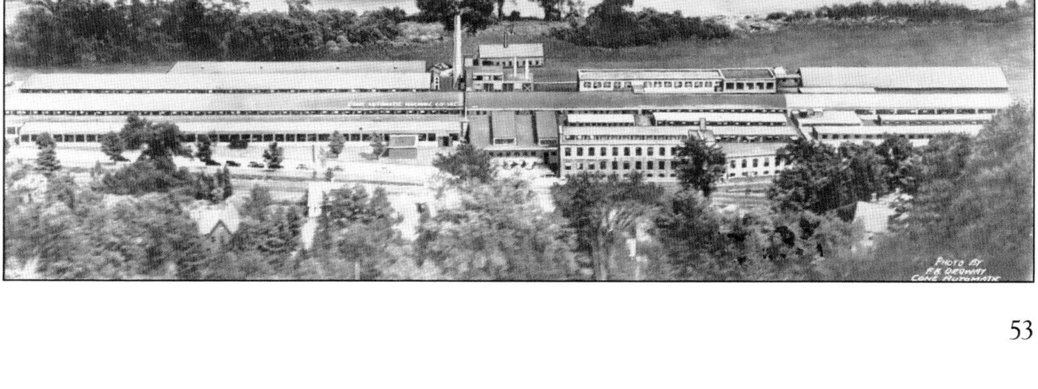

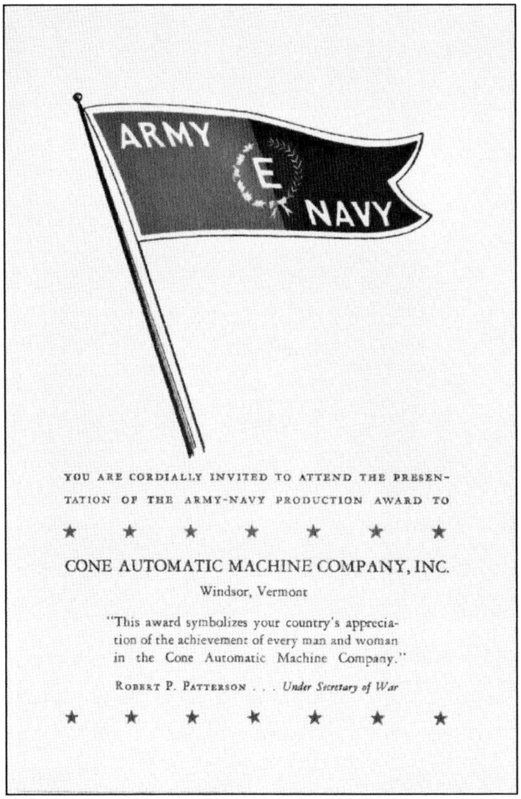
ARMY E NAVY

YOU ARE CORDIALLY INVITED TO ATTEND THE PRESENTATION OF THE ARMY-NAVY PRODUCTION AWARD TO

★ ★ ★ ★ ★ ★ ★

CONE AUTOMATIC MACHINE COMPANY, INC.

Windsor, Vermont

"This award symbolizes your country's appreciation of the achievement of every man and woman in the Cone Automatic Machine Company."

ROBERT P. PATTERSON . . . *Under Secretary of War*

★ ★ ★ ★ ★ ★ ★

On Tuesday, August 25, 1942, the Cone Automatic Machine Factory was presented with the Army-Navy Production Award. Presented to them by Under-Secretary of War Robert P. Patterson, it expressed the country's appreciation to every man and woman for their services. It was a very high honor given only to those who exhibited exceptional performance. There were many speeches and addresses, the raising of the flag, and then a performance by the Cone Automatic Machine Company Band.

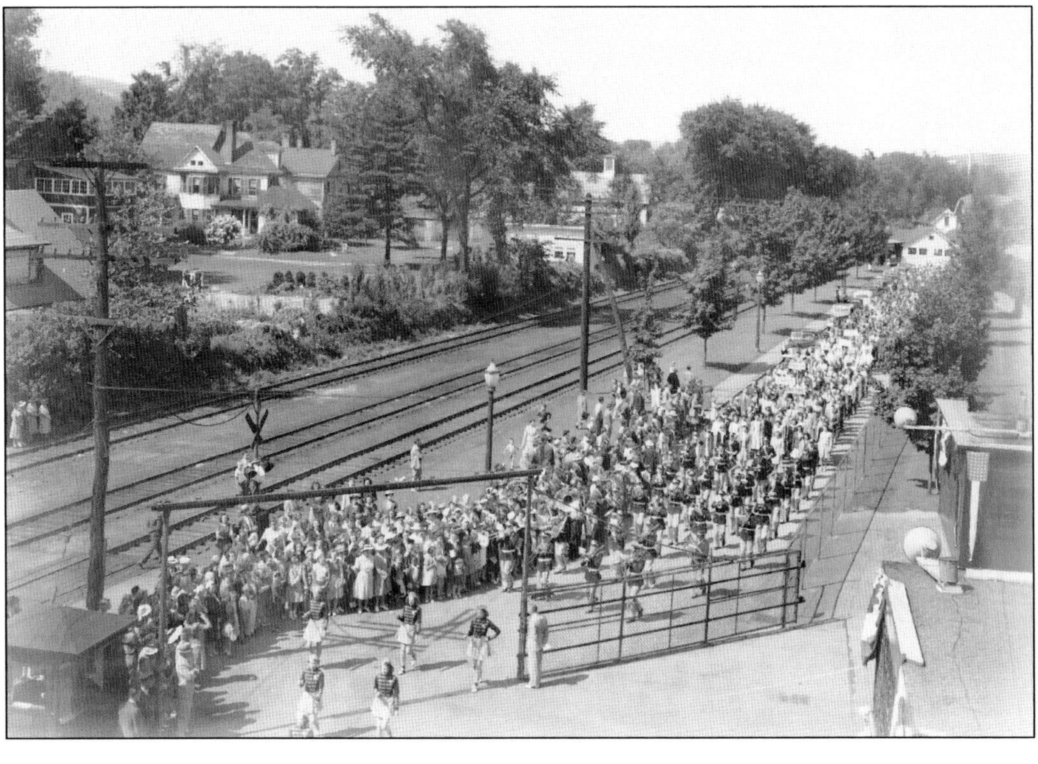

This 1953 photograph was published in the Labor Day edition of the Cone Automatic company newsletter. Walter Dewey, age 81 at the time the photograph was taken, was born in 1872. He worked in a variety of jobs at Cone before being promoted to foreman of the casting department, holding that position for 22 years.

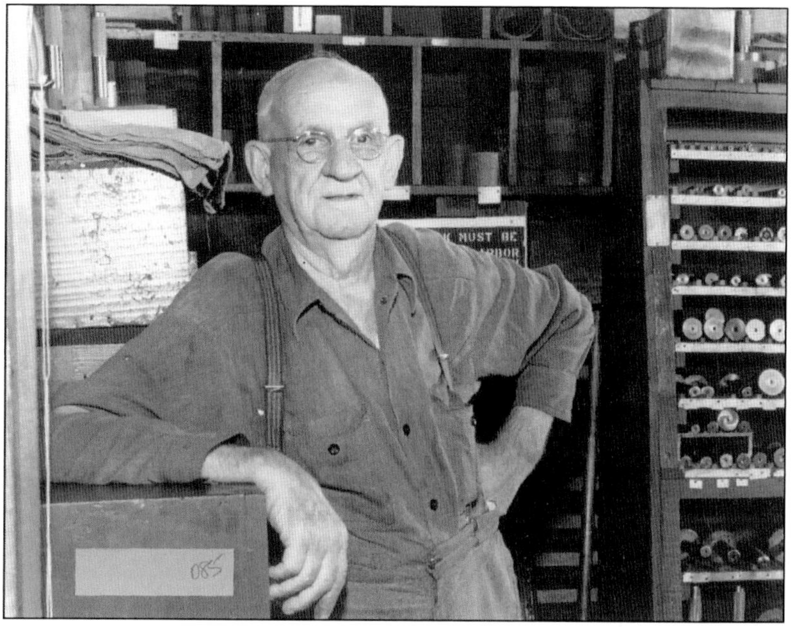

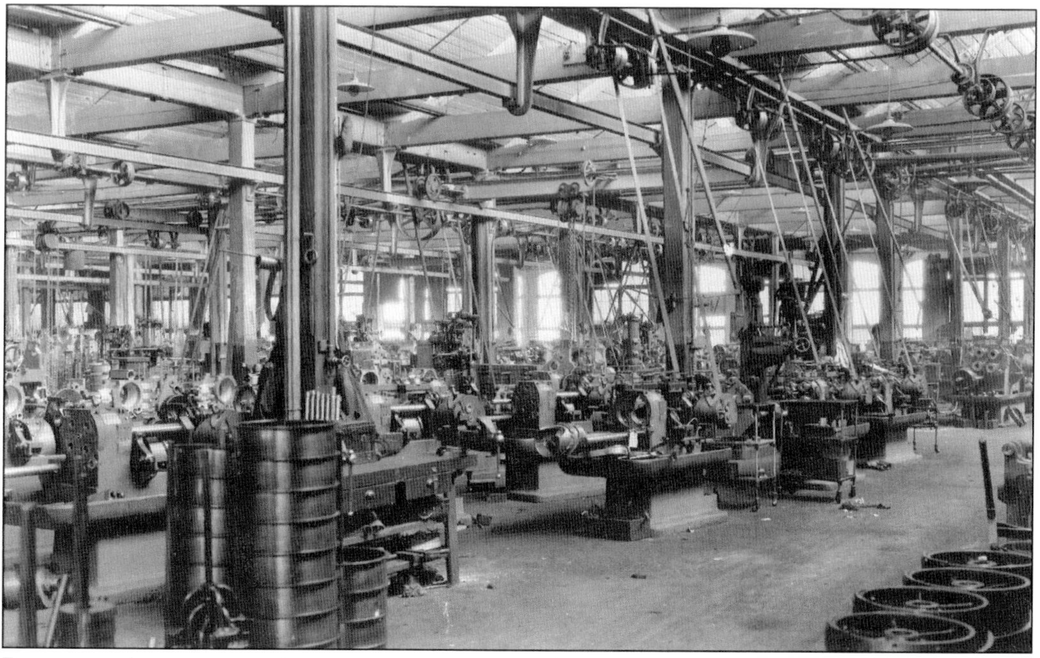

Dewey was later promoted to another position in the grinding department. The caption to the newsletter photograph read, "Mr. Dewey, you are an inspiration to every man and woman employed at Cone's. The youngsters in the plant could achieve greater heights by following your footsteps and using your record of achievement as a beacon to their own future." Word is that he spent many happy years in this grinding room.

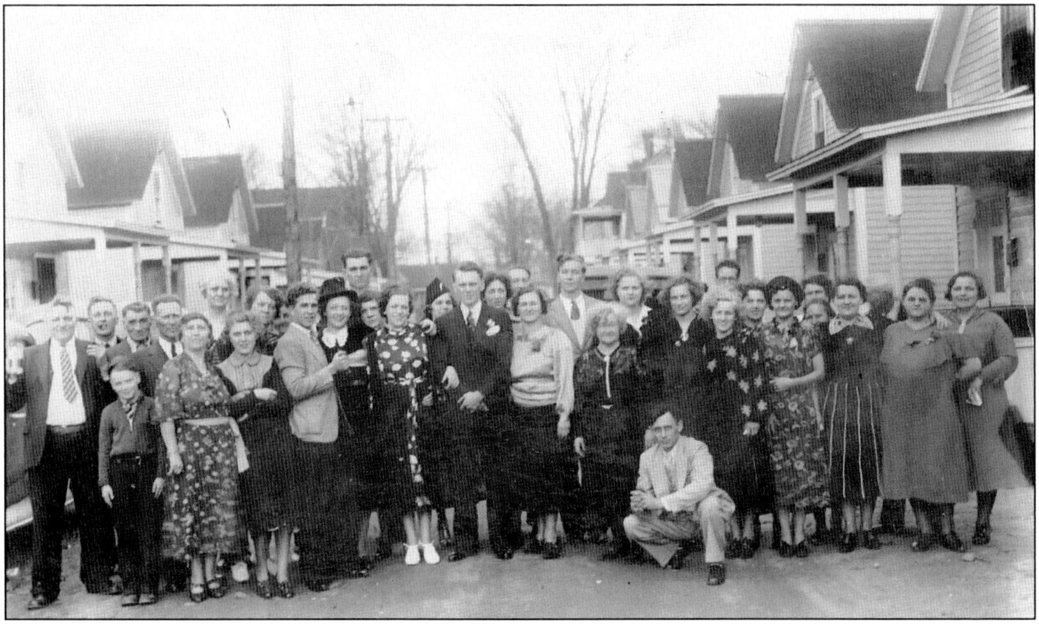

As workers immigrated to America, many chose to settle together in areas where they could find work. Called "Little Warsaw," these homes were built to house the Cone factory workers, many of whom came from Poland. Pictured is a traditional Polish wedding celebration on Jarvis Street in 1937. In attendance were Joe White, John Haurelick, and Kay Puskta, who later married Joe White.

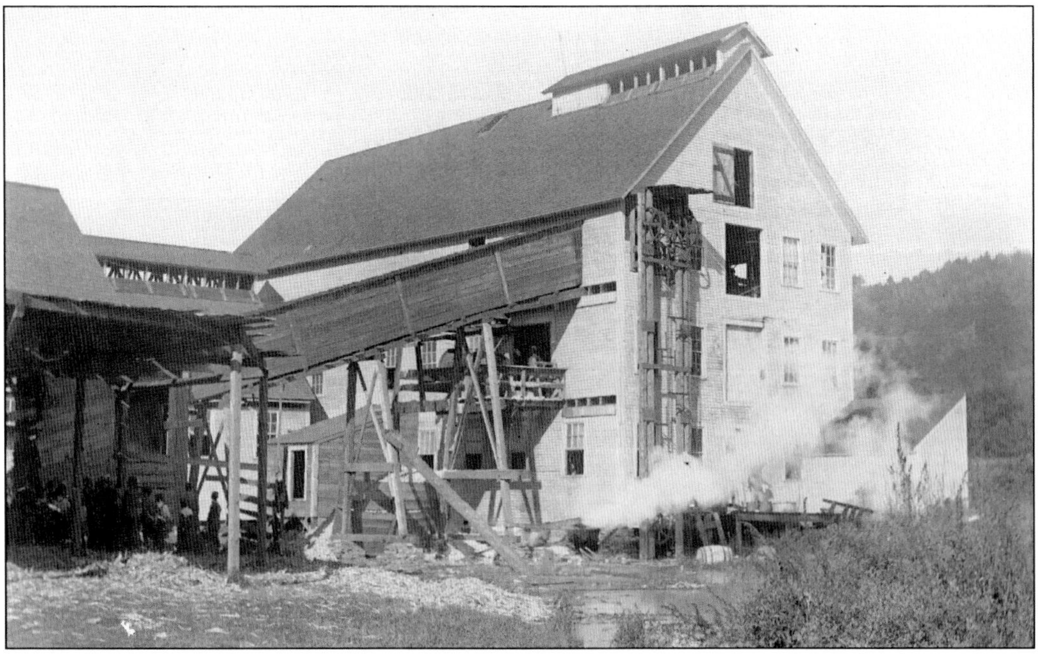

The Windsor canning factory, which operated from 1895 to 1932, was said to be the largest of its kind in the world. The complex consisted of four buildings and gave local farmers a profitable outlet for their significant corn harvests. In August 1905, the factory was producing 40,000 cans per day. In one month, a total of 720,000 cans of a variety of vegetables were produced.

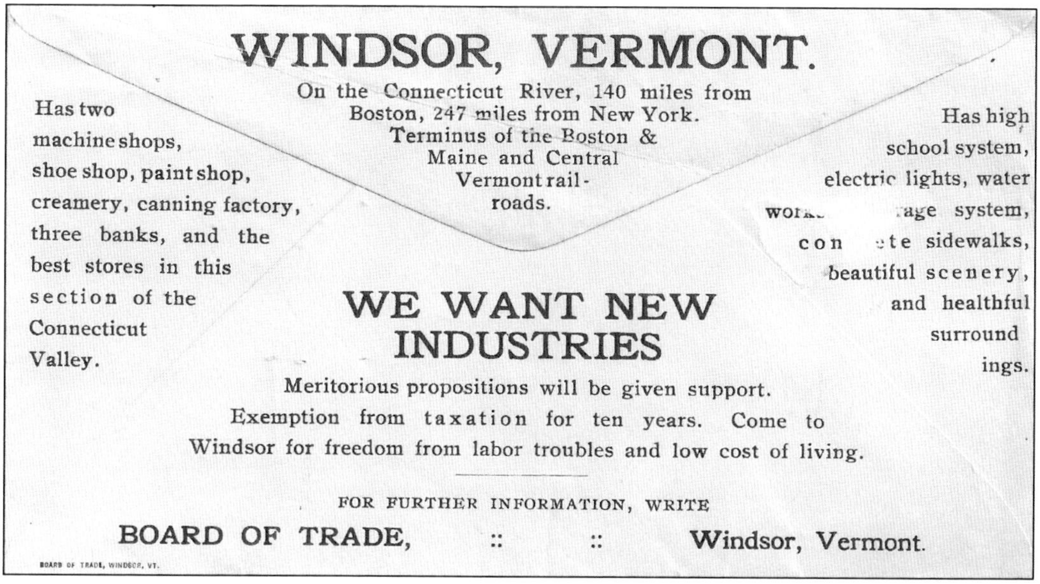

Then as now, towns in Vermont were hoping to attract new businesses, both by drawing attention to amenities available in town and by highlighting features and benefits of doing business there. In this case, a bit of humor was used to draw attention to the desire and need for new industries. It must have worked, as industries from shoe and scale manufacturing to canning and machine industries all came to town in the 19th and first half of the 20th centuries.

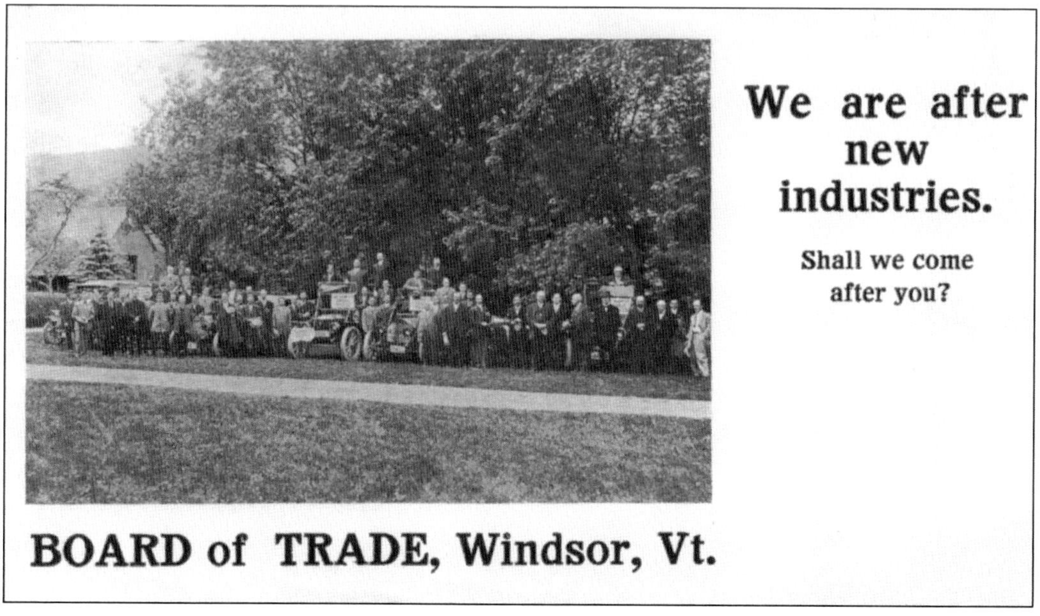

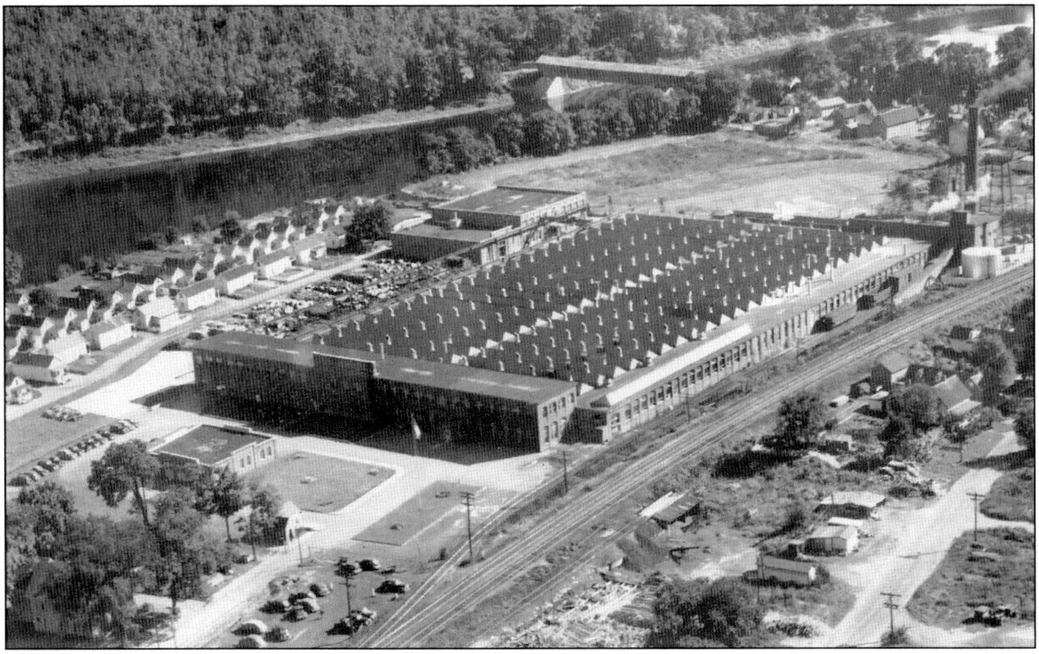

Goodyear Tire and Rubber moved to Windsor in 1936. The initial hiring rate was 25¢ per hour, though wages steadily increased. World War II created a surge in the need for Goodyear's products. Half of their production was devoted to rubber heels and soles for paratroopers' boots. They also produced 100,000 inflatable life vests and two million breather tubes for gas masks. Hard times fell upon Windsor when Goodyear closed its doors in 1986.

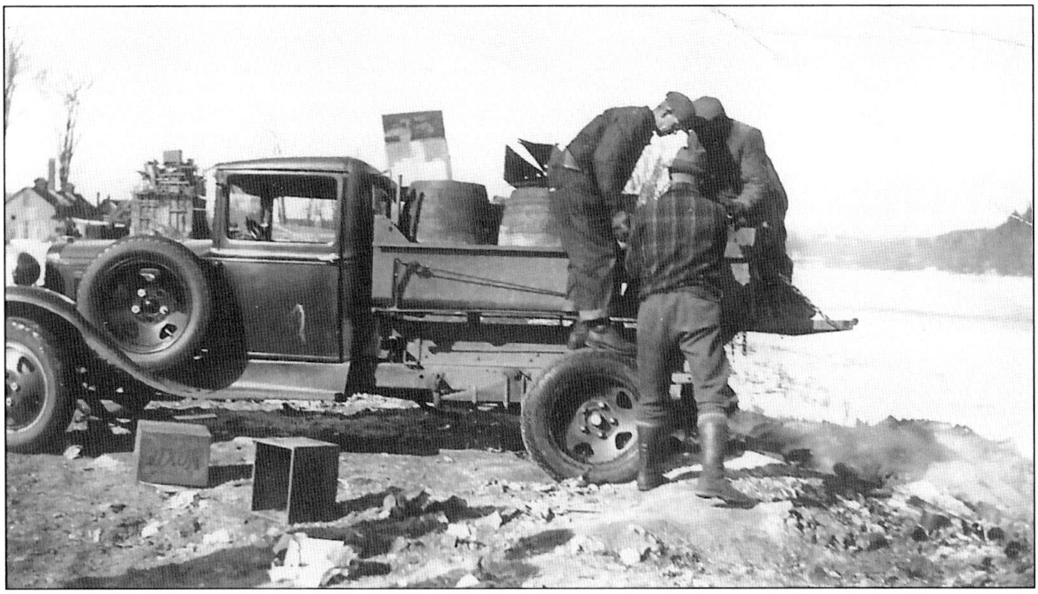

A more notorious sort of manufacturing also occurred in Windsor. During Prohibition, just as in many other parts of America, people experimented with homemade wines made from practically anything they could harvest. Others contented themselves with classic bathtub gin, while the affluent procured their alcohol from Canada. Pictured are several employees of William Ayers dumping moonshine into the Connecticut River.

Five

"I LOVE A PARADE" AND THE MERCHANTS OF MAIN STREET

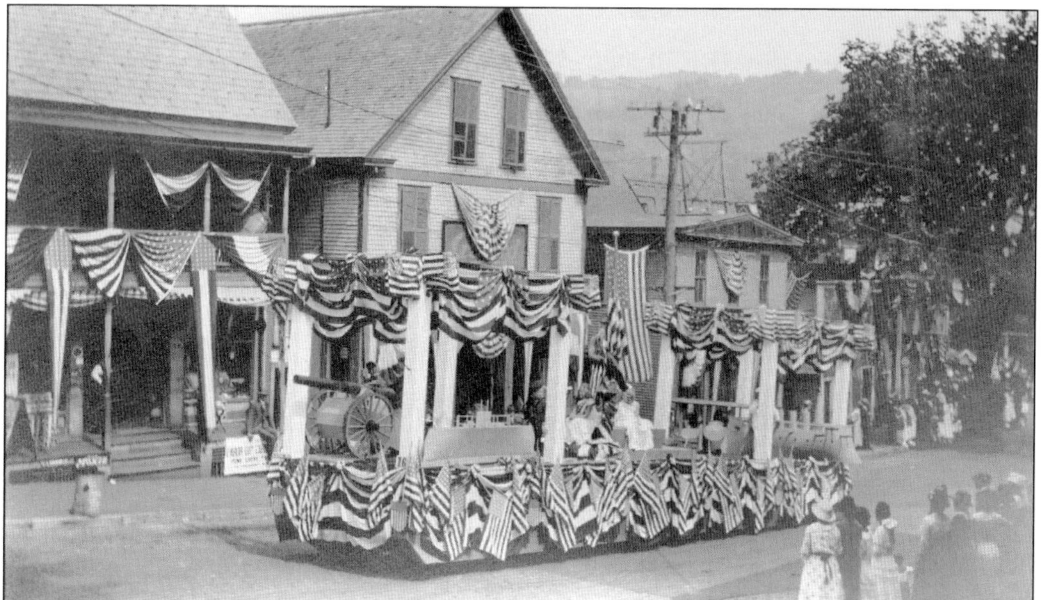

The Pageant of the Allies was the focal point of Windsor's Welcome Home Day celebration for veterans of World War I. On August 16, 1919, nine months after the signing of the treaty to end the war, the daylong program began with reveille at 7:00 a.m. and the Windsor military band performance at 9:00 a.m. The crowd looks on as a float makes its way up State Street.

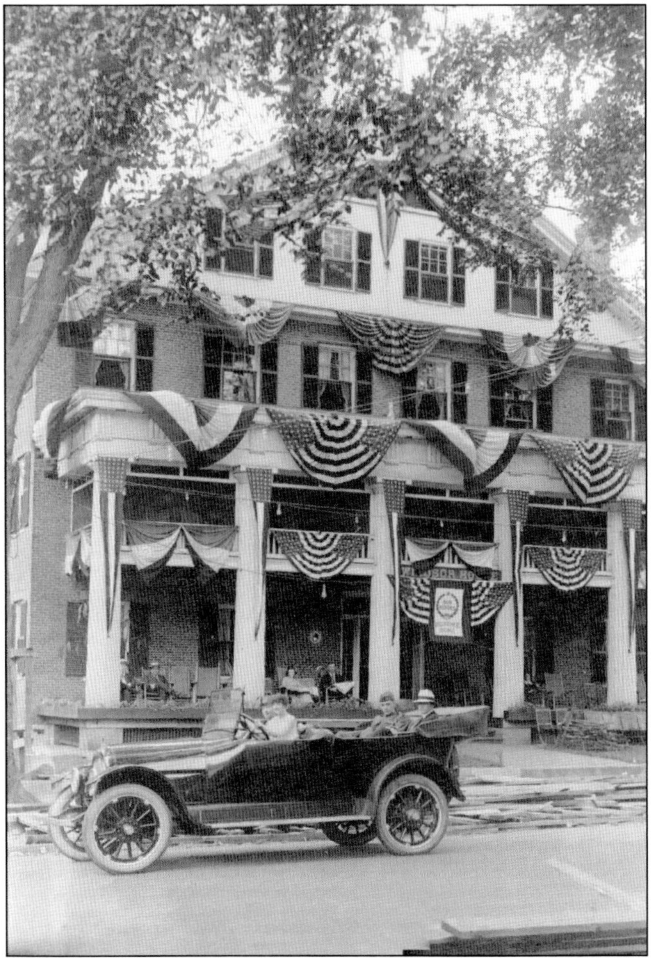

Heading up the welcome home parade for the veterans of World War I is the lead car, driven by a woman! James Dewey, resident architect at the National Machine Company plant, designed the large white arch. Each float and participant in the parade passed through this grand entrance, like a halo consecrating the joyous procession heading towards Main Street.

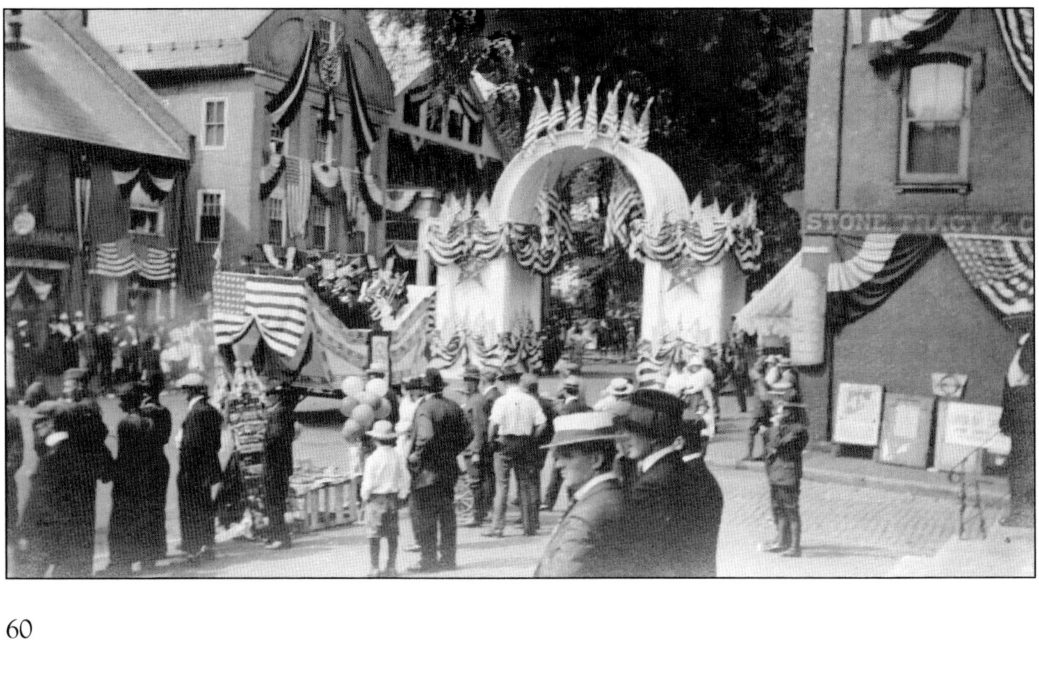

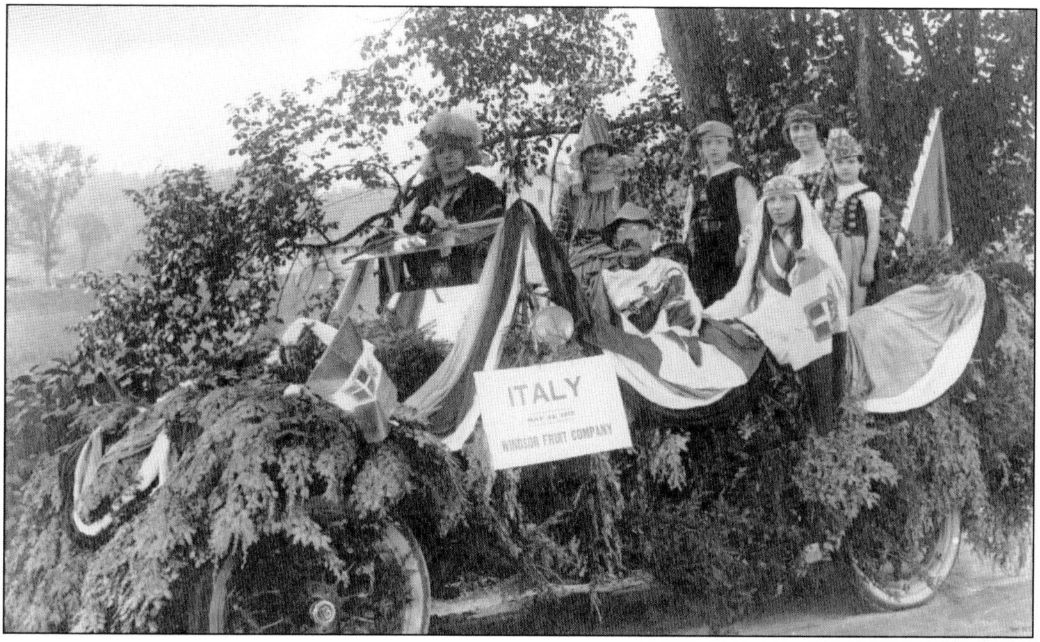

The Bianchi family, who owned the Bianchi Fruit Company, sponsored the Italy float. Louie Bianchi is driving with his wife, Ermina (sitting second from right), and their daughter Mina (far right). Their prominent family marker on the hill in the Ascutney Cemetery is carved and adorned with lush fruits and vegetables, the icons of the family business.

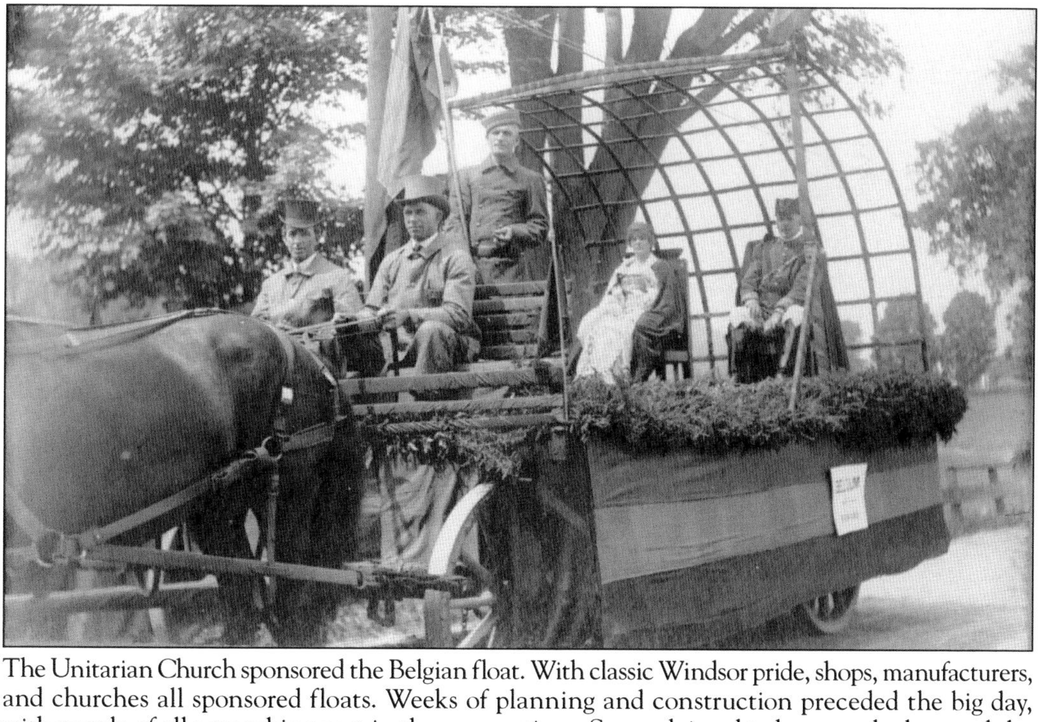

The Unitarian Church sponsored the Belgian float. With classic Windsor pride, shops, manufacturers, and churches all sponsored floats. Weeks of planning and construction preceded the big day, with people of all ages taking part in the preparations. Some claimed to have worked around the clock to complete their contributions.

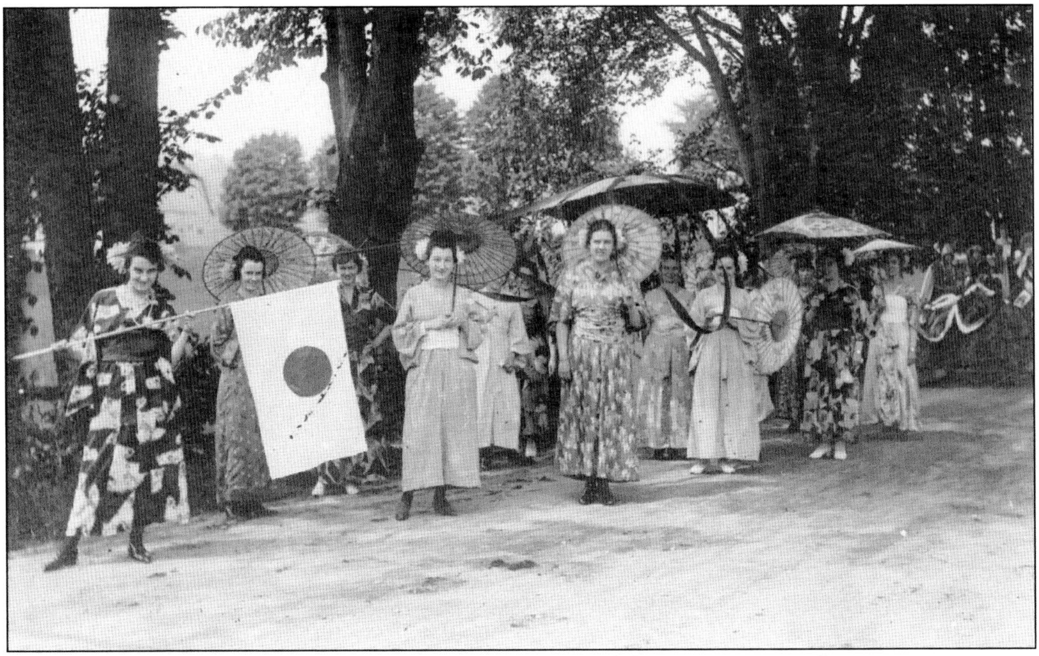

The Unitarian Junior Alliance sponsored the float celebrating Japan. These women are an example of the great effort that went into the parade. The attempt at accurately representing the costumes of each nation for this huge celebration kept needles stitching for weeks before the big day. Everyone's talents were employed, and the event was talked about for months.

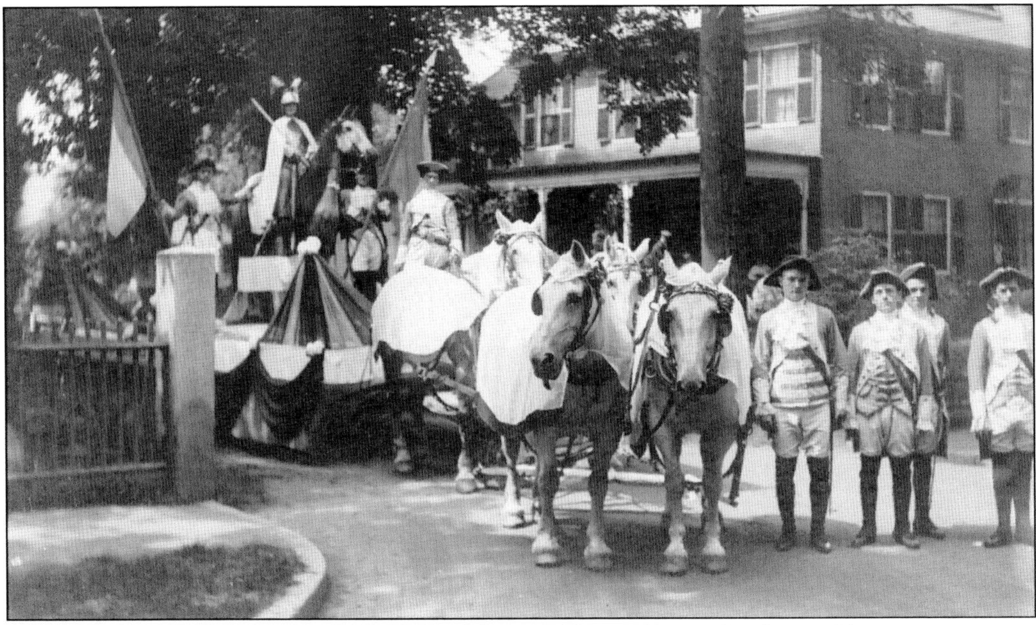

The Catholic Church presented the float celebrating France. Dressed as Joan of Arc, townswoman Louise Costello sat proudly atop the horse in the French procession. The day continued with a luncheon for the veterans, a meeting of the Windsor Post of The American Legion, a baseball game between Windsor and the neighboring town of Claremont, and finally a street dance that lasted well into the evening.

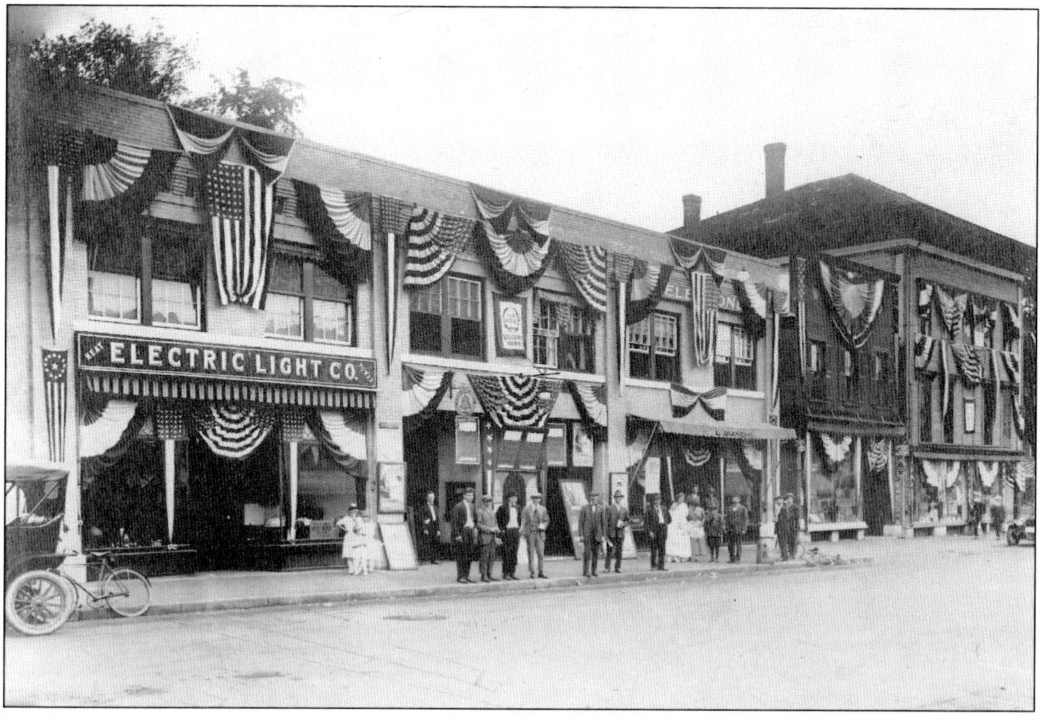

In a long shot looking North, a bedecked Main Street embraces the shops and shopkeepers lining up to view another of the many parades that made their way through the center of town. The new electric company, Bell Telephone, and the Bianchi Fruit Company filled the storefronts. James Conlin and James Callan were the proprietors of the corner store at the intersection of Bridge and Main Streets.

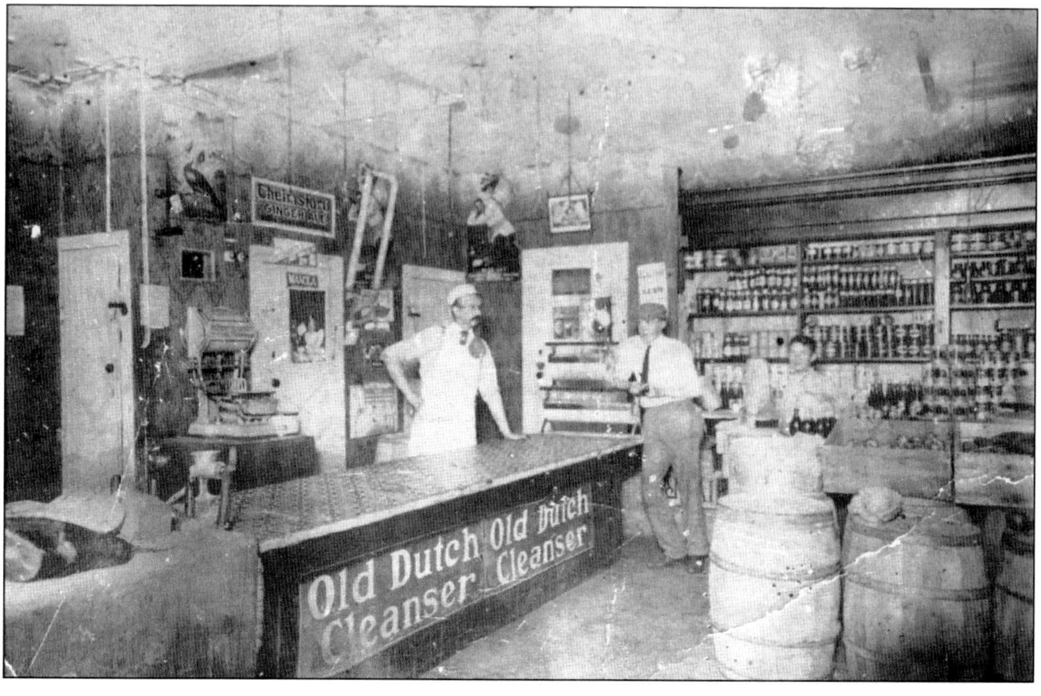

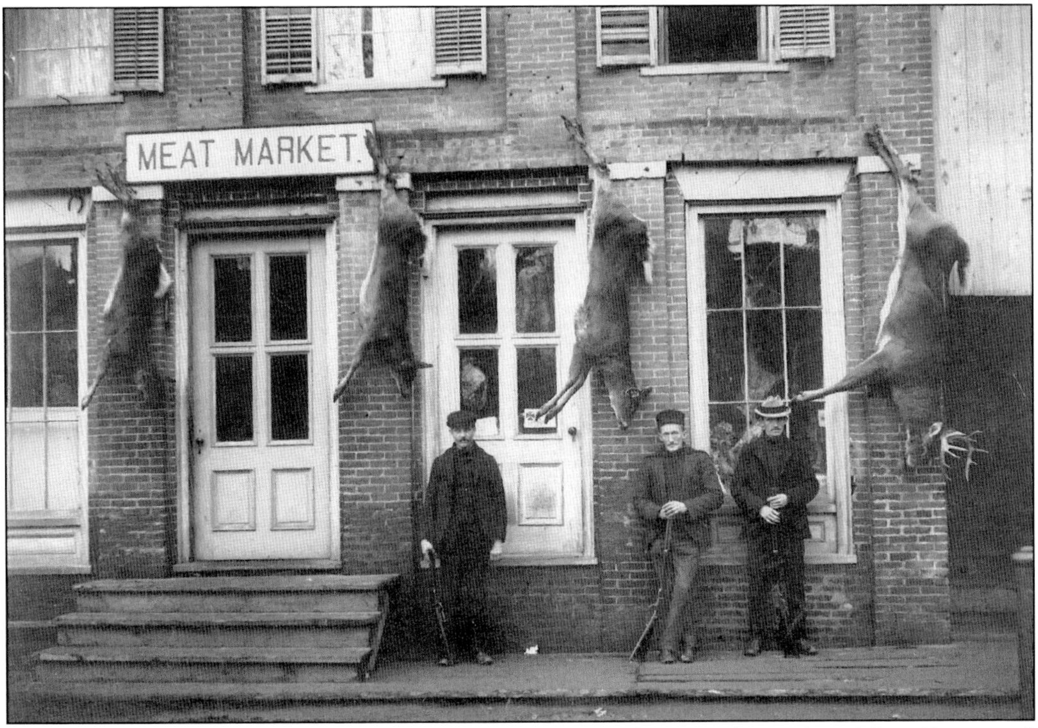

The Windsor Market, also known as the Jarvis Meat Market, was located on Main Street and owned by Peter Jarvis. Customers knew that the meat was fresh, as the "catch of the day" was sometimes exhibited outside the shop. Local farms provided the pork, lamb, and beef, while local hunters were the source for venison. Below, as one of the Jarvis Market wagons stops at the top of Union Street, he meets a customer and makes a delivery. Barely two blocks from the location of the shop, deliveries of this kind provided the personalized customer service that was a hallmark of conducting a proper business in Windsor.

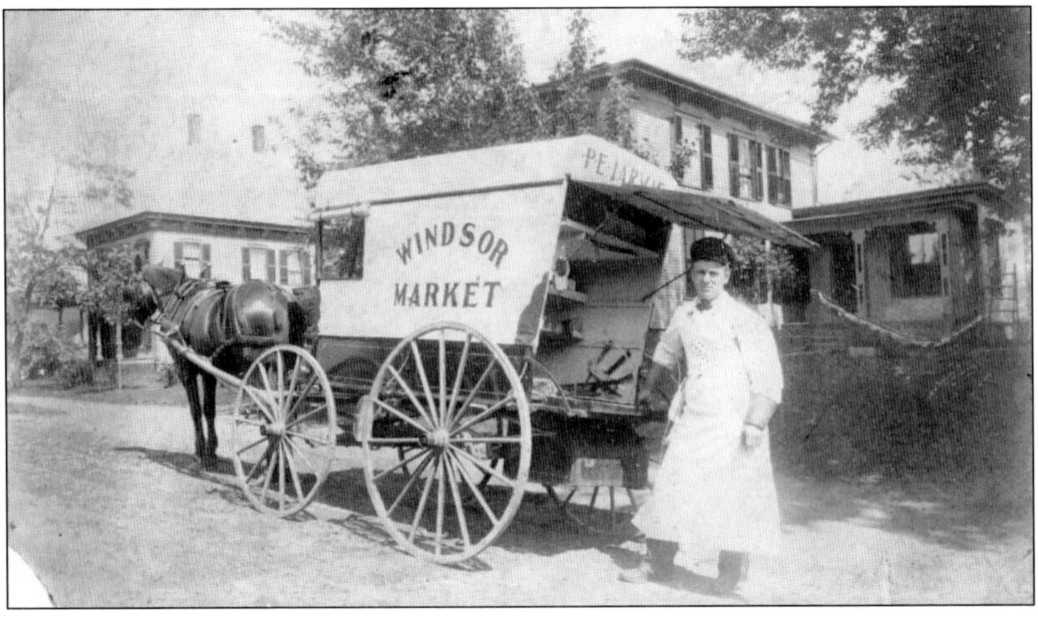

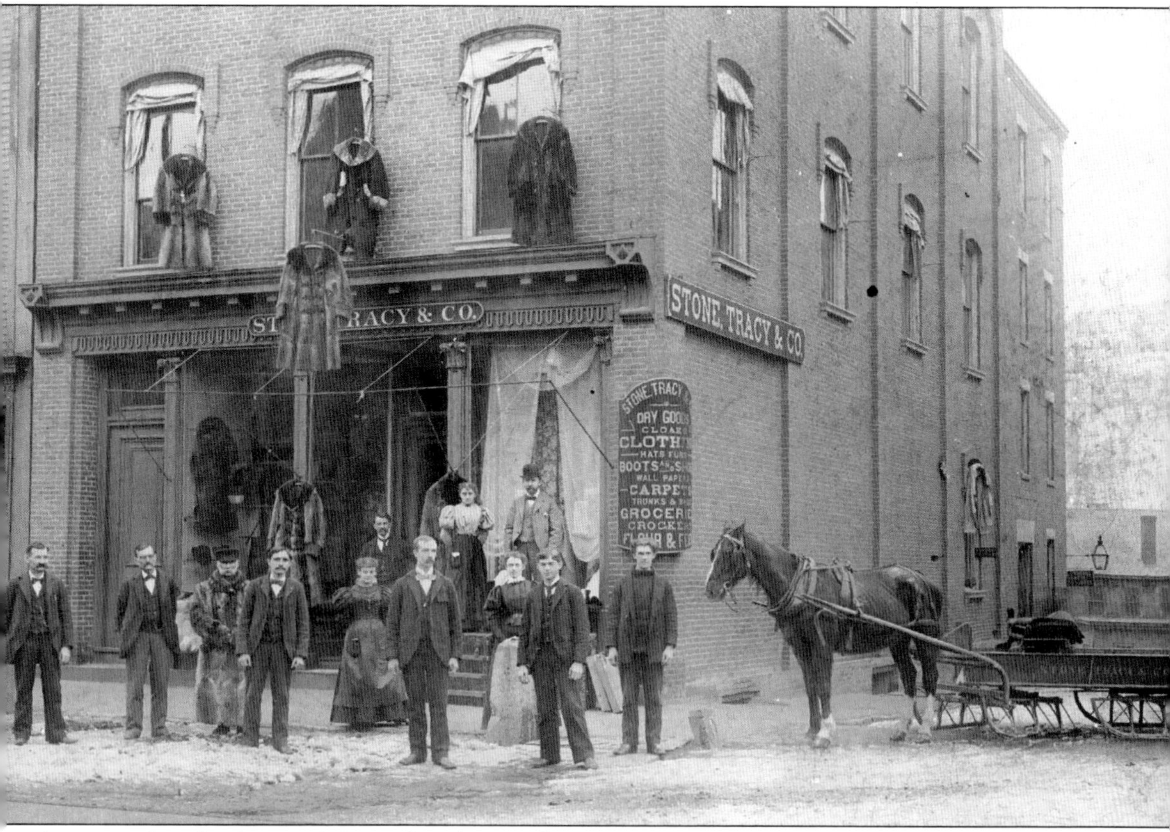

A notice placed in *Spooner's Journal* read, "Windsor Store For Hats Samuel Patrick Jr. begs leave to inform his friends, customers, and the public that he has just received from Boston a fashionable and elegant assortment of Gentlemen's superfine and first quality BEAVER HATS together with a variety of Ladies BEAVER BONNETS of the latest fashions with elegant trimming for the same; consisting of black and drab Ostrich Plumes, Gimp &c &c. He has on hand an exclusive assortment of castor, knap'd & felt HATS for men and boys; all of which are made of the best stock, and will be sold very cheap for cash, fur, country produce, or on a liberal credit. Please to call at his old stand next door south of Patrick's Tavern in Windsor. (Monday, 19 Oct., 1818)." Similar merchant traditions continued through the 1800s.

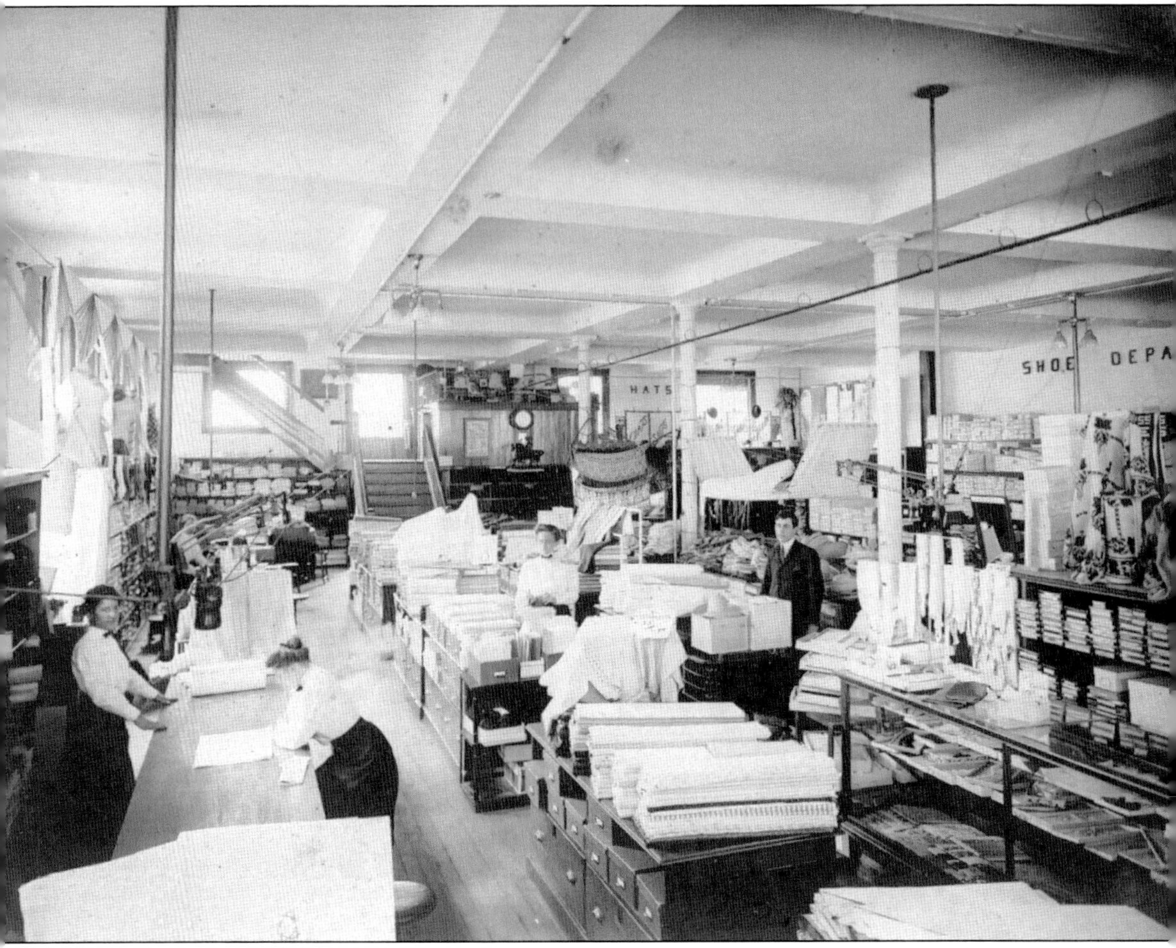

Tuxbury and Stone was a first-class department store that opened on Main Street in 1887. Occupying two floors and a basement, it sold dry goods, men's and women's clothes, shoes, groceries, household items, and furnishings such as furniture, carpet, and wallpaper. It later became Fowle and Brown, followed by Fowle and Johnson, as family members bought and sold their partnerships in the business. The Stone-Tracy Block, which still occupies its place on Main Street, was another dry goods store just to the right of Tuxbury and Stone. A little neighborly competition never hurt, as the succession of stores passed through several generations. Names, provisions, and offerings changed through the years, but the one constant was the family of merchants dedicated to supplying quality goods to the town. Today, the interior retains the original balcony, bead board, and exquisite details.

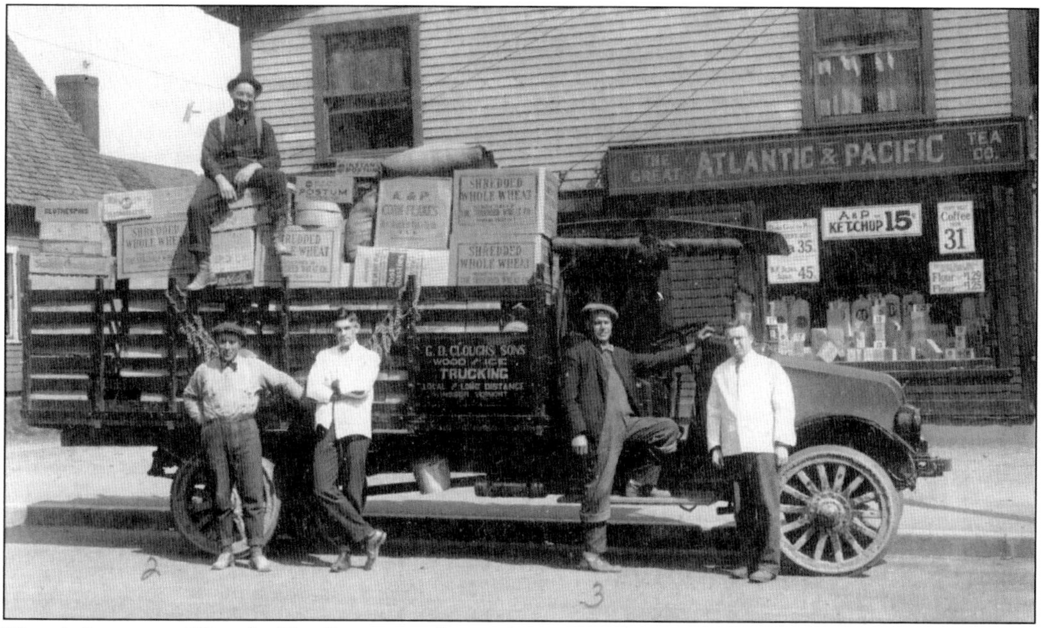

The Atlantic and Pacific Tea Company, better known as the A&P, occupied a space at the south end of Main Street not far from the Windsor-Cornish Covered Bridge. Eric Clough is seen on top of the delivery wagon, with Joe Marcott on the left, and Ed Harding third from left.

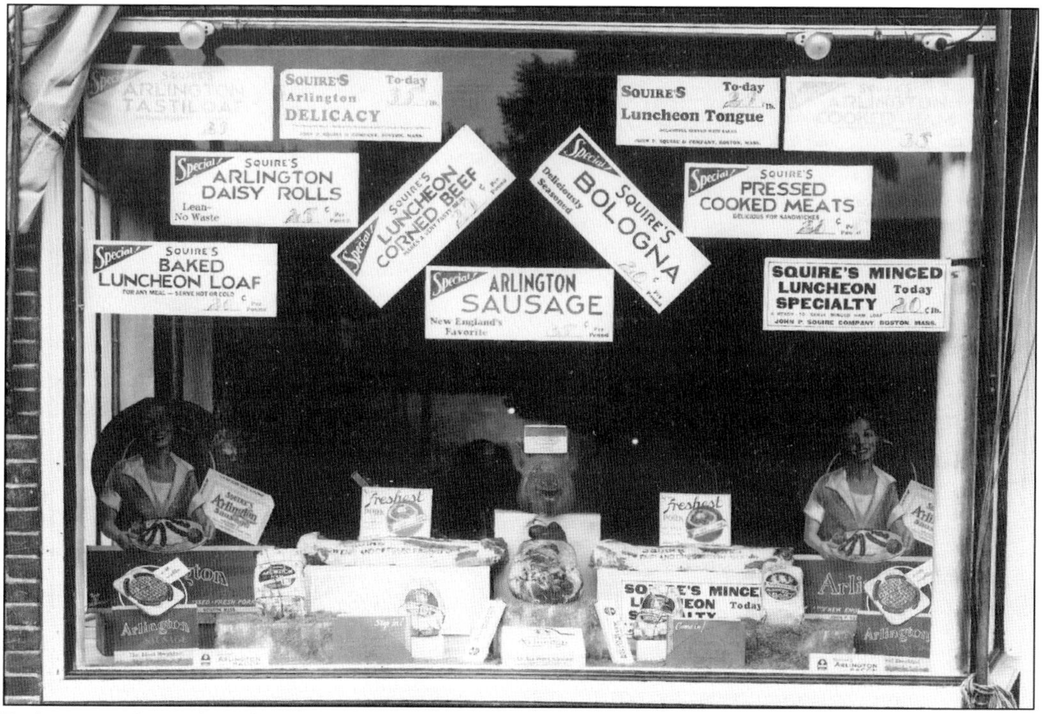

Delicacies abound as the groceries of the day are advertised in the shop windows. Merchants enthusiastically embraced the new style of graphics and images, which are now thought of as classic American design. There were many mouths to feed and much money to be made during the prosperous times enjoyed by Windsor in the early 20th century.

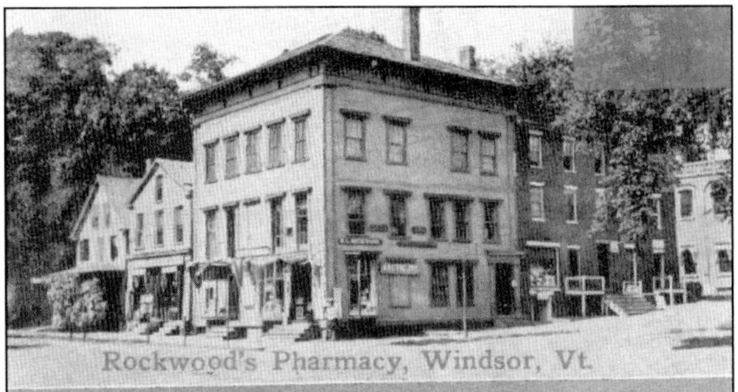

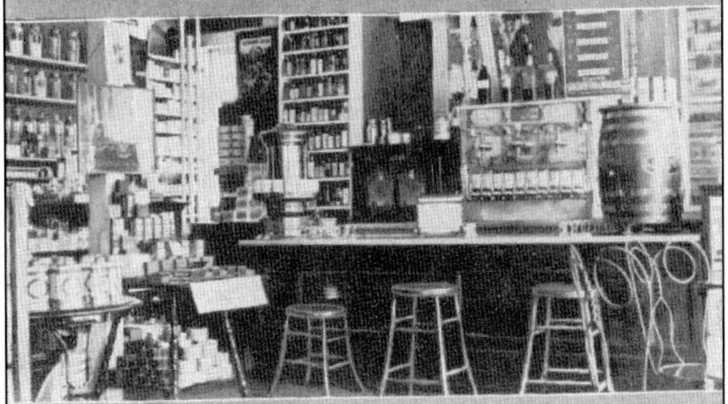

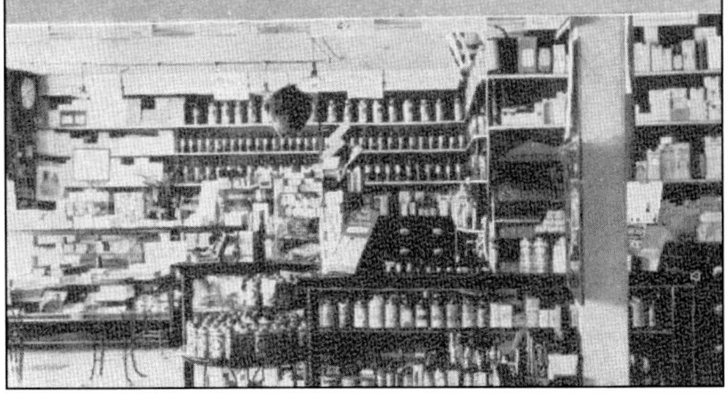

Dr. Joseph Stiles most likely built his pharmacy during the 1870s or 1880s and continued to run it until it changed hands. Purchased by Gilbert Davis, the name changed to the Davis block. Mr. H. Rockwood succeeded Dr. Stiles, garnering praise for his high quality offerings and custom compounding abilities. It passed through several hands before being purchased by Tom and Mary Kelly in the early 1940s. Kelly's grandnephew Ted White owned it until it was destroyed by fire in 1990.

Merchants in the 1950s included Cinderella's Spa (under the awnings), which was a favorite soda fountain and bakery, and Myers Department Store just beyond that. Beth Bishop was a very fancy shop. In 1955, it closed and moved to Cape Cod, where the shop still exists today in the town of Orleans. Across the street was the Blue Haven Grill, a popular stop on the way home from a hard day's work. Fifty cents bought a shot and a beer.

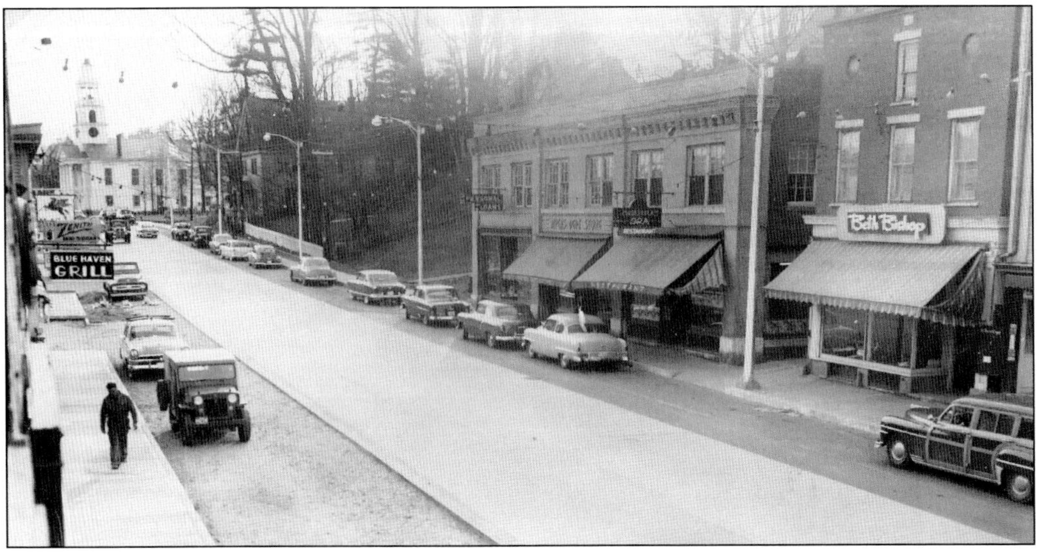

Six

The Good, the Bad, and the Vermont State Prison

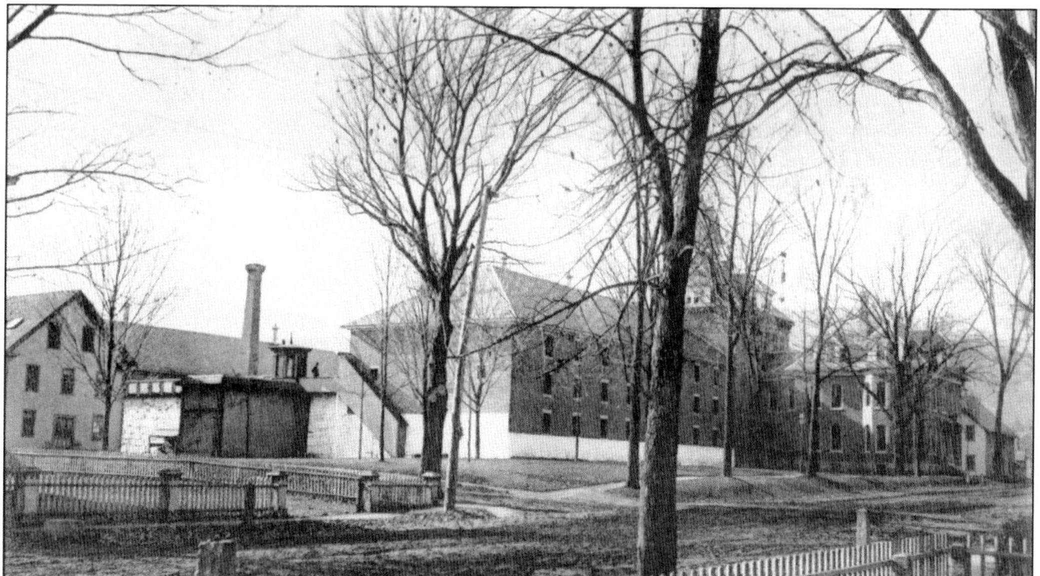

The Windsor State Prison was the most modern of penal institutions in the early 19th century, offering classes and training to its residents. They even served fresh produce harvested from their gardens. Construction began in 1807, when Pres. Thomas Jefferson was still in office. It opened in 1809, the year that both Abraham Lincoln and Charles Darwin were born. It used 5,000 tons of local granite and was located just off Main Street.

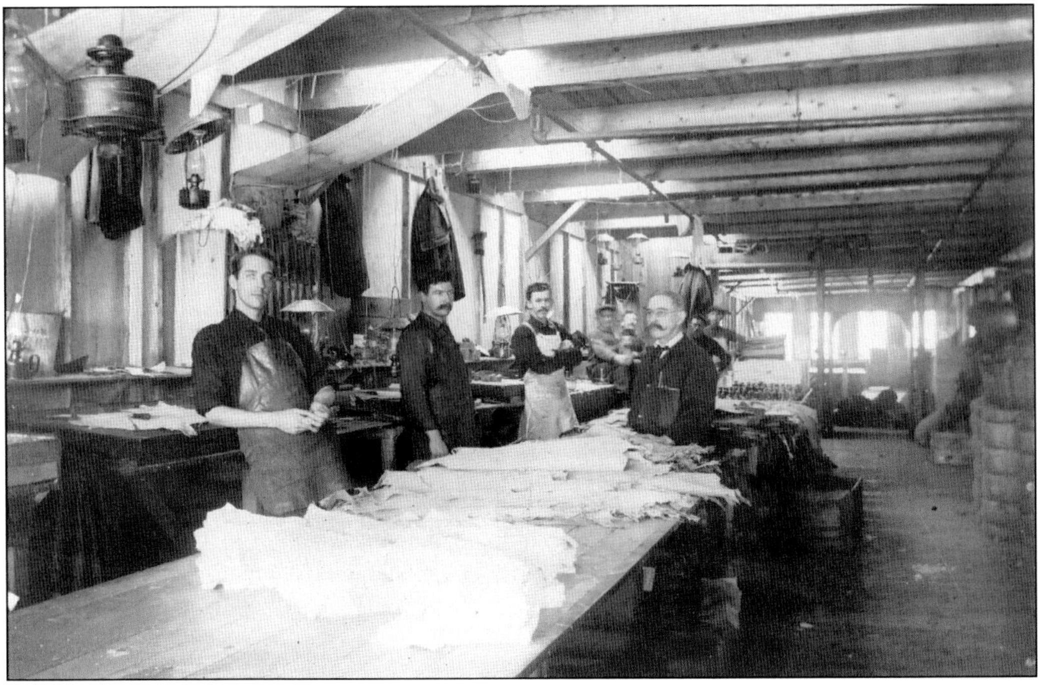

With forward-thinking prison overseers, the prison became a very productive manufacturing center. It housed a carpentry shop and cotton weaving facility, which produced over 41,000 yards of cloth from 1812 to 1813. The shoe factory pictured was operated by A.E. Mann and Company and was adjacent to the Windsor State Prison. Employing an average of 200 men and women in the shop, the cutting and fitting was done here. The shoes were then completed and sent over to the prison for finishing. These workers seem only mildly pleased to be having their photographs taken.

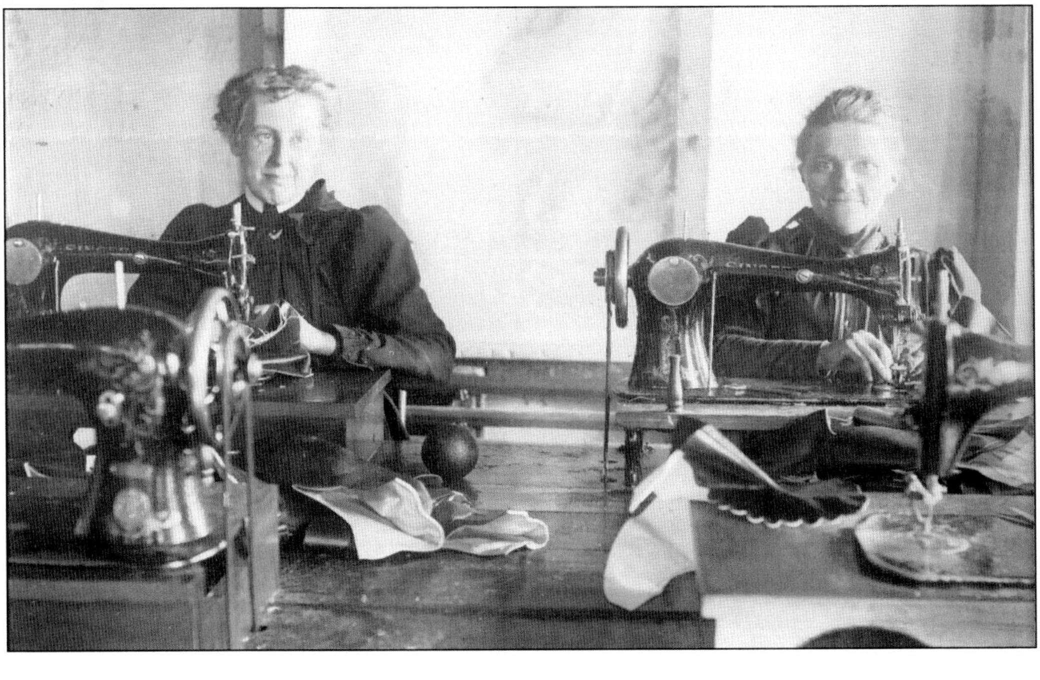

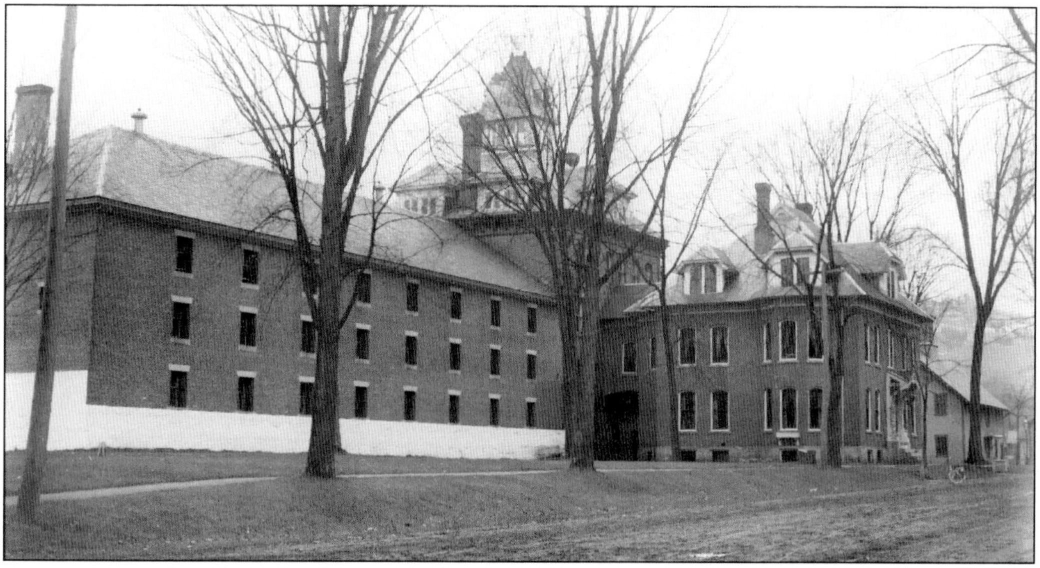

A notice regarding the prison that appeared in an 1815 edition of *Spooner's Journal* said, "Goods For Sale. Sewall Cutting, Contractor for the Vermont State Prison, has for sale at the State Prison Ware House: Ginghams, Shambrays, Stripes, Apron Checks, Bed Ticking, Sheeting, Shirtings, Table Cloths, Pocket Handkerchiefs, Flannels, Shuttles, and Cotton Yarn of almost every colour. All of which articles will be kept constantly for sale and at as low a rate as they can be purchased at any Factory in New England. N. B. Grain, Wood, Butter, Cheese, received in payment for the above, and the market price allowed." In the 1830s, the prison also manufactured Hubbard's pumps, and in 1842, they were manufacturing Robbins and Lawrence gun parts. Inmates also had other duties, such as grounds keeping and working the fields. The corn was harvested at the farm and shucked by the residents. (Courtesy Correctional Photo Archives.)

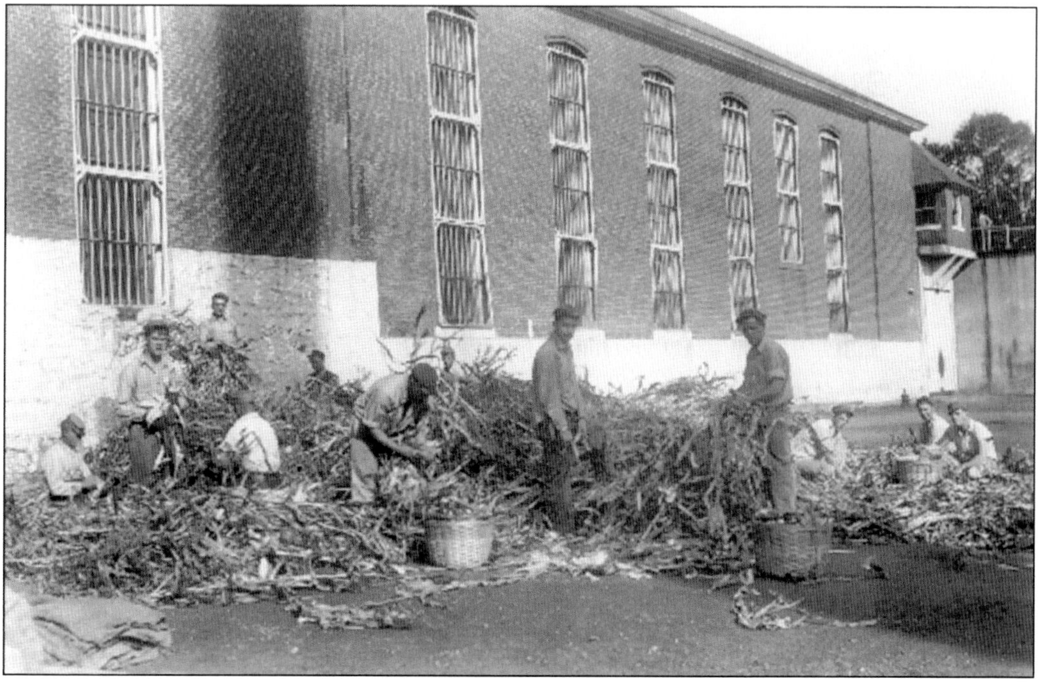

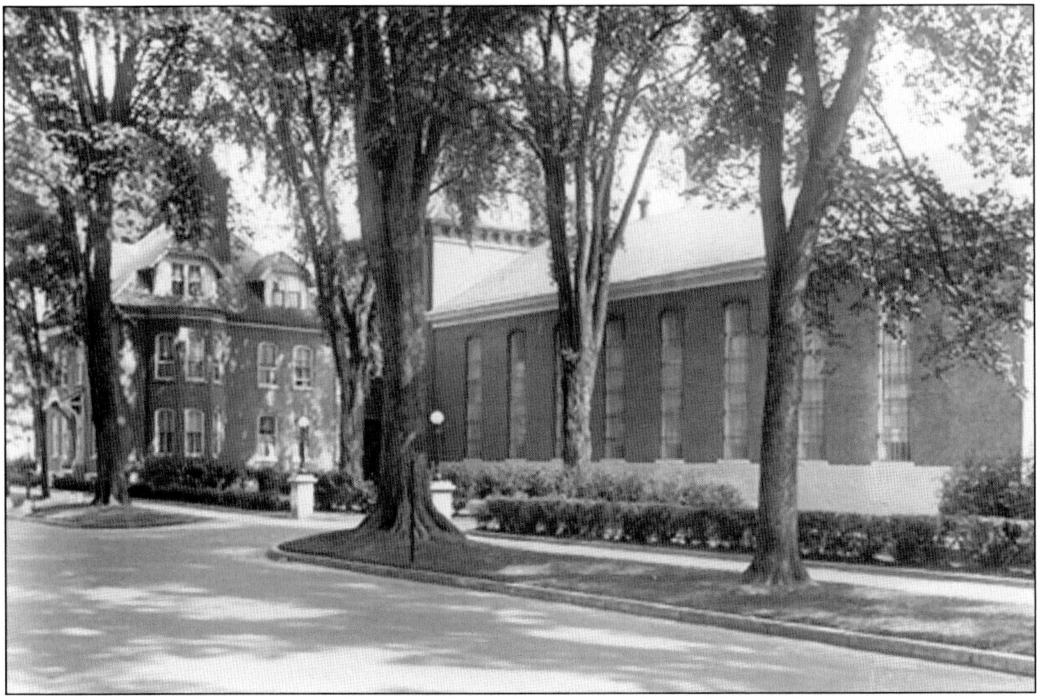

When it first opened, the prison was a popular tourist attraction. Public tours were conducted on Thursdays, and tickets were sold separately for those interested in viewing the scheduled hangings. Records show that sometimes the events would draw more than 1,000 pairs of curious eyes in a single week. Situated right downtown and bordering some of the finest residences in town, the building was truly a part of the community. There were also adjoining farmlands that produced dairy products and produce for the prison. (Courtesy Correctional Photo Archives.)

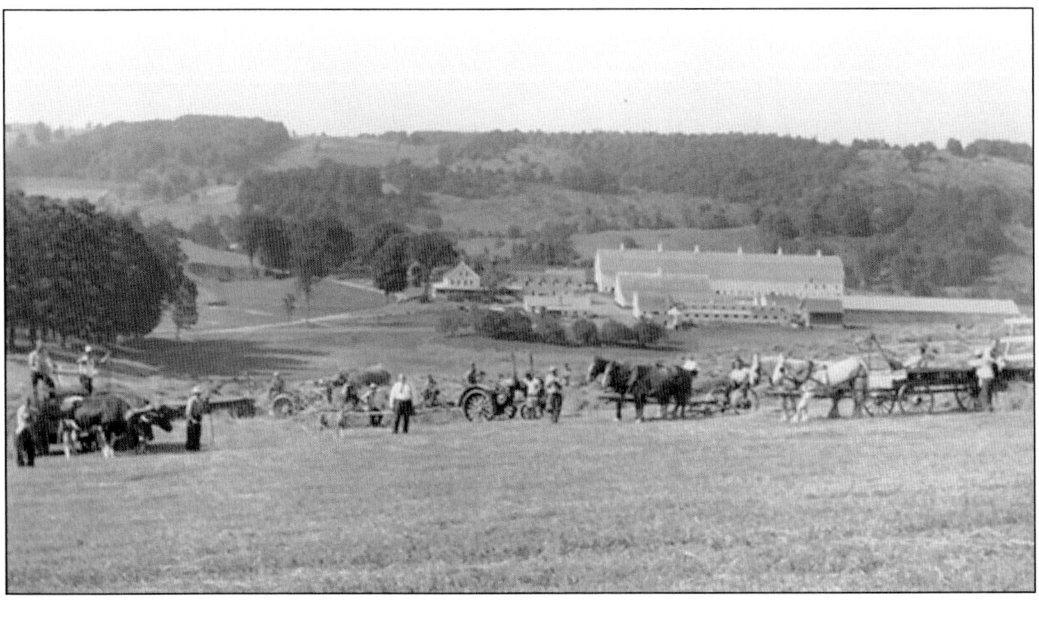

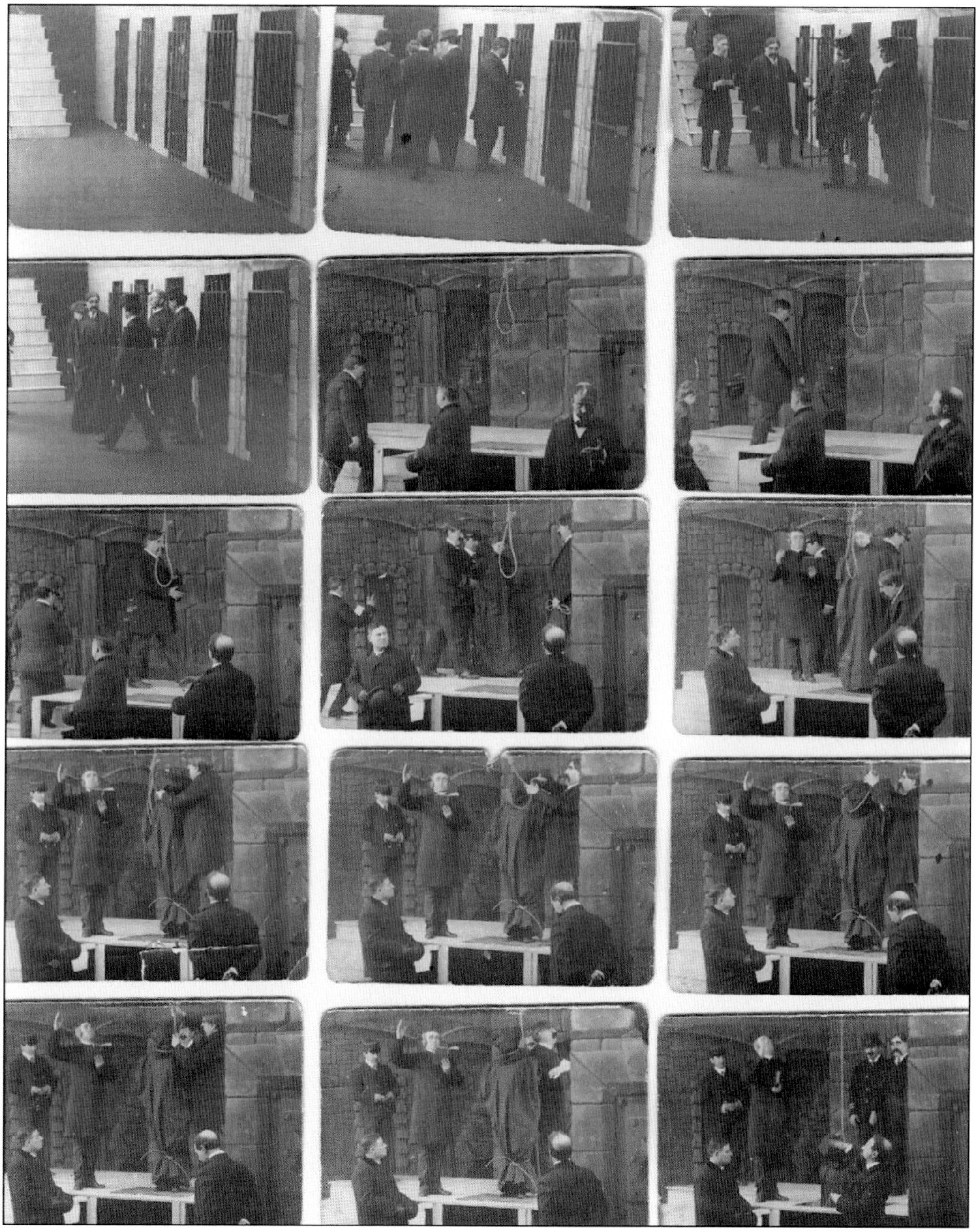

In 1905, an unforgettable hanging took place. Mary Rogers and her boyfriend were convicted of killing Mary's husband, Marcus Rogers. During her trial, she stated that she was pregnant, hoping to avoid the death penalty. Ignoring her claim, she was hanged, but later found to have been pregnant. The hanging was documented in a series of photographs showing her leaving her cell and every step of the way to her final destination. She was the last woman to be hanged at the Windsor Prison gallows. (Private collection.)

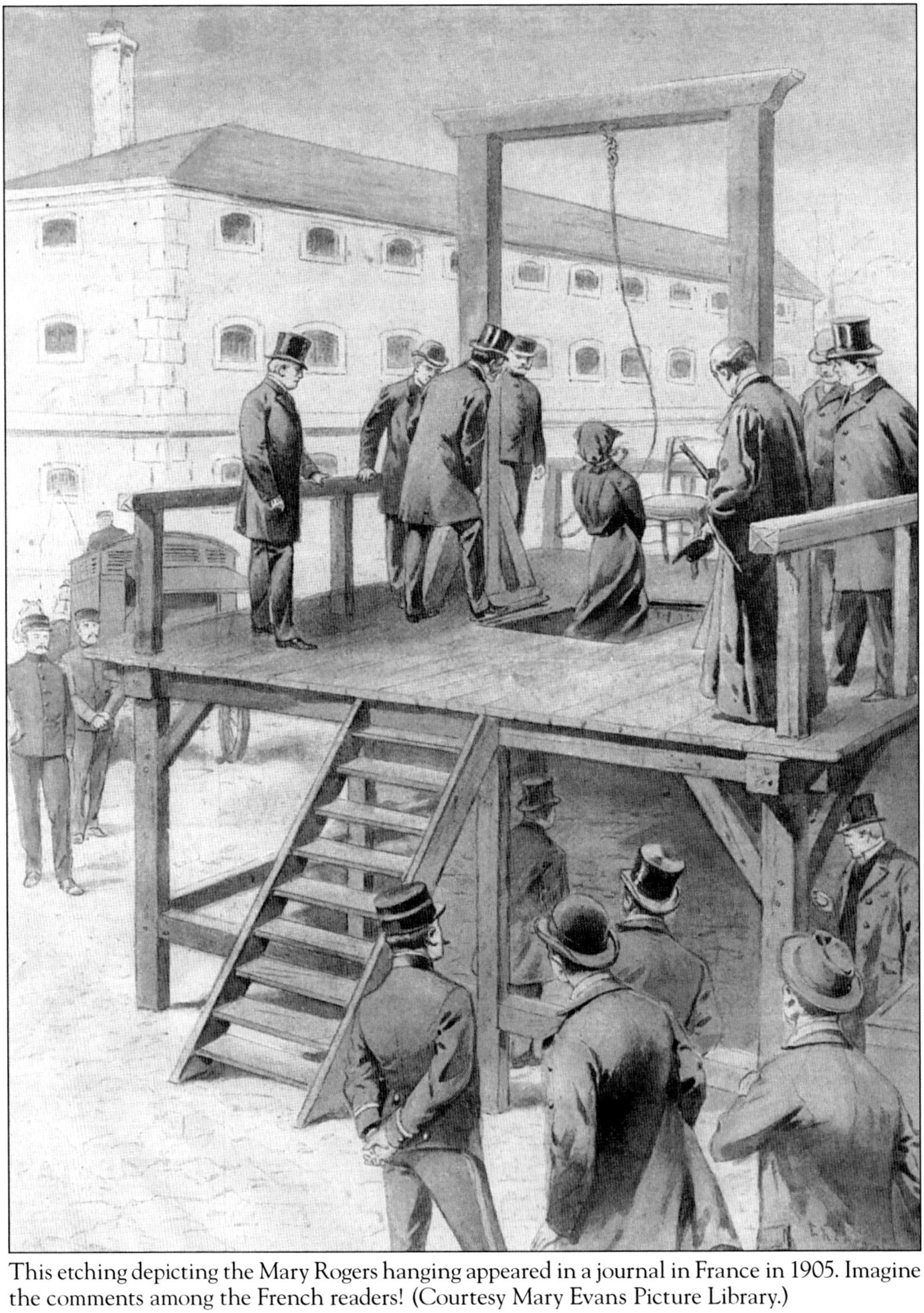

This etching depicting the Mary Rogers hanging appeared in a journal in France in 1905. Imagine the comments among the French readers! (Courtesy Mary Evans Picture Library.)

Seven

People of Note, Men of Letters

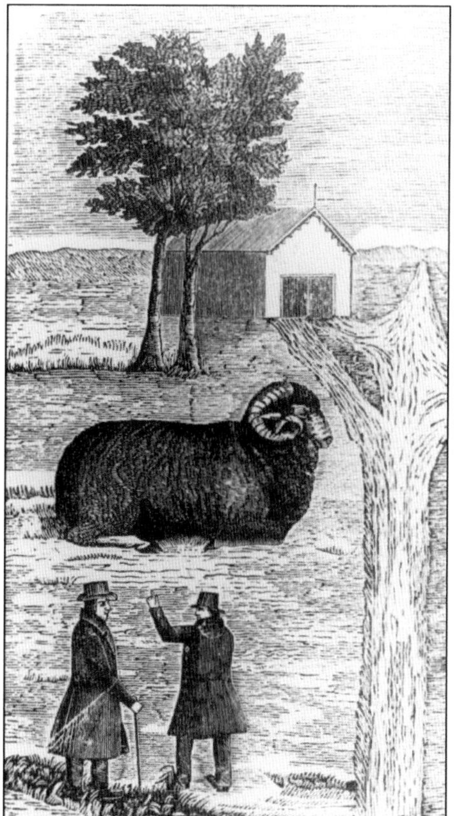

In 1810, Vermont resident William Jarvis was the American consul at Lisbon, Portugal when he purchased 2,000 Merino sheep. He sent them back to Vermont via various means of transportation, thus beginning the 30-year reign of a thriving wool industry. In 1823, there were three woolen mills in the area. By 1827, there were almost 7,000 sheep grazing on the pastures of East and West Windsor. Jarvis's home later became the Jarvis Inn. (Courtesy Vermont Historical Society, Barre.)

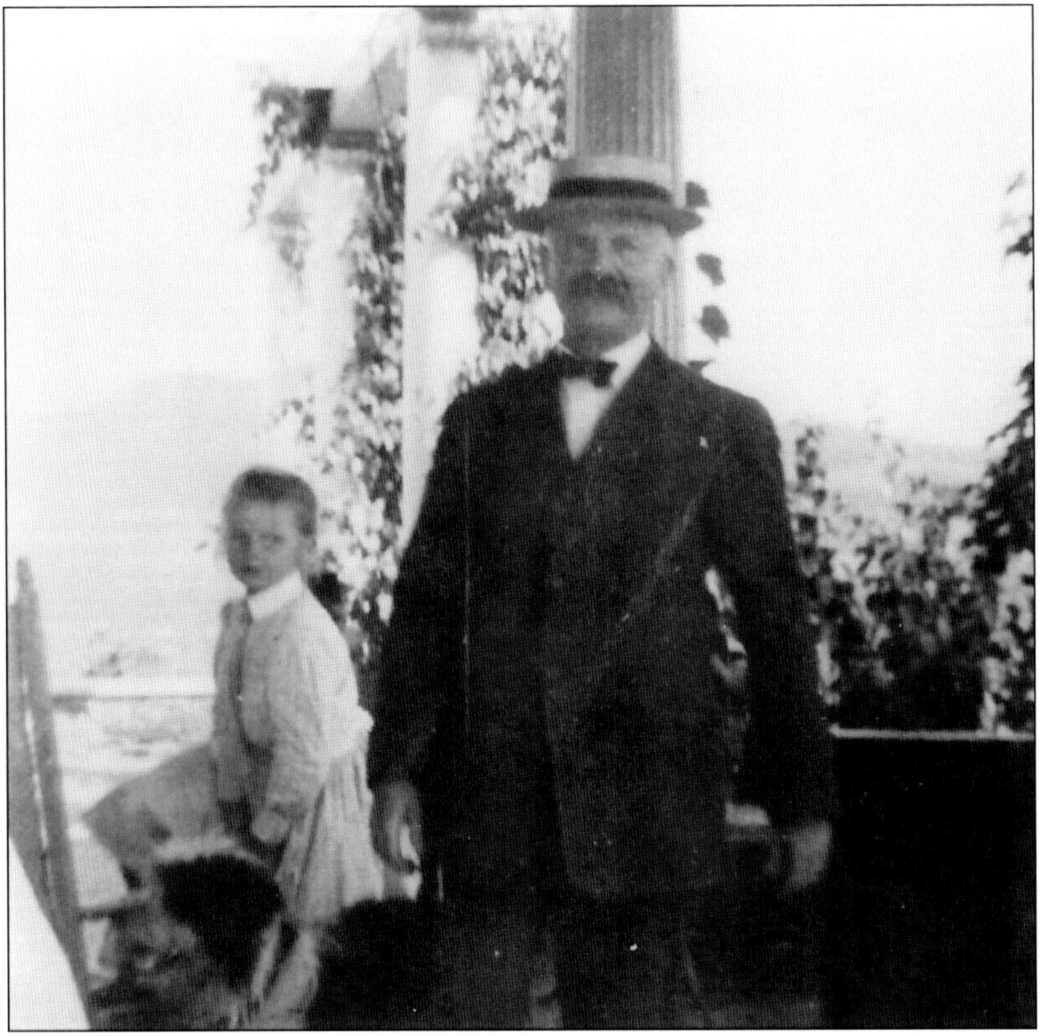

Maxwell Evarts, son of William Evarts, inherited the family property. In 1902, he built a country estate called Juniper Hill Farm on a 300-acre parcel overlooking the town. Maxwell was a prominent New York City attorney and general counsel to the E.H. Harriman Railroad. Harriman was a frequent guest in his home, and thanks to his affiliation with the railroad, Maxwell Evarts had his own private railcar. He began a breeding program on his farm that helped save the Morgan horse, the revered and truly American breed. Well connected in many circles, Maxwell Evarts was also the grandson of Roger Sherman, the only man to have signed all four of the founding documents of the United States of America.

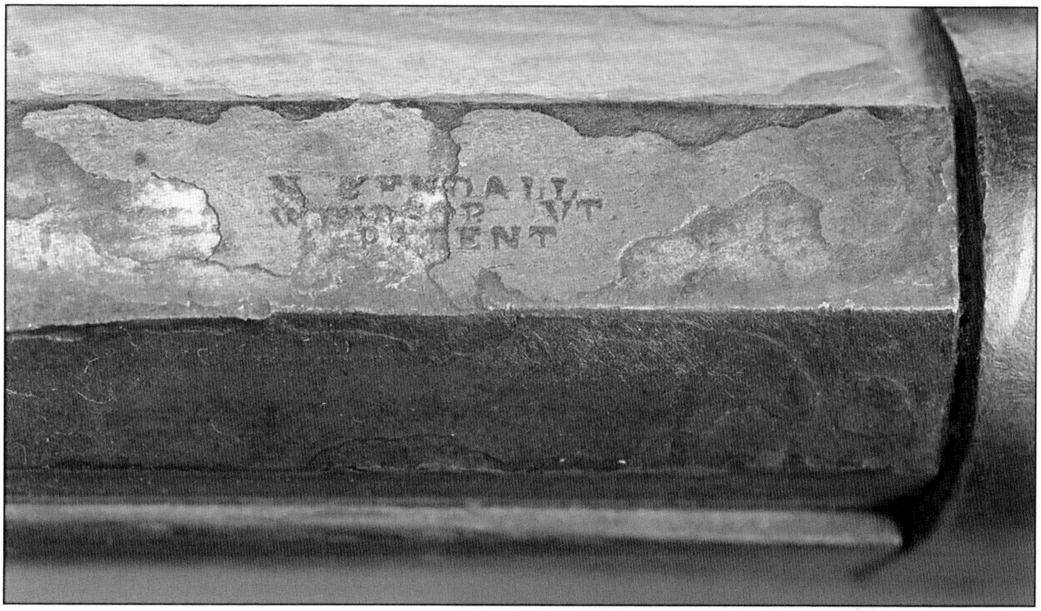

Nicanor Kendall, inventor of the underhammer rifle, became a part of Kendall, Lawrence and Robbins in 1844. Kendall left the company in 1847, several years after completing the government contract for an initial 10,000 guns. Due to the cancellation of a later contract in 1857, the company went bankrupt. Kendall died in 1861. (Courtesy American Precision Museum.)

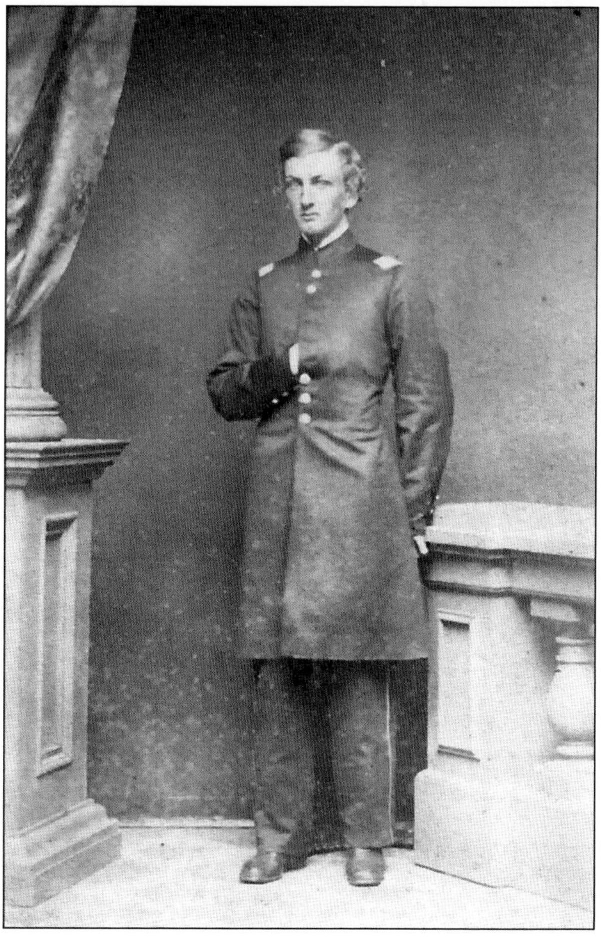

First Lieutenant Albert Sabin of the 1st US Infantry was stationed in Leavenworth, Kansas, during the summer of 1862. In the spring of 1863, he was selected by famed Civil War general James Blunt to transport treasure to Santa Fe. He died in Windsor in September 1863.

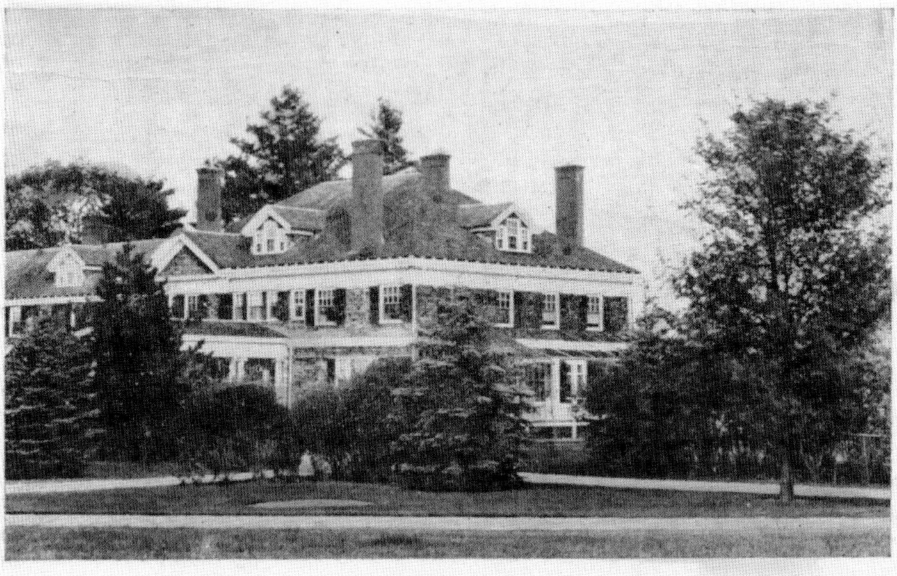

Published by Frank M. Wright Residence of F. A. Kennedy, Windsor, Vt.

Frank Kennedy arrived in Windsor in 1895. Known as the "cracker man," his company produced the biscuits that sustained thousands of troops during World War I. Having made his fortune by selling his company to the National Biscuit Company (NABISCO), Kennedy became the gentleman farmer of Windsor. Kennedy's mansion, Buena Vista, sat on a plateau that overlooked the river. He gradually added a golf course, outbuildings, a creamery, a henhouse, a sawmill, extensive gardens, and an apiary. He had a large riding rink as well, which he generously offered for the annual Windsor Corn Shows from 1911 to 1914. Reportedly, John Phillip Sousa's marching band performed at one of the shows. He established the Windsor Electric Light Company in the former Robbins and Lawrence armory, which was owned and operated by Kennedy until his death in 1925. This gasoline engine was inside his private powerhouse.

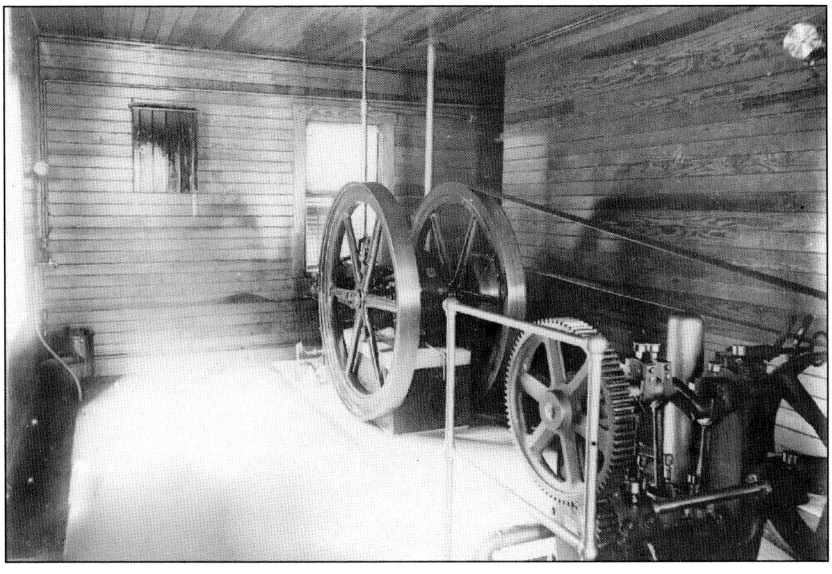

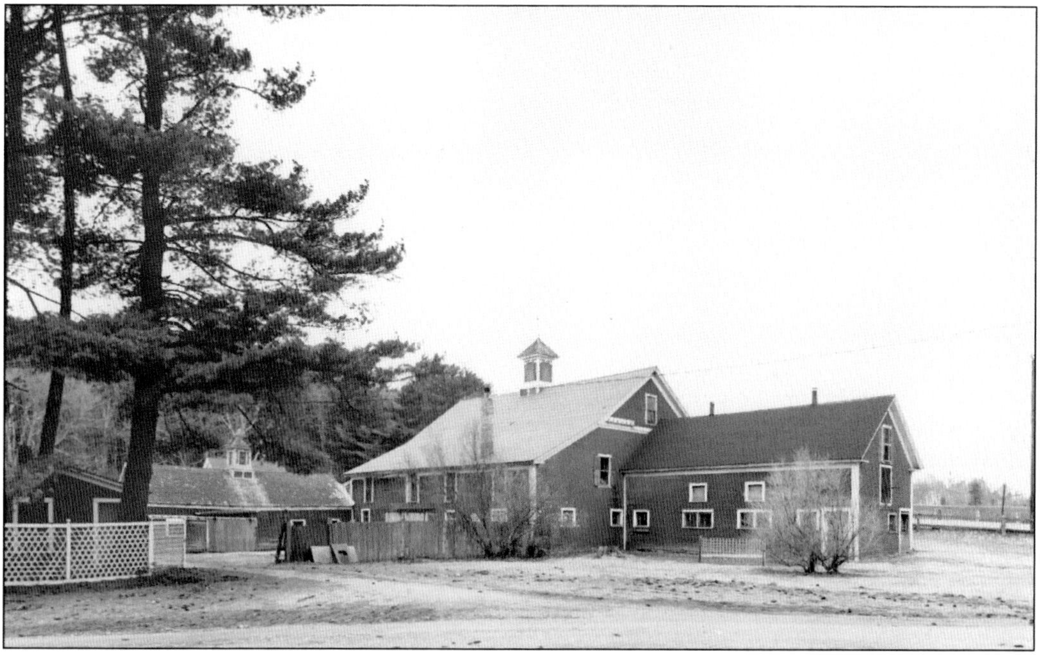

The site of these imposing barns from the Old Bailey Farm was at one time also home to the Dressler Barns. Once a resident of Windsor, vaudeville actress Marie Dressler owned a large home and barn complex across the road. She was famous for her role in the 1933 comedy *Tugboat Annie*, costarring Wallace Beery. Dressler won an Academy Award in 1931 for her role in the film *Min and Bill*. She later became active in the women's suffrage movement and was the first woman to appear on the cover of *Time* magazine. Dressler used the barn, located near her summer home Pine Tops, in Windsor, as a stable for her many horses and named the complex Windsor Farms.

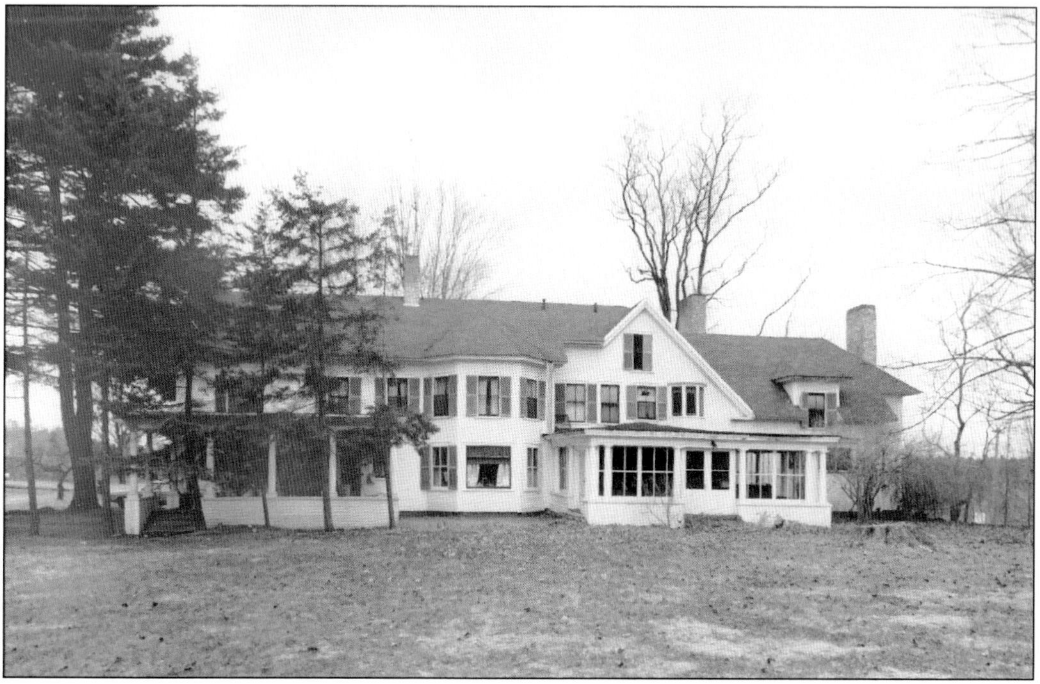

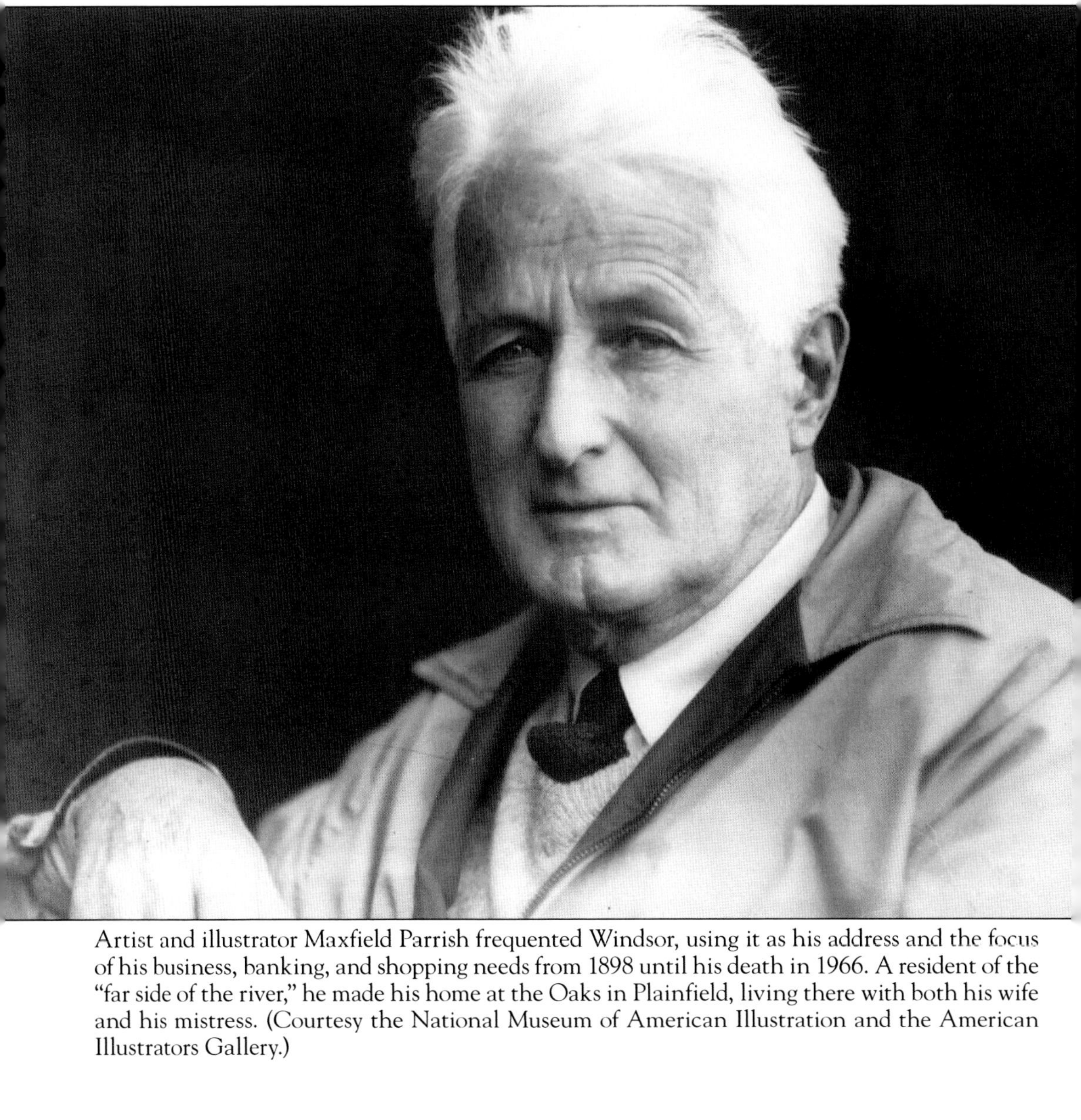

Artist and illustrator Maxfield Parrish frequented Windsor, using it as his address and the focus of his business, banking, and shopping needs from 1898 until his death in 1966. A resident of the "far side of the river," he made his home at the Oaks in Plainfield, living there with both his wife and his mistress. (Courtesy the National Museum of American Illustration and the American Illustrators Gallery.)

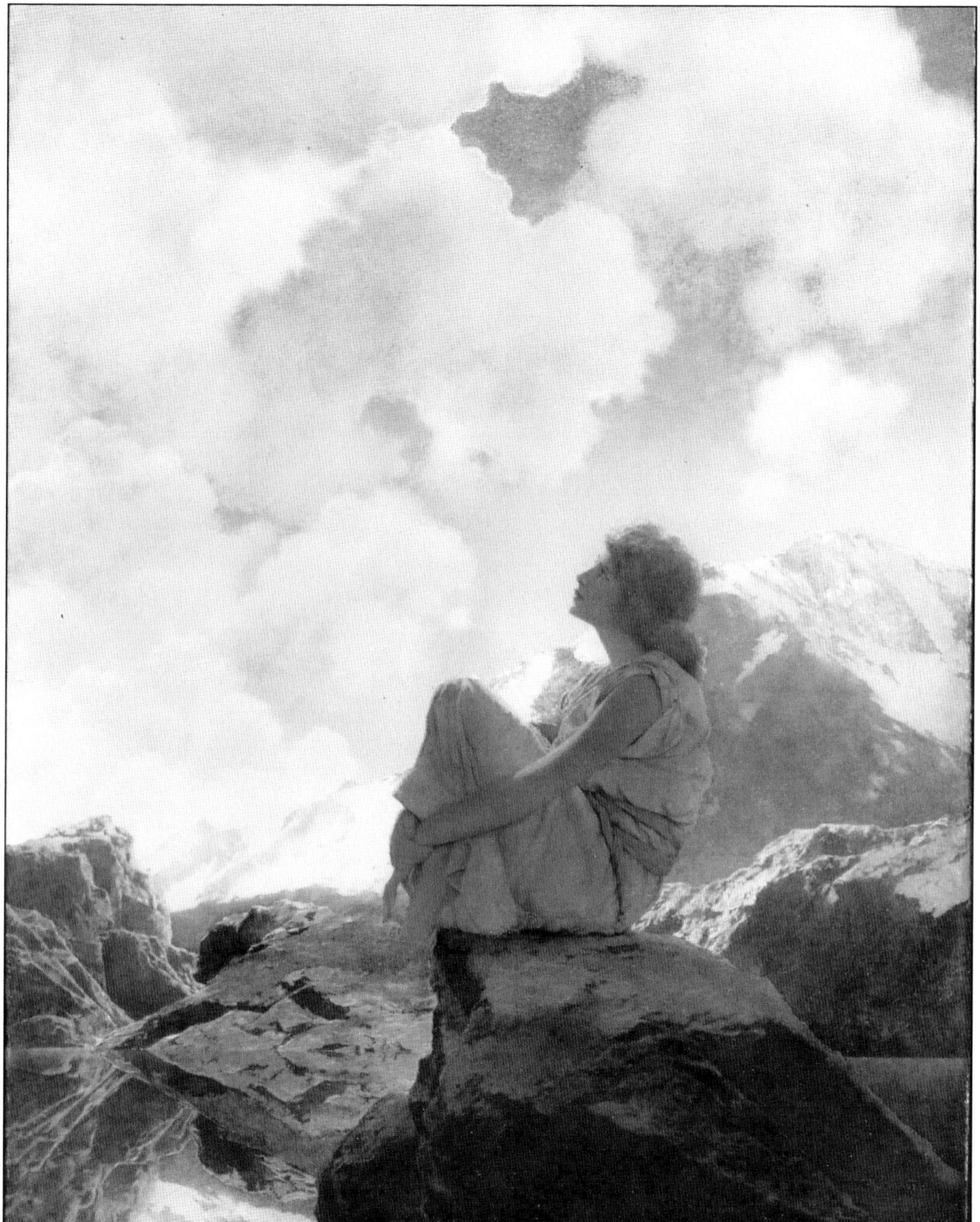

Maxfield Parrish's style of painting was unique for its luminosity, and he was instrumental in creating America's Golden Age of illustration. Often thought of for his exquisite blues, he was paid tribute with the naming of a color called Parrish blue. In yet another connection to Windsor, his signature is found on a deed for the purchase of the Solon-Mower House on Ascutney Street, said to be the residence of his muse and love interest Sue Lewin. (Courtesy the National Museum of American Illustration and the American Illustrators Gallery.)

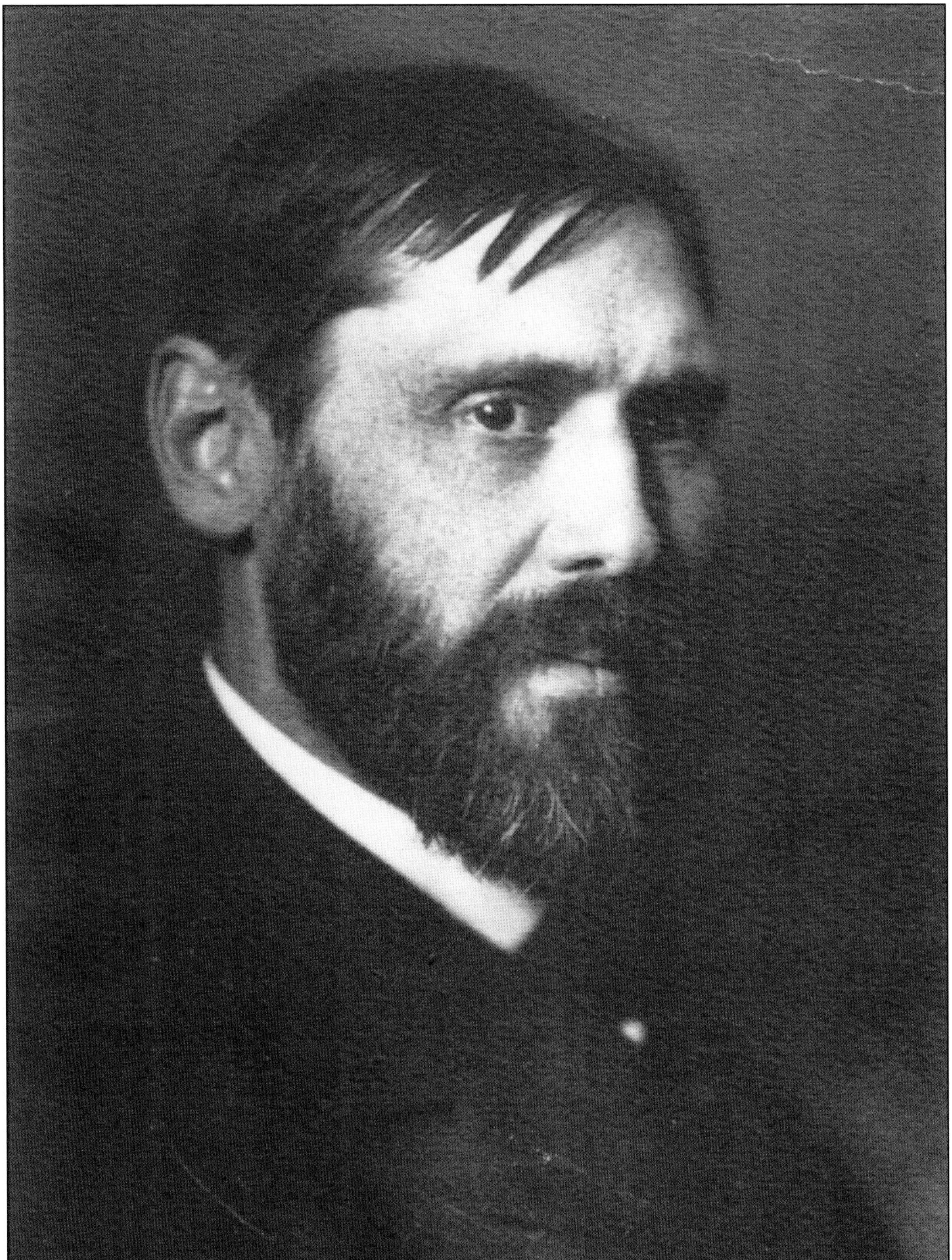

Kenyon Cox was a muralist who summered in Windsor and was associated with the Cornish Colony of artists and August Saint-Gaudens. Cox studied with William Merit Chase at the Art Student's League in New York City. He was married to illustrator Louise King Cox, with whom he created the murals decorating the Liberal Arts Building at the 1893 World's Columbian Exposition in Chicago.

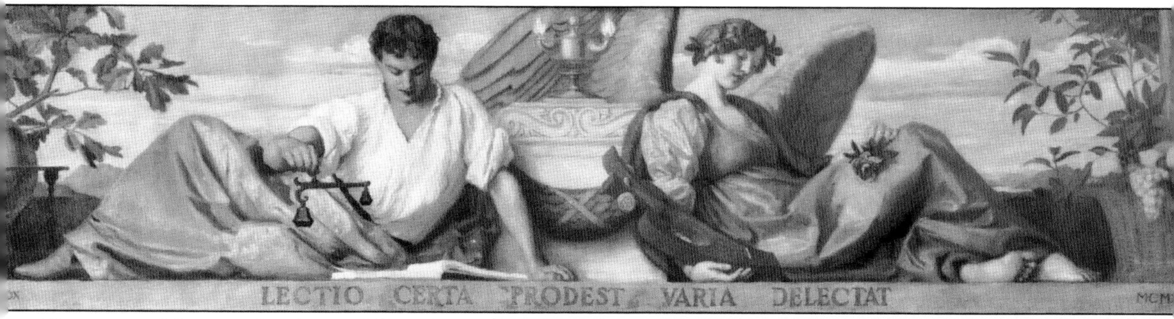

Kenyon and Louise Cox's son Allyn Cox, also a muralist, painted this mural above the mantelpiece in the Windsor Public Library. He was paid $13 to cover his expenses, and spent the summer completing it prior to his fellowship at the American Academy in Rome. Sherman Evarts, an official of the library at the time, provided the Latin inscription, "Lectio certa prodest varia delectat," which translates as "Accurate reading profits, varied reading delights." Cox's work was commissioned throughout New England. Many commissions were for the US Capitol Building. In 1975, he completed a commission for the US Senate of a mural illustrating the first moon landing. Cox was honored for his adept depictions of major events in American history and hailed as the "American Michelangelo." Though they shared a name, he was not related to the Archibald Cox family, also residents of Windsor. (Courtesy David Westby.)

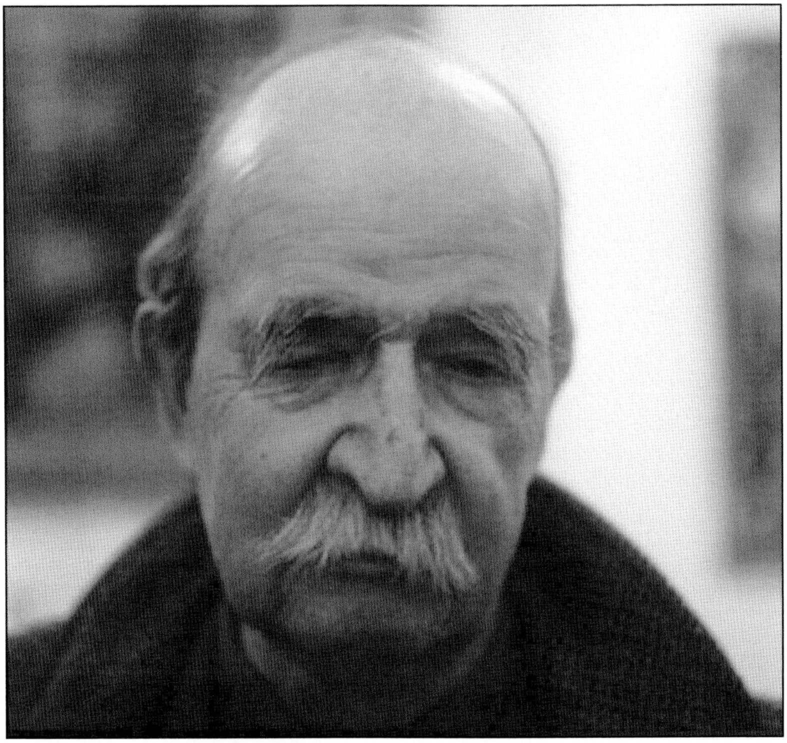

Sydney Edward Dickinson was an artist who retired in Windsor. He studied with William Merit Chase at the Art Students League in New York, where he later taught painting. He also taught painting at the National Academy of Design in Washington, DC. His portraits of John D. Rockefeller and New York Mayor Fiorello Laguardia, among others, hang in the Corcoran Gallery and the Art Institute of Chicago. (Courtesy Nikos Kalamaris.)

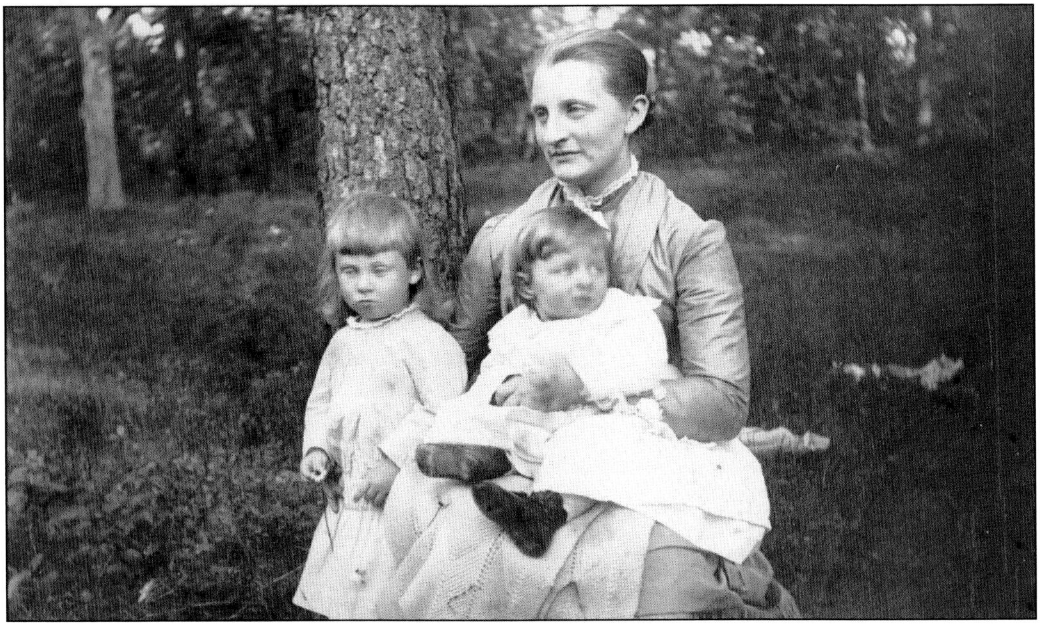

Maxwell Evarts's grandson Maxwell Perkins was a renowned and beloved editor at New York's Scribners and Sons Publishers. Respected and revered by writers and colleagues, he brought to light the work of a new literary generation, including Hemingway, Fitzgerald, and Wolfe. He owned the house at 26 Main Street in Windsor and was the uncle of Watergate special prosecutor Archibald Cox. Maxwell is pictured on the right with his mother and brother Edward in this very early photograph.

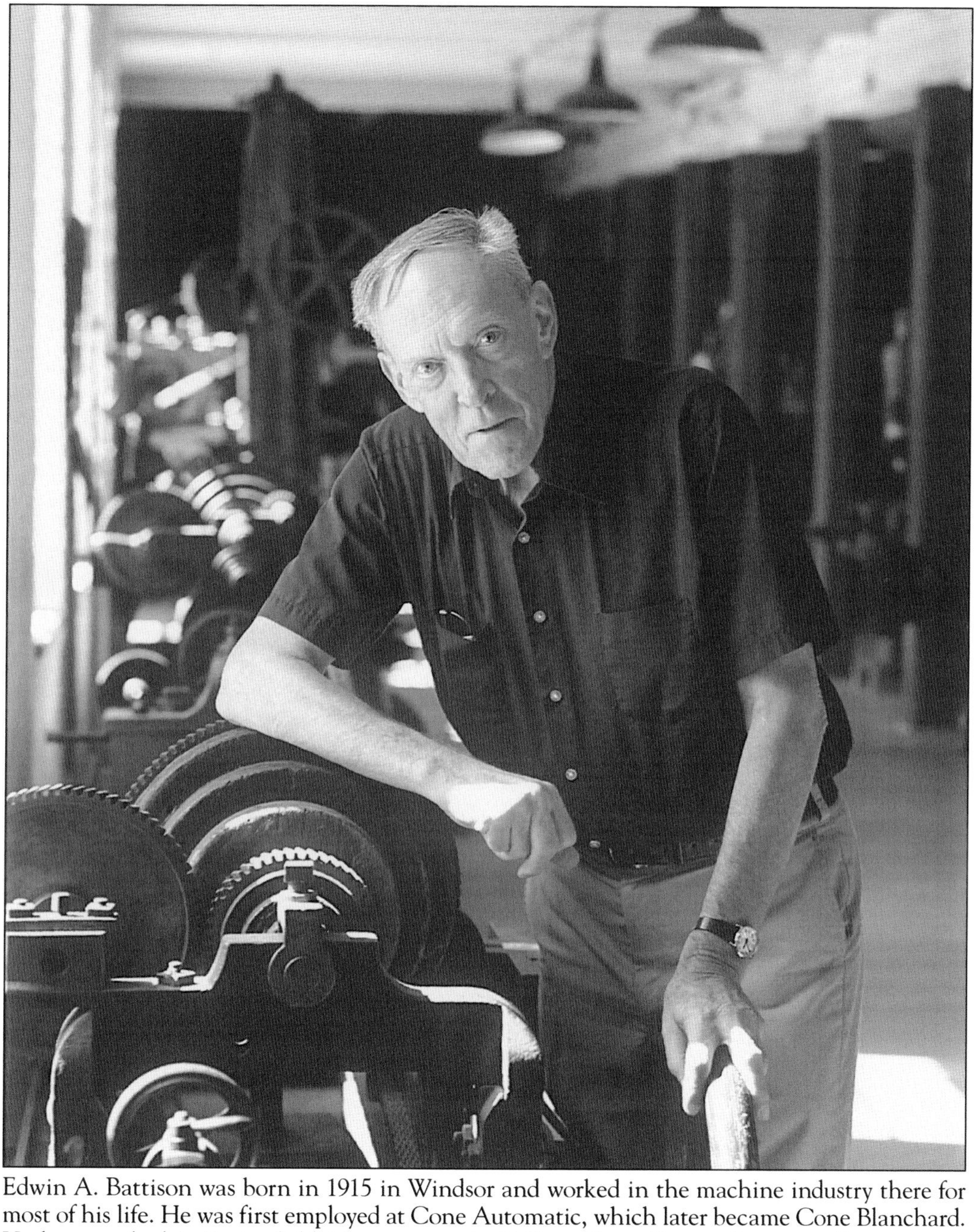

Edwin A. Battison was born in 1915 in Windsor and worked in the machine industry there for most of his life. He was first employed at Cone Automatic, which later became Cone Blanchard. He later worked in Springfield, Vermont, at the Fellows Gear Shaper Company. Battison was a collector of machines and tools and would frequently visit the Smithsonian Institute to do research on his acquisitions. When the curators realized he knew more than they did, he was hired by the museum. Battison held the position of curator of mechanical engineering at the Smithsonian Institute of History and Technology in Washington, DC, until 1977. He founded the American Precision Museum in Windsor in 1966 while still working in Washington. His legacy to Windsor was the establishment of the museum and the collection he amassed to fill it. (Courtesy American Precision Museum.)

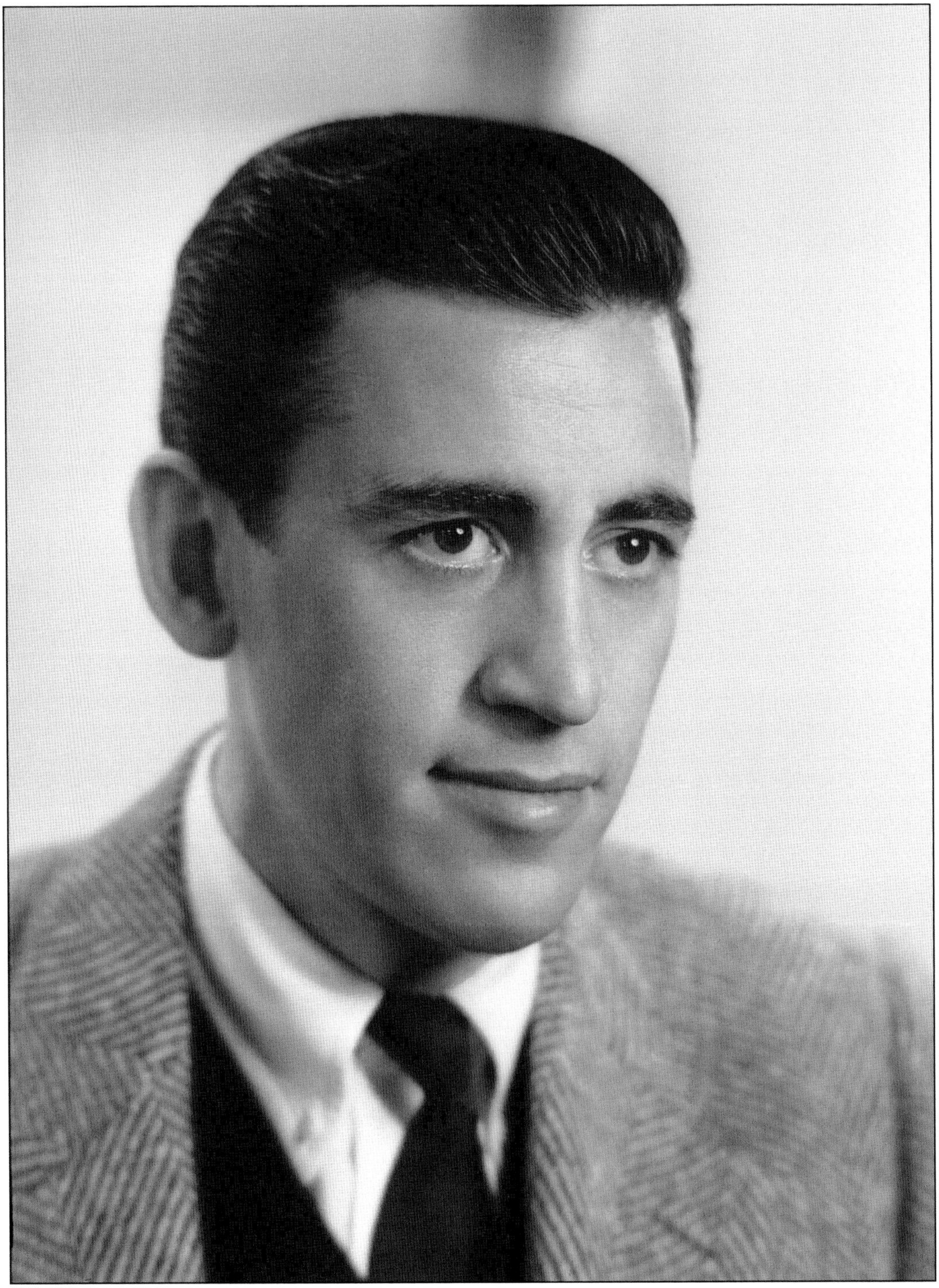

Although Windsor cannot claim him as its own, J.D. Salinger frequented the town and was often seen on Main Street. Salinger, author of *The Catcher in the Rye*, regularly ate breakfast at the Windsor Diner and shopped at the local grocery store. His home was across the river in Cornish, New Hampshire. (Courtesy of The Lotte Jacobi Collection, University of New Hampshire.)

Eight

Places We Remember, Though Some Remain

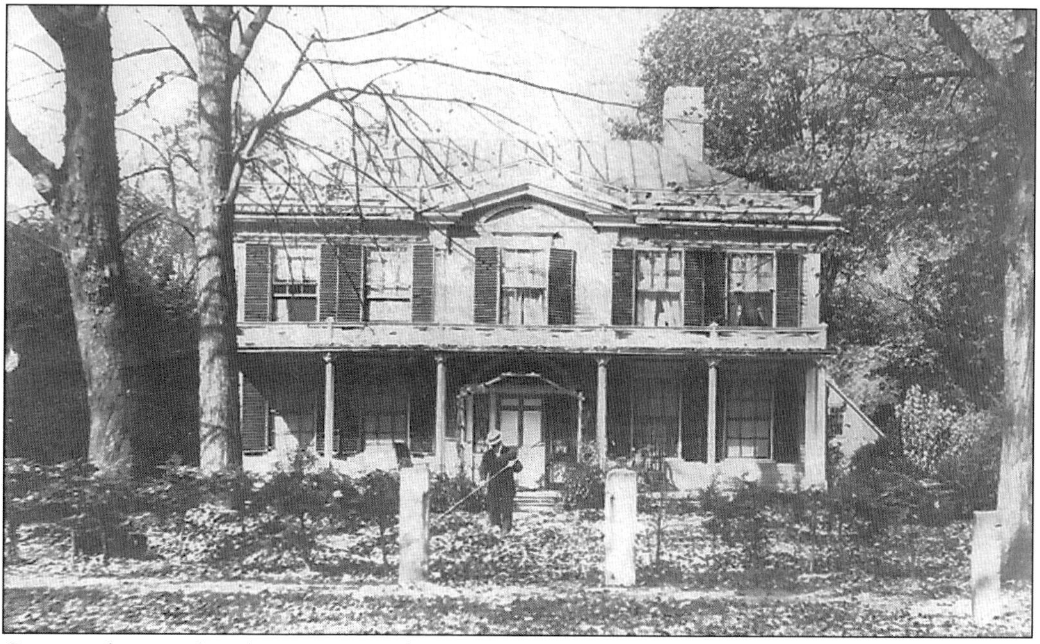

Gone and somewhat forgotten are the many homes, schools, churches, and shops that were destroyed by natural disasters, fires, or floods, or in the name of progress. Here are some as they were, and others whose outlines have become shadows of memory, preserved only in photographs. The Hubbard House, designed by Asher Benjamin, is gone.

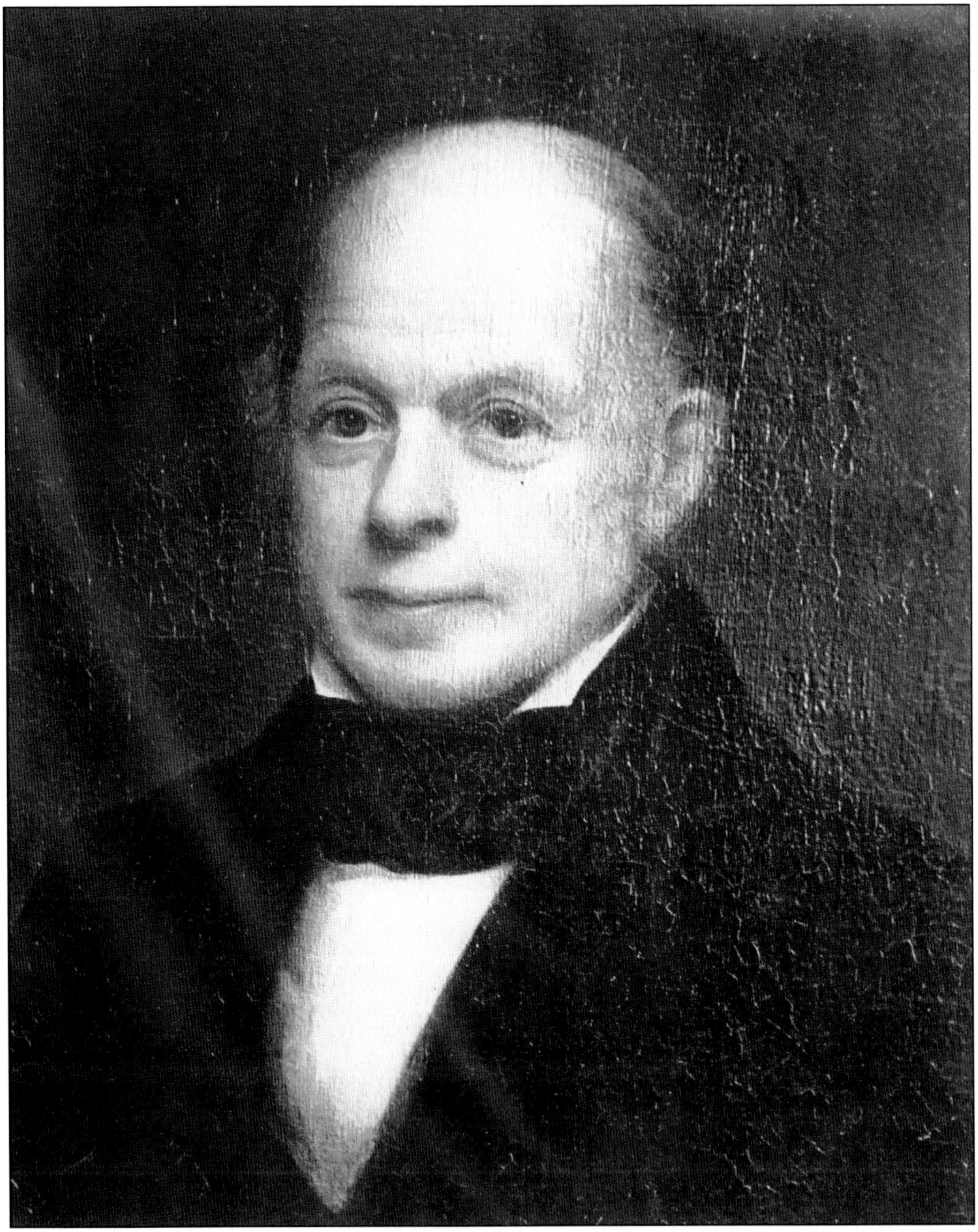

Noted architect Asher Benjamin moved north from Boston and resided in Windsor for several years. During that time, the architect designed several gorgeous homes in Windsor and in the neighboring town of Hartland along with the Old South Church on Main Street.

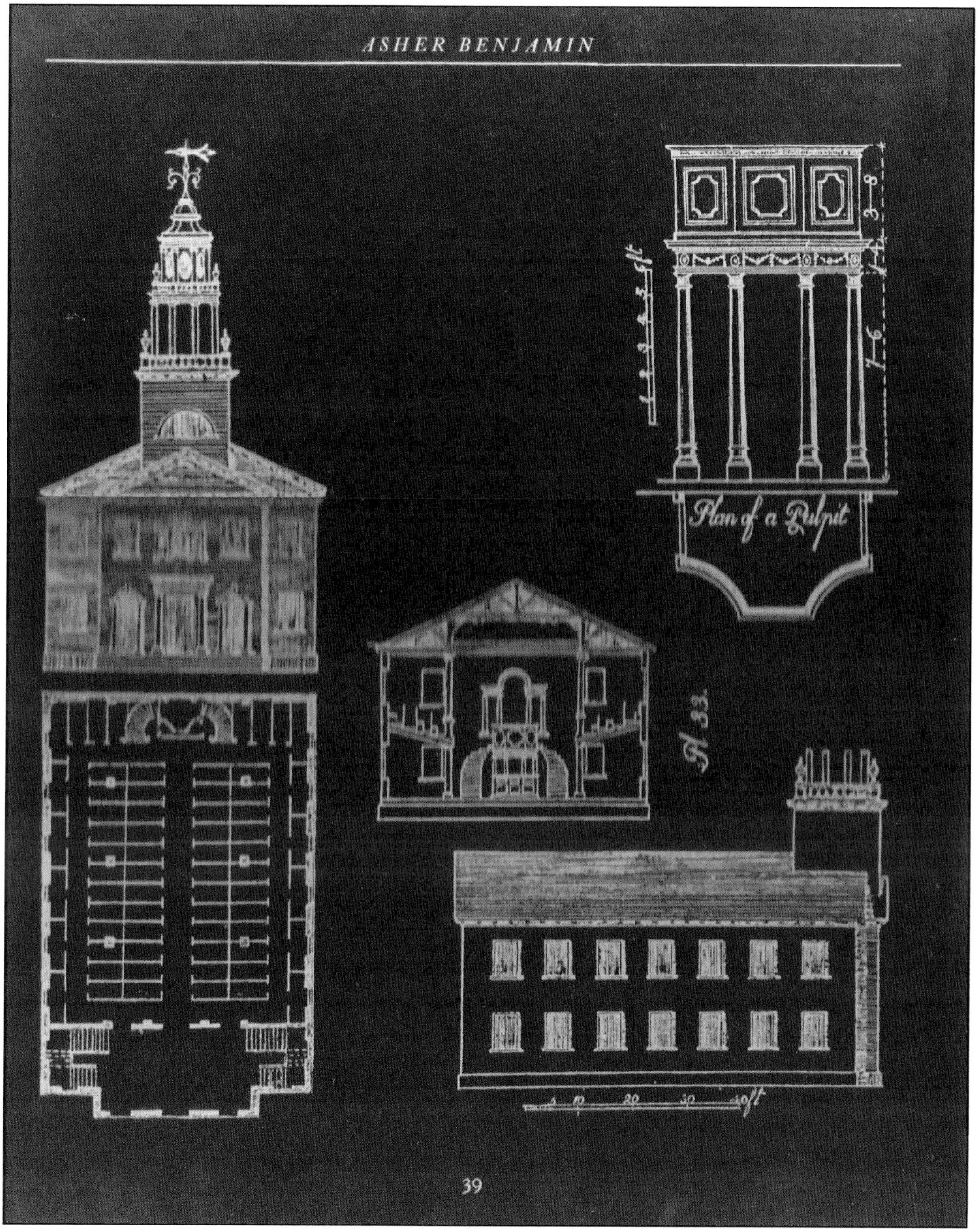

Benjamin authored a number of builders' guides and pattern books that functioned as catalogs of ideas, architectural history, and inspiration for local builders. These books provided drawings and advice for building complete houses with exquisite details for spiral staircases, doorways, mantels, and other architectural niches. (Courtesy Historic Deerfield Inc. Deerfield, Massachusetts.)

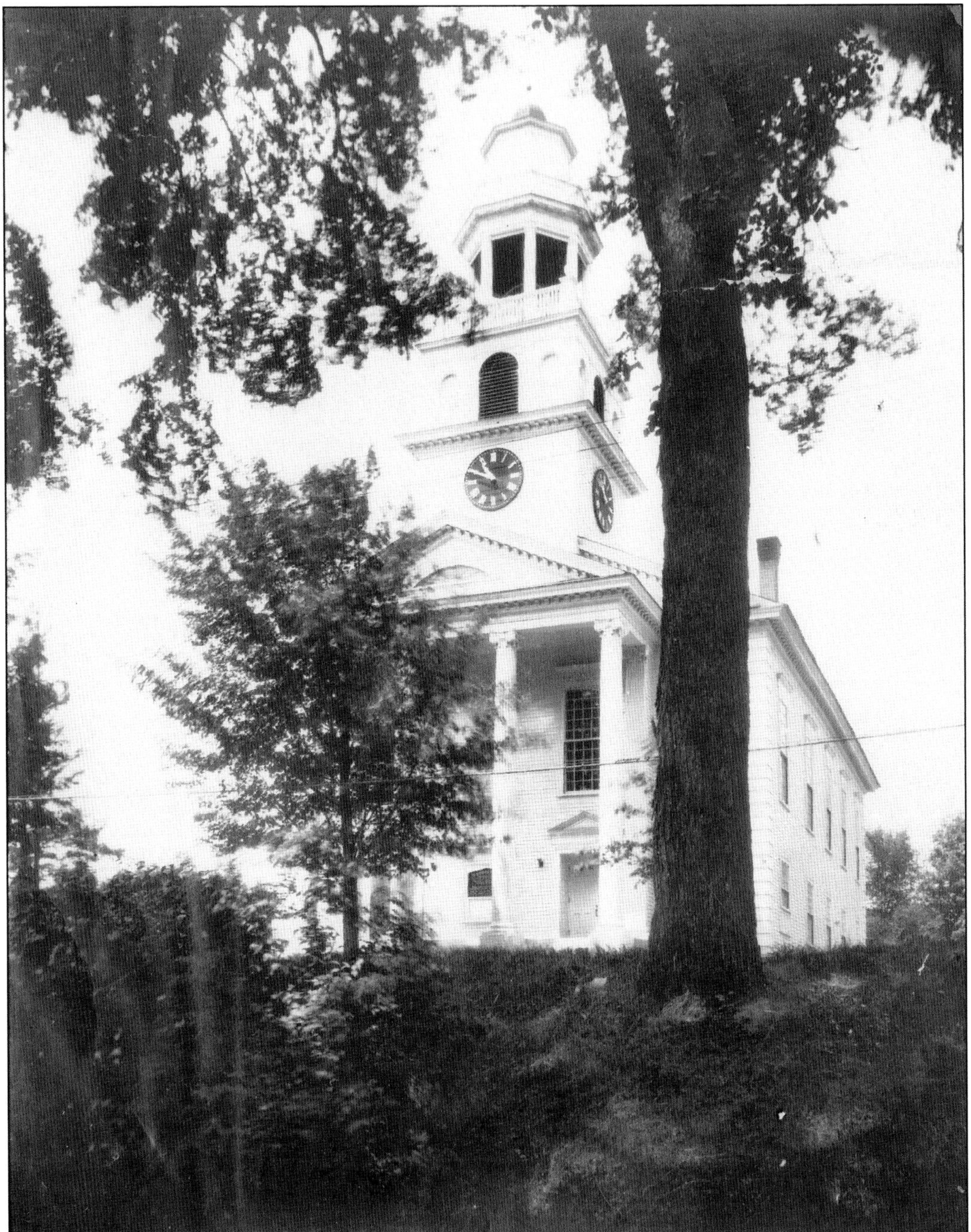

Perhaps Benjamin's best know project in Windsor is the Old South Church. Built in 1798, the church embodies the history of the founding of the town itself. The design followed Benjamin's own architectural guides, most closely resembling his basic design for a meetinghouse. The original building cost $5,000 to construct and had no columns. Overall, the church remains as it was built in 1798, when it was touted as the most sophisticated building in Vermont. It had one of three organs built in Windsor by Lemuel Hedge. A clock was added in 1818, a bell in 1844, and a portico in 1922.

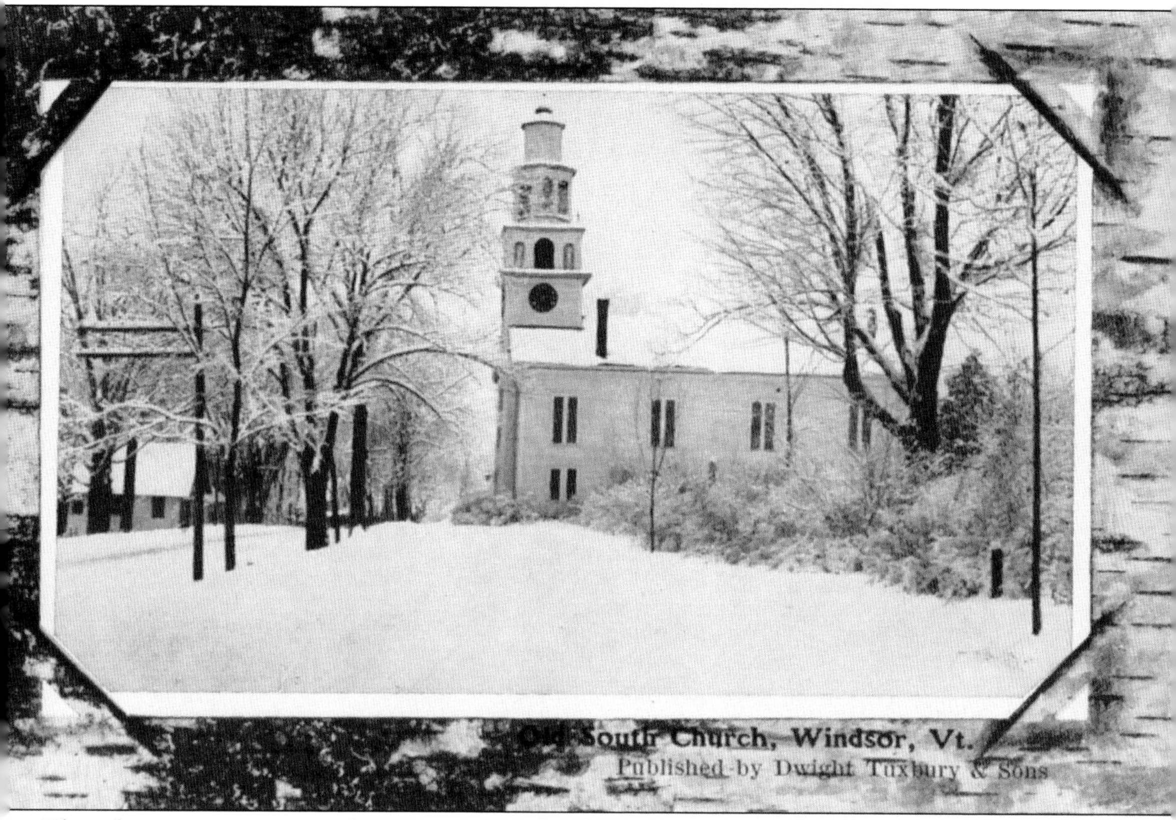

The adjoining cemetery is the resting place for the many names that built and sustained the town over three centuries, including Hubbard, Hoisington, Blood, Tracy, Stone, Pettes, Curtis, Spooner, Sabin, Thompson, and Jacob. A bond dated 1768 and archived among the town's historic documents states that the first reverend, James Wellman, was to be paid his salary either in money or in "grains, pork, beef or a day's labor."

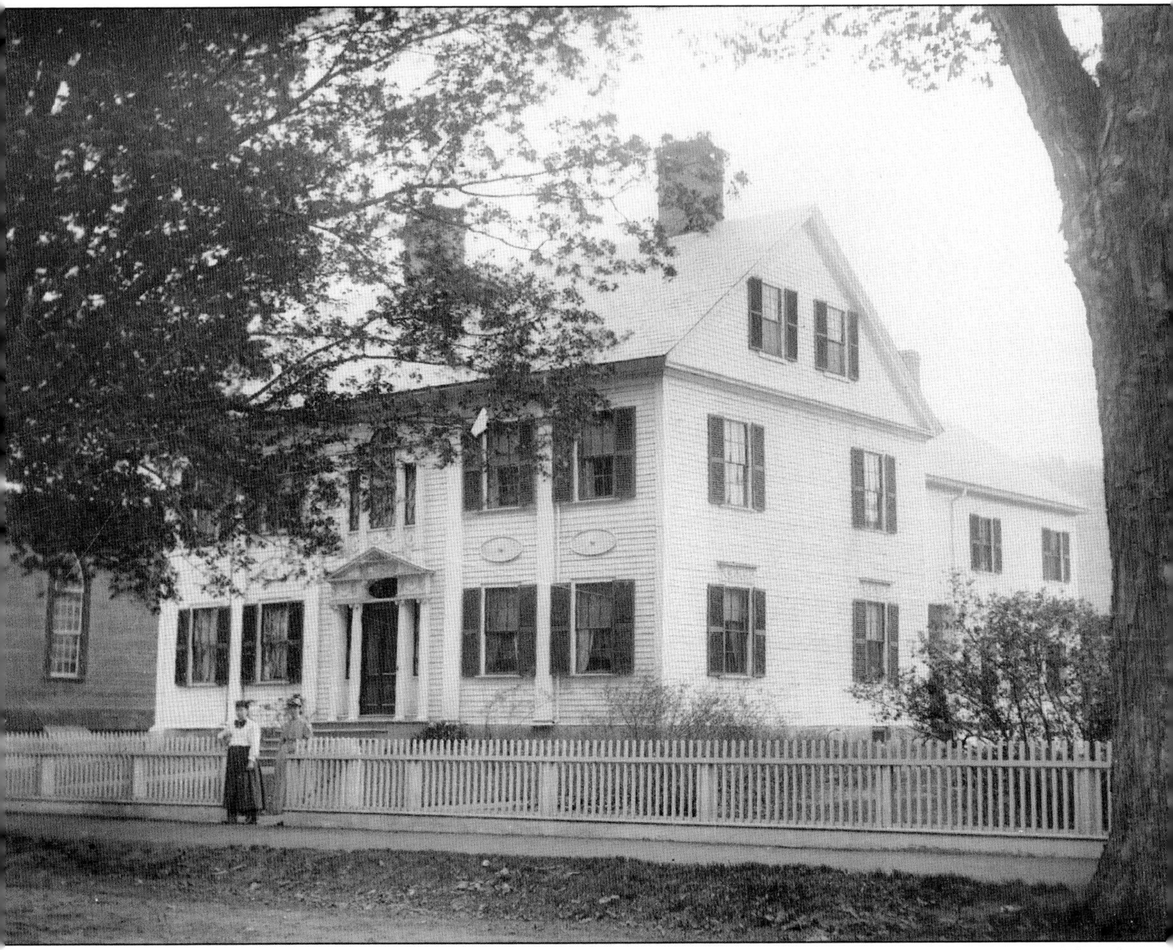

The Fullerton House was designed by Benjamin and built in 1800 by Judge Jonathan Hubbard. One of three private homes built by Benjamin in Windsor, the exterior was a great example of his attention to detail. The interior of the house was extremely well documented and also well detailed. Few such thorough records of a home interior of this caliber from the period remain intact.

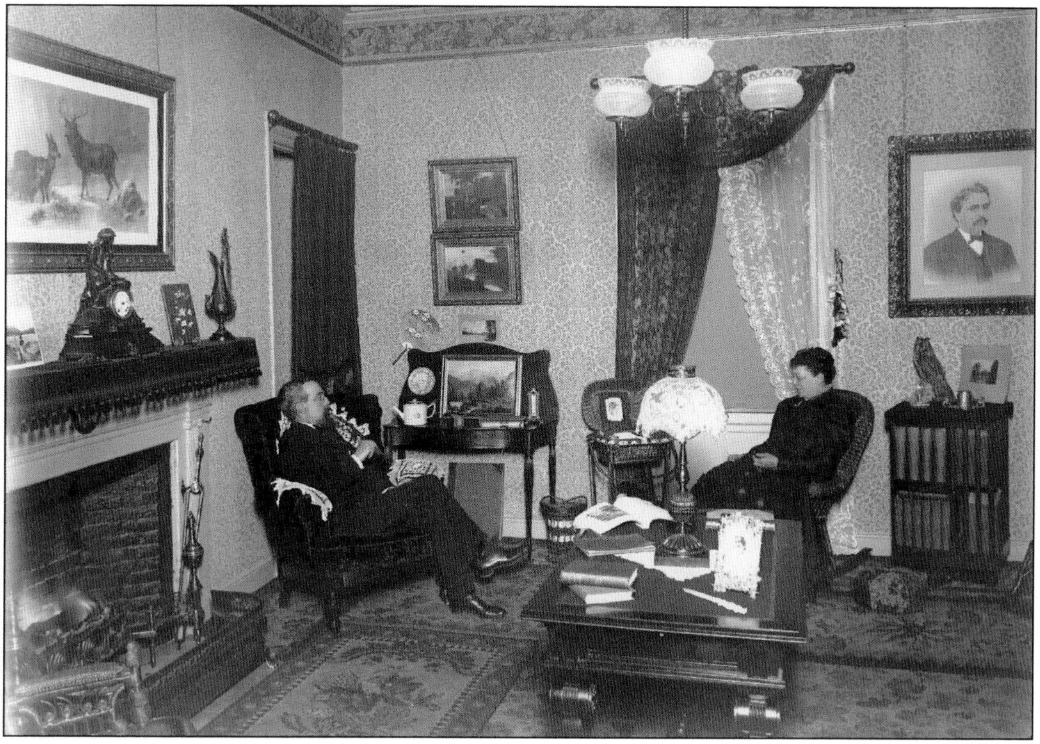

Willima and Melinda Fullerton are pictured above relaxing in the south parlor, which is complete with hand painted wallpaper and lush textiles of the period. Benjamin cited his sources and inspiration with the utmost detail. Drawing from buildings in Rome and Athens, architectural historian Talbot Hamlin wrote, "he more than any other person is responsible for the character we roughly call late colonial." Below, the dining room in the Fullerton House had a sideboard that was reportedly brought to Vermont from Kentucky by oxcart.

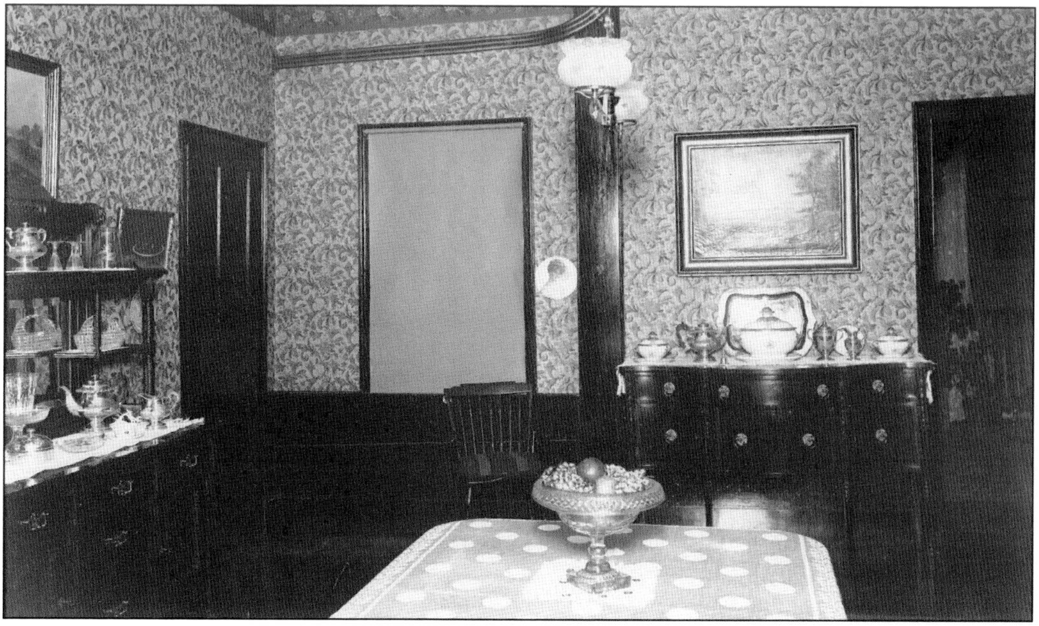

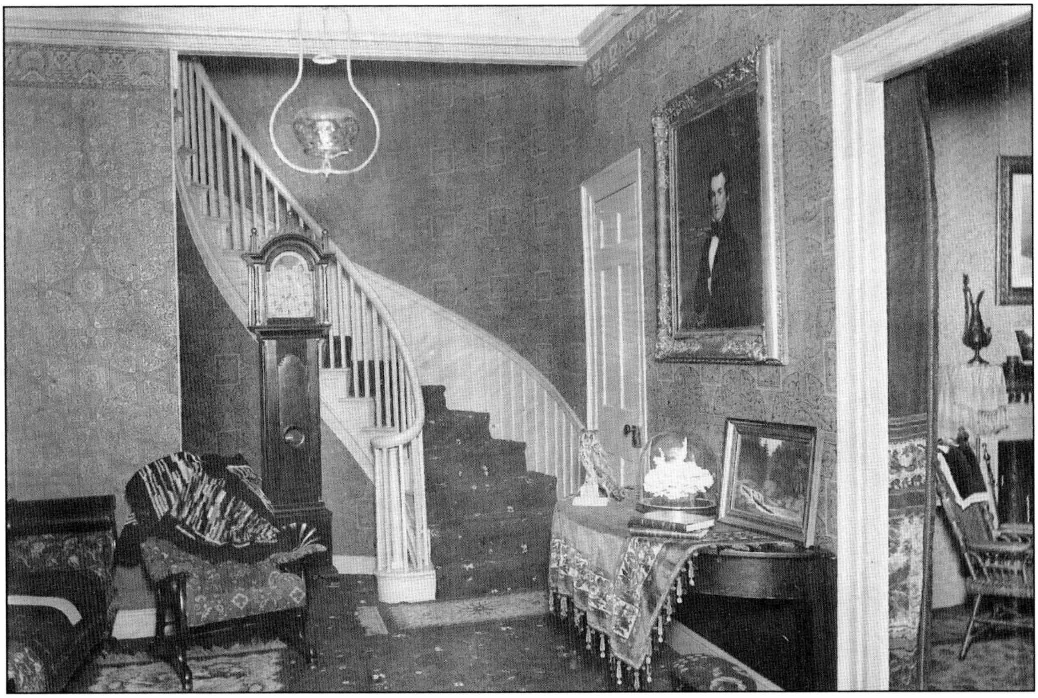

The front hall of the Fullerton House featured a turned wood banister, which was a signature of Benjamin's residential work. A similar one can be seen in his design of a brick Federal in Hartland, Vermont. Called The Sumner-Steele Mansion, it is located several miles north of Windsor. Built around 1811, it is perched high on a hill overlooking Hartland Three Corners. Several Windsor houses, including Stoughton House on Main Street and the 1806 Col. Jesse Lull House in Windsor, have similar stairways inspired by Benjamin. Many followers of his work throughout New England were inspired by his designs and building guides.

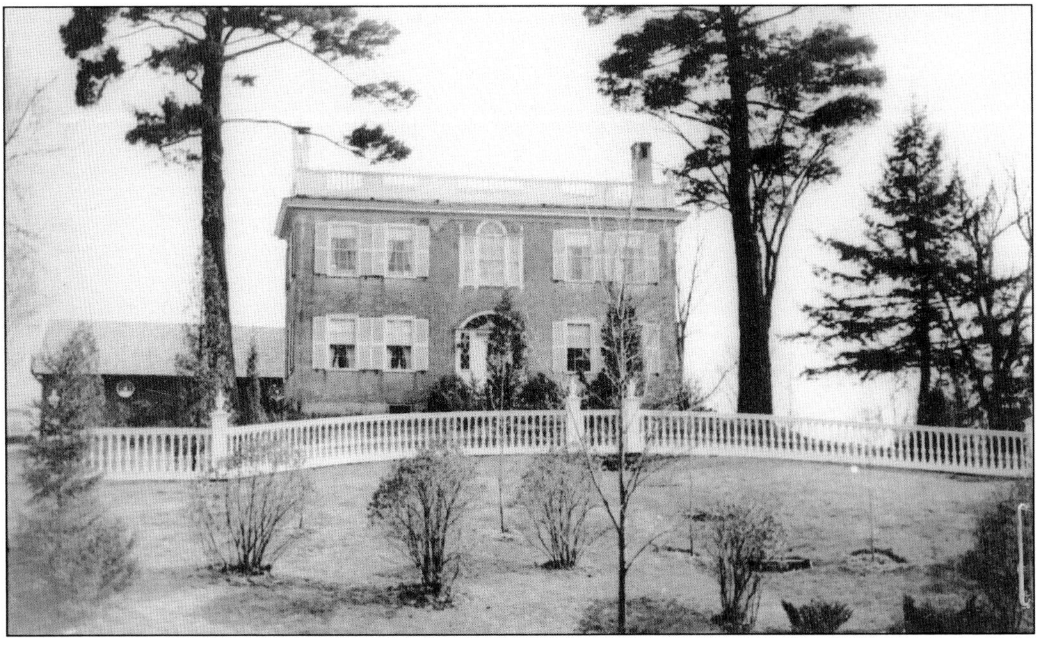

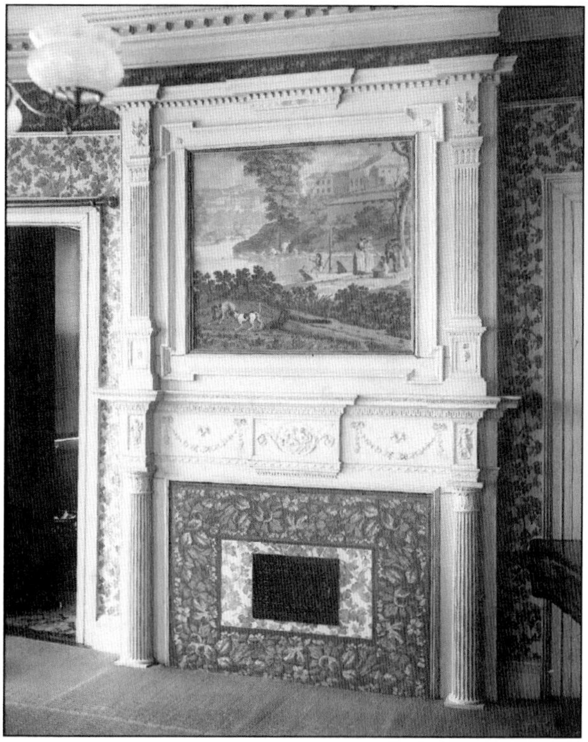

The fireplace in the north parlor of the Fullerton House shows the interior detailing for which Benjamin was known. Destined for demolition in 1936, the house was relocated and rebuilt by the Bloomingdale family in New Canaan, Connecticut. When the family was in residence, it formed the center of the Bloomingdale Estate. The main part of the house remains intact, but has been added onto in all directions. In the summer and fall, the Fullertons spent afternoons relaxing on the side porch.

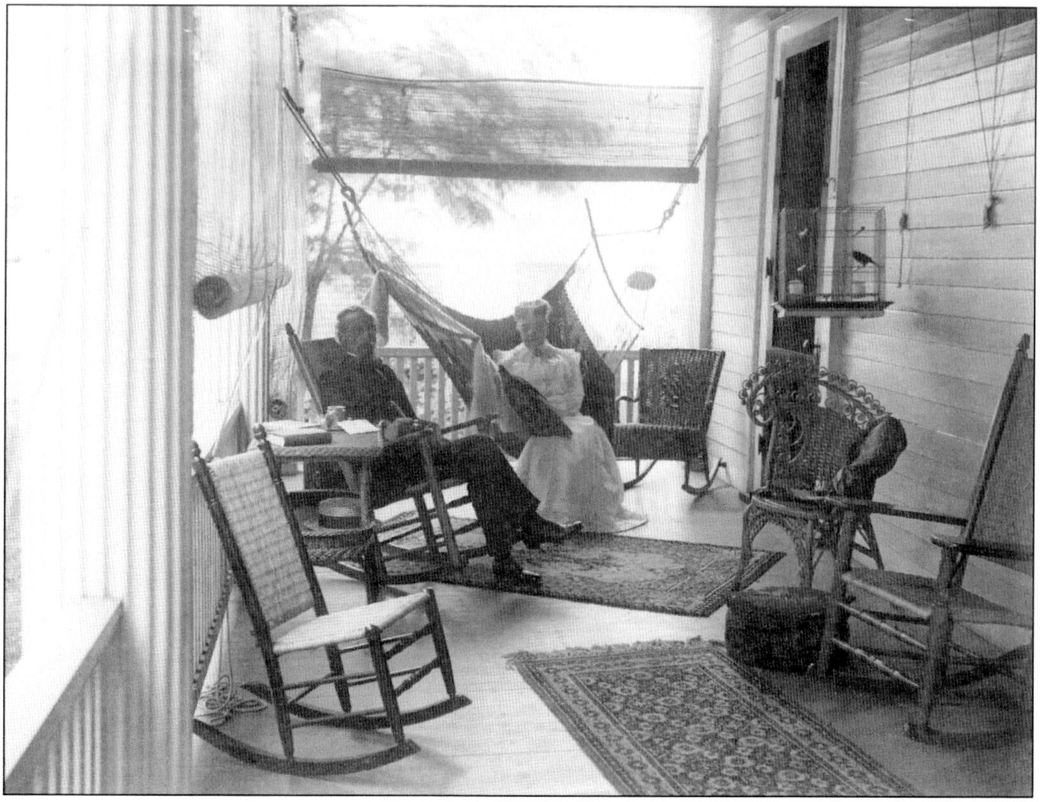

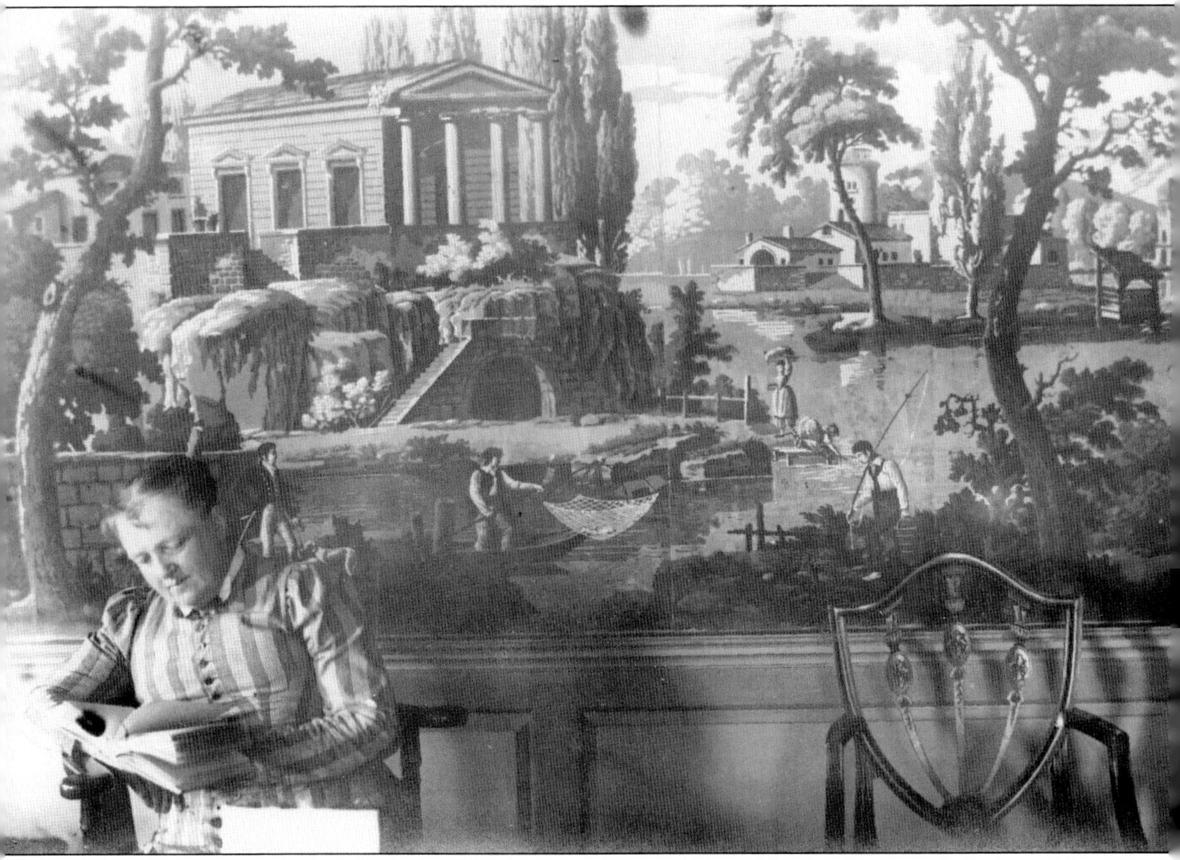

Mary Phelps, daughter of Doctor Phelps, sits reading in front of the hand-painted scenic wallpaper of the period. Doctor Phelps was Windsor's medical examiner and physician to the town poorhouse. He was also a partner in the recipe for Paine's famed celery compound. An activist in the area of social welfare reform, he devoted much of his time to reviewing and improving the conditions of the poor and infirm. He was instrumental in the rebuilding of the poorhouse to include better living arrangements, better food, and better care.

Thomas Emerson built Stoughton House in 1833; however, he soon lost his fortune, along with the fortunes of many other Windsor residents, in the Panic of 1837. The house was attached, and Emerson was escorted to the Woodstock jail. Sewell Belnap, known as "the Napoleon of Railroads," caused the house to meet the same fate in 1849 when the mansion was sold to settle debts caused by unwise investments. (Courtesy Historic Homes of Runnemede.)

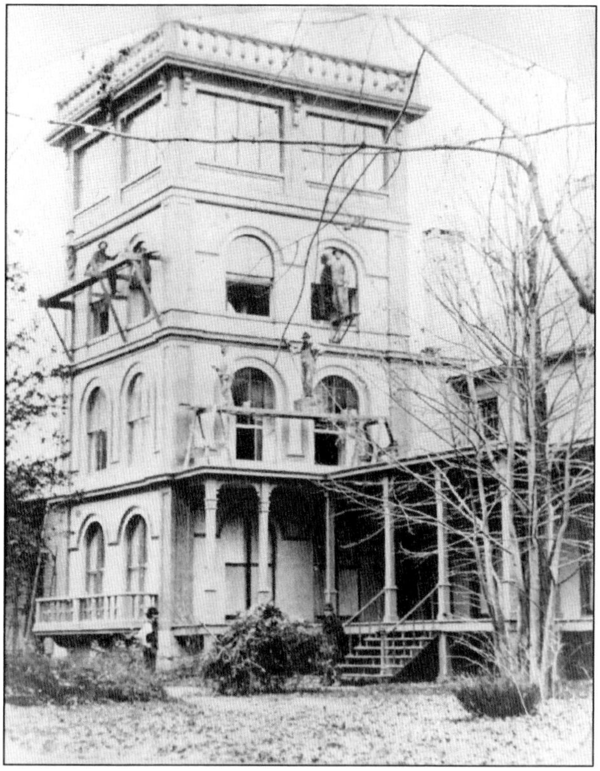

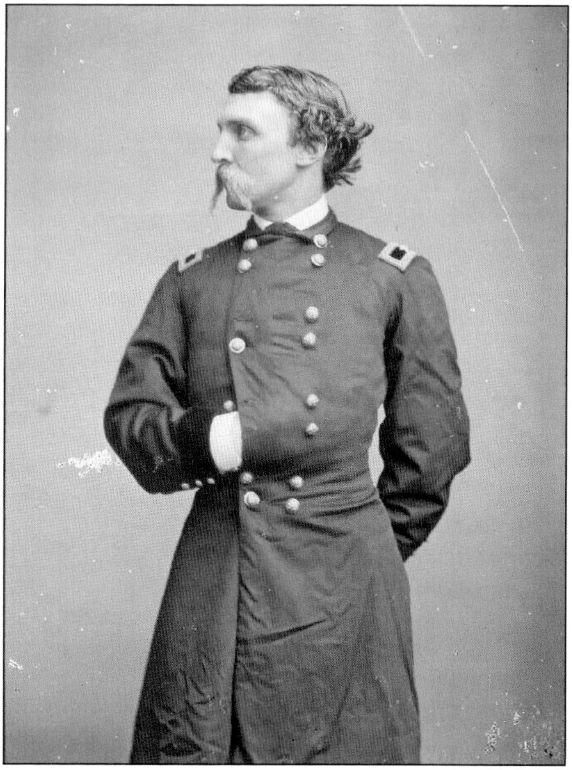

The third time was the charm when Edwin W. Stoughton, a prosperous attorney from New York, purchased what became the Stoughton House and restored beauty to the house and gardens. His carriages, accompanied by coachmen and footmen, were frequently seen downtown. Fond of entertaining on a grand scale, Jenny Lind performed at musicals held in the drawing room. President Hayes was also a guest, and in 1877, Hayes more than returned the favor by appointing Stoughton ambassador to Russia.

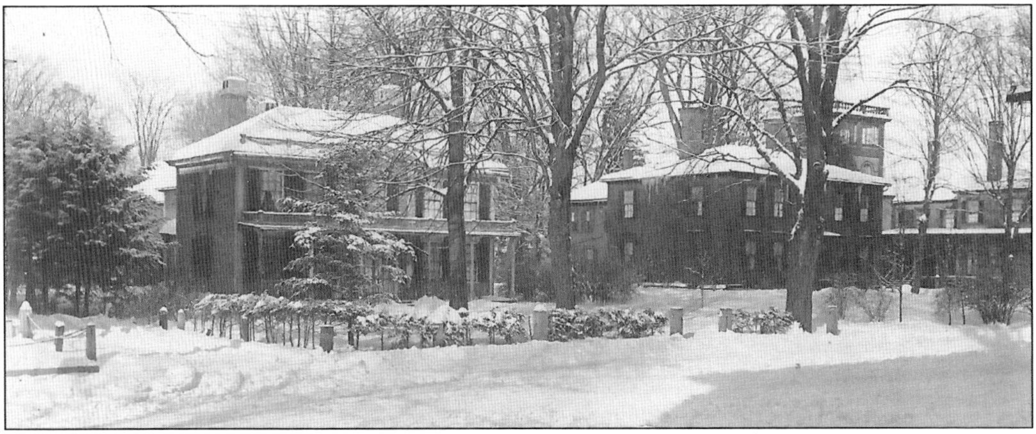

Hubbard is the house on the left, Lane House is in the middle, and Stoughton House is on the right. Of these three, only Stoughton House remains.

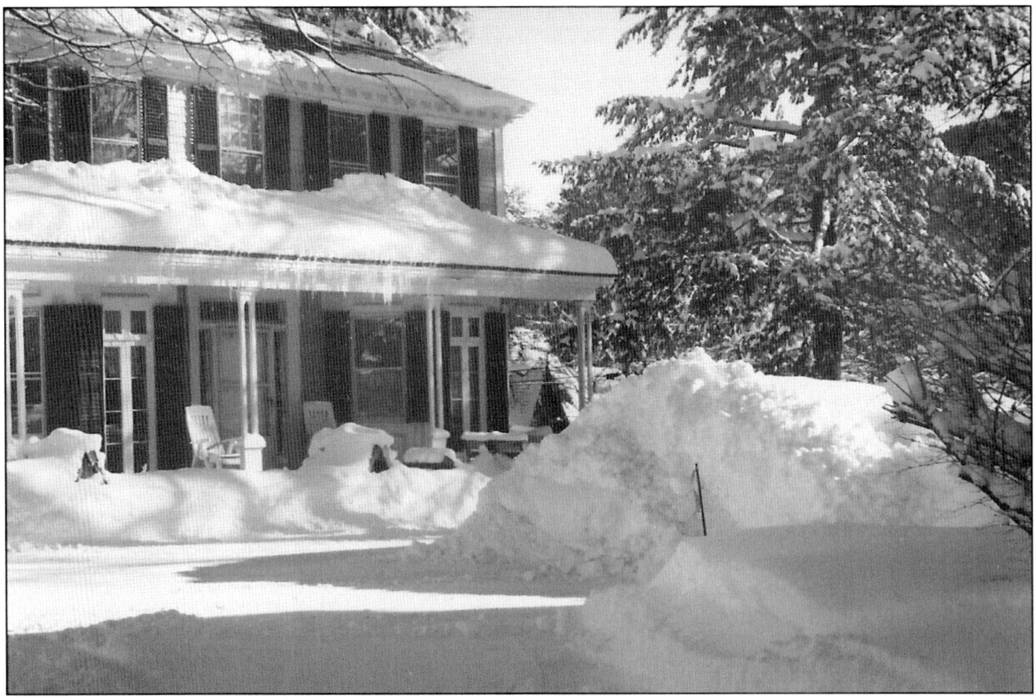

Built in 1796 and purchased by William Evarts in 1851, this home became known as the "White House," as it hosted presidents Hayes, Harrison, and Roosevelt. In addition to holding the position of secretary of state under Hayes, William Evarts served as attorney general under Andrew Johnson and as a senator from New York. It is one of the three homes that now comprise the Historic Homes of Runnemede, a residential facility for seniors. (Courtesy Historic Homes of Runnemede.)

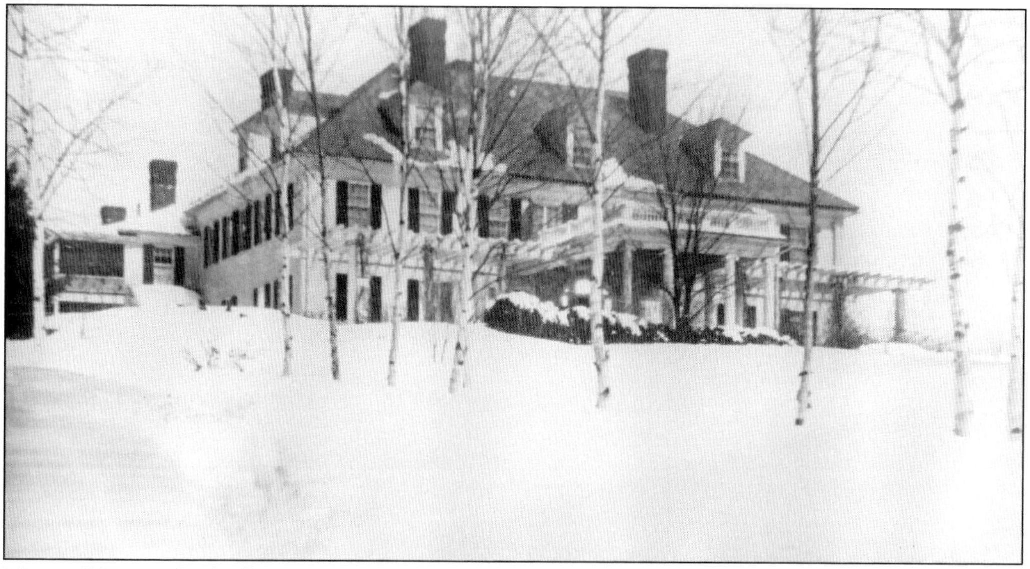

Maxwell Evarts built the mansion known as Juniper Hill Farm in 1902 on land that had been purchased by his father, William Maxwell Evarts. The colonial revival mansion, built as a summer cottage, overlooks Paradise Park and Lake Runnemede, the "in town" estate created by his father. This grand cottage was completed at a cost of $100,000. Maxwell, a Yale graduate like his father, William, was a prominent attorney and president of the Windsor National Bank. He was also lead counsel to the Union Pacific Railway. While in residence, Maxwell continued entertaining in the tradition of his father. The dining room has seated presidents Teddy Roosevelt and Calvin Coolidge. It is now the welcoming destination of the Juniper Hill Inn.

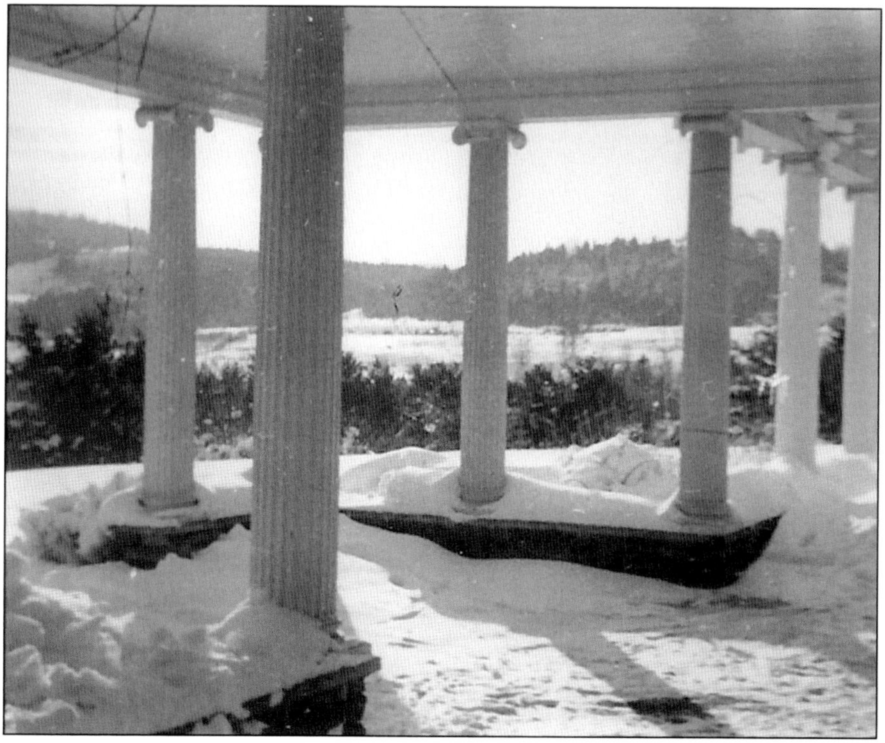

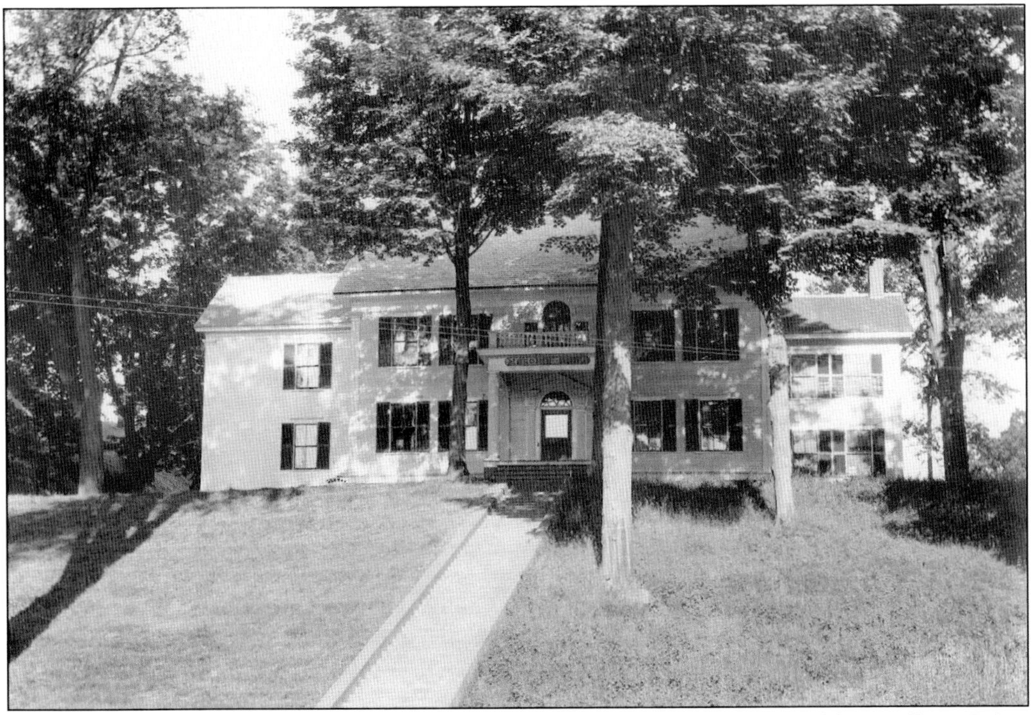

Capt. Nathaniel Green Leonard built the Leonard-Sabin mansion in 1791. Sold to William Sabin some 60 years later, the house was nearly consumed by a fire in 1881. Sabin, one of the largest property owners in Windsor at the time, rebuilt the house after the fire and then moved to the Whatnot House north of town. In the early 19th century, the Sabin house became the famous Windsor Female Academy, visited in 1817 by President Monroe. In 1919, George Gridley, inventor of the Gridley Automatic Lathe, rebuilt and restored the mansion.

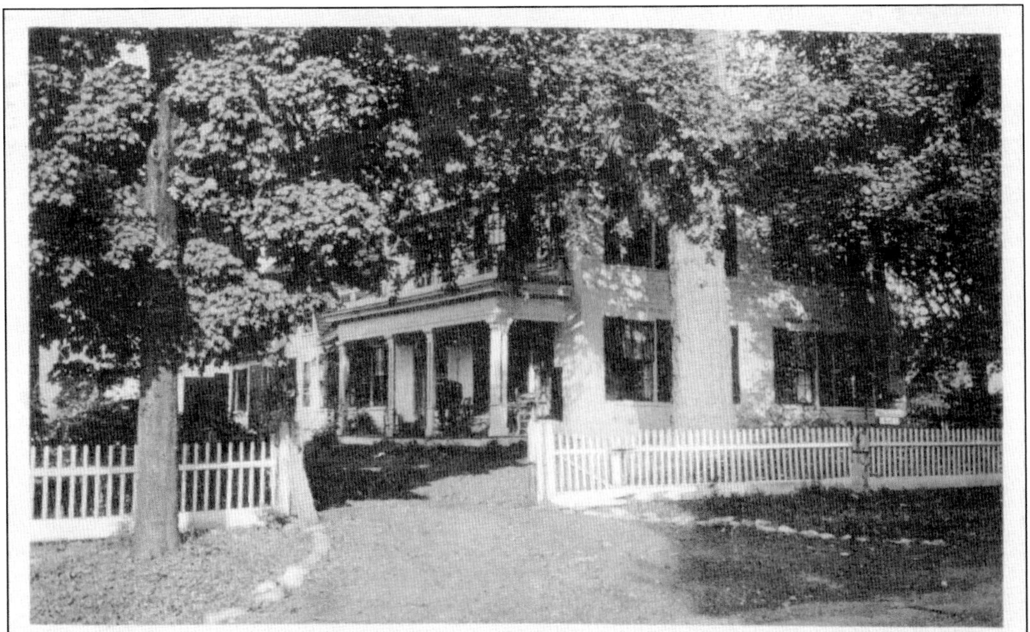

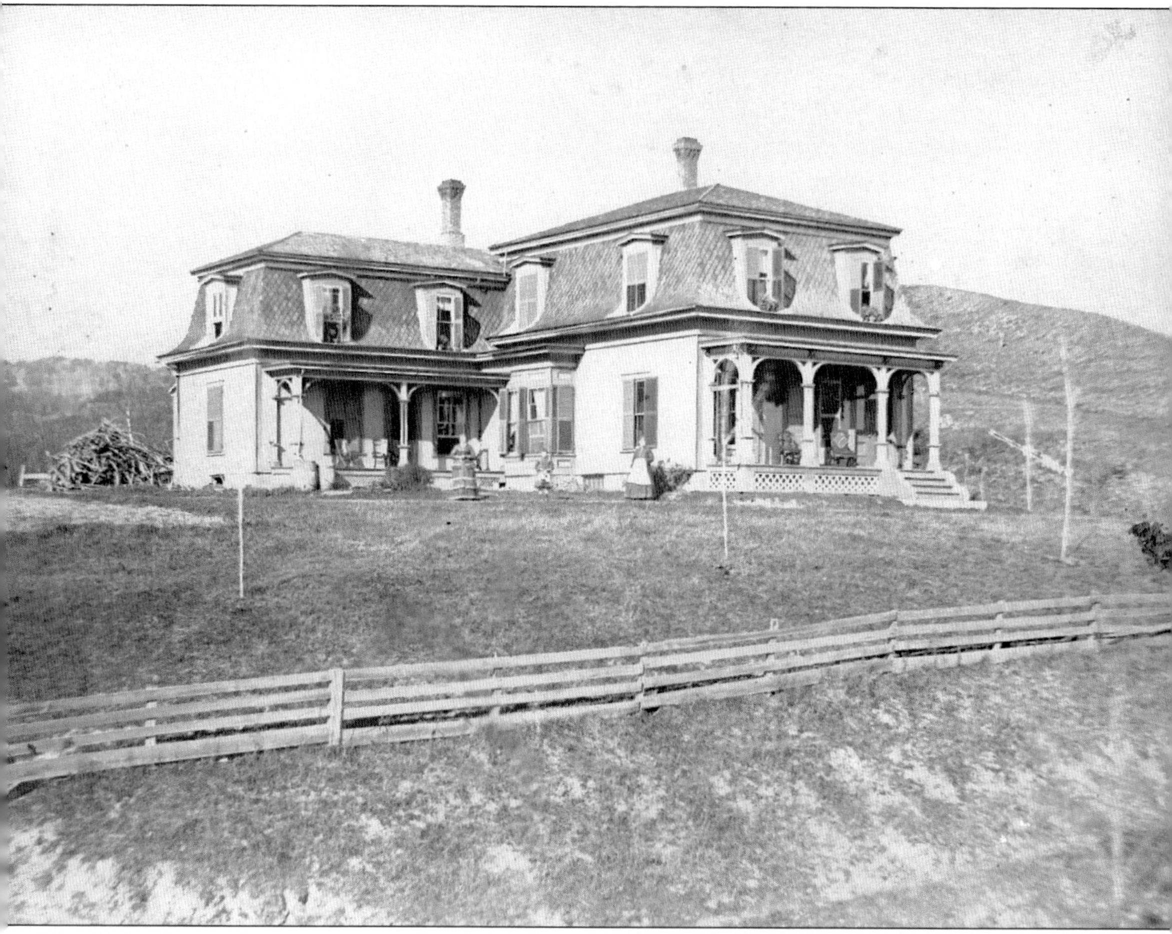

The Solon-Mower house, seen in this 1876 photograph, was built in 1874. Now surrounded by trees and other homes, it was briefly owned by Maxfield Parrish between 1936 and 1939 and is said to have been home to his muse, Sue Lewin. One can see her in many of Parish's paintings costumed as the Pied Piper and other colorful characters.

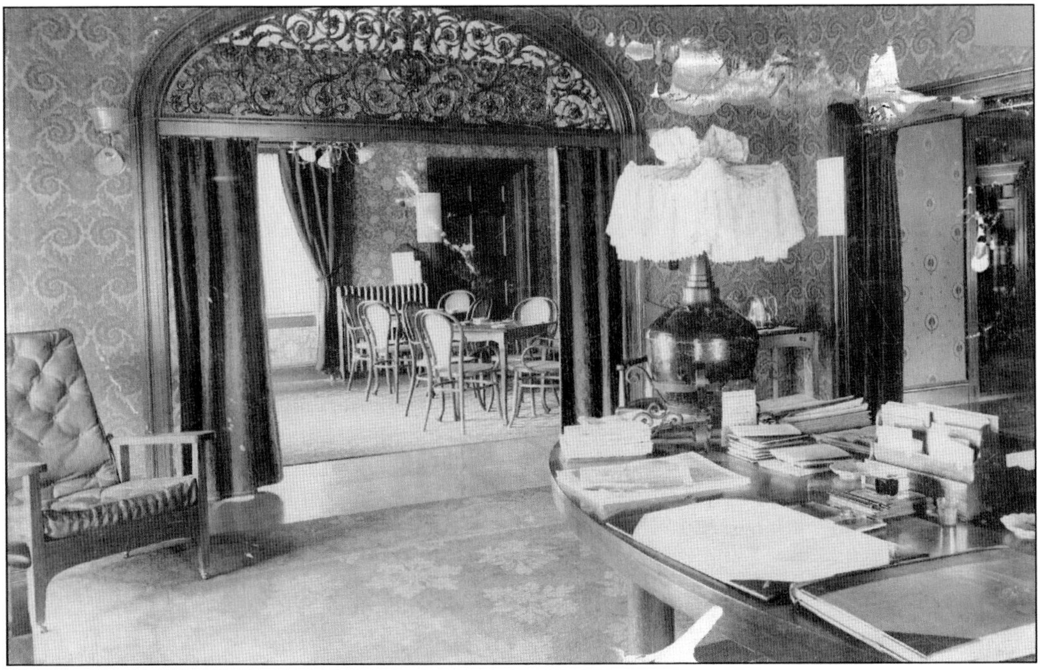

What is currently known as the Windsor House began its life as Pettes's Coffee House in 1800. Capt. Joseph Pettes came to Windsor from Amherst, Massachusetts, and purchased the land from Stephen Conant. Pres. James Monroe and the Marquis de Lafayette were both entertained here. After it burned in 1836, it was rebuilt as a hotel and public house and reopened in 1838. In the latter half of the 19th century, it was said to have had 50 newly furnished rooms and impeccable food—the best between Boston and Montreal.

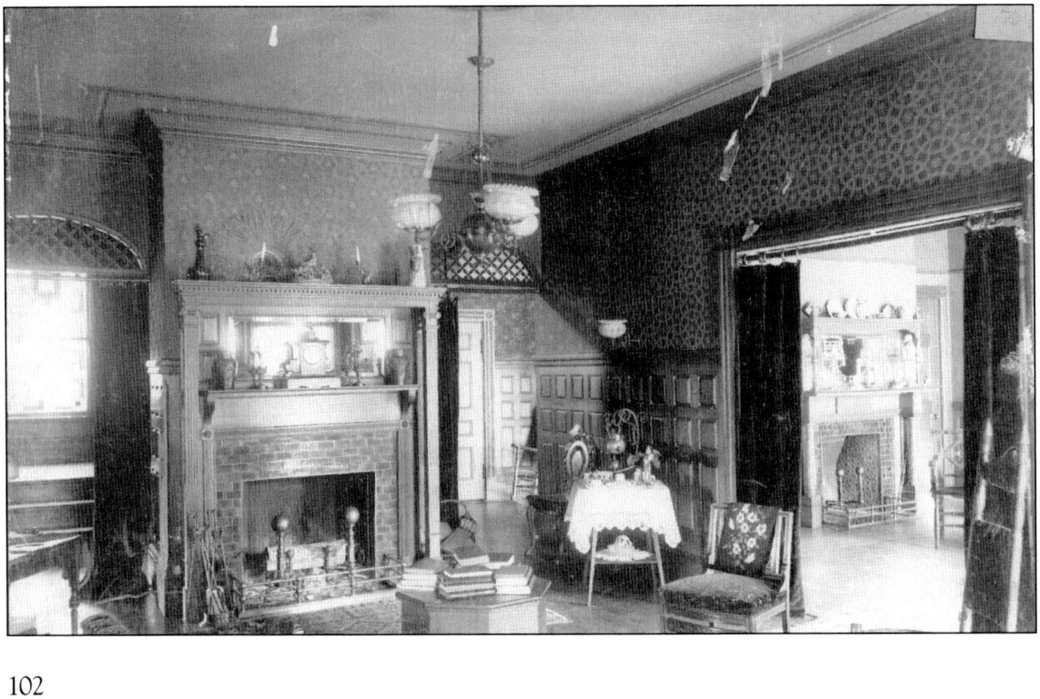

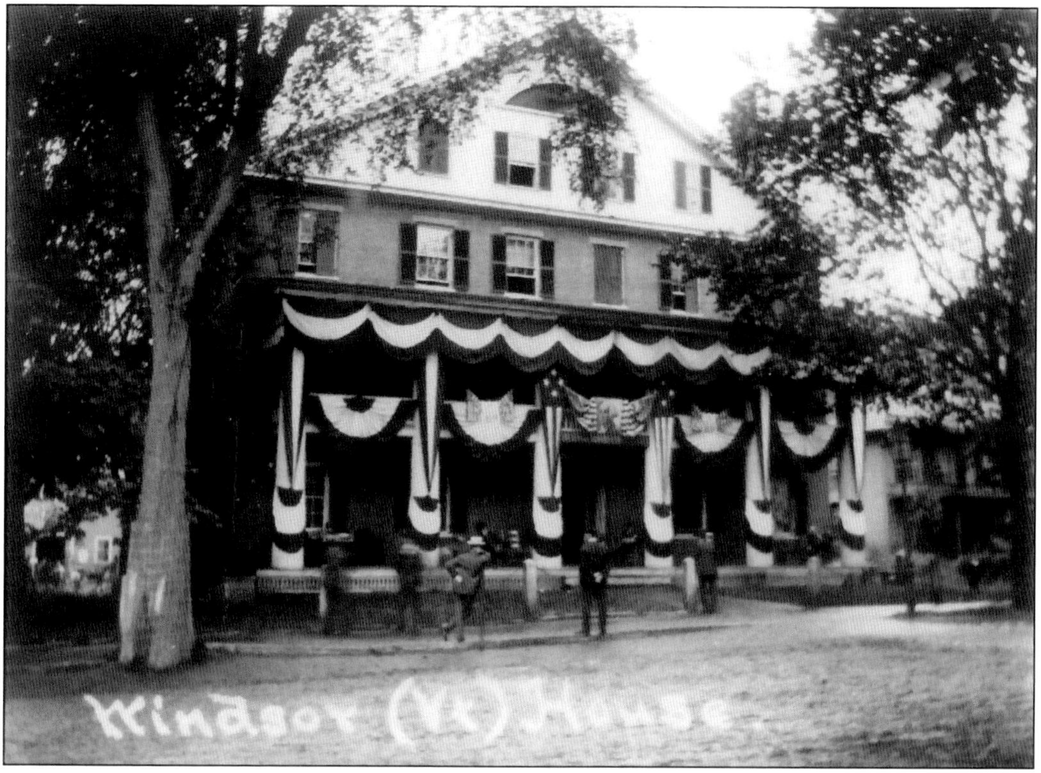

Draped in bunting to welcome President Roosevelt when he came through town in 1902, the Windsor House was slated for demolition in 1971. The rapid formation of Historic Windsor Inc. saved and preserved it. Today, it remains an imposing presence on Main Street and now has a spot on the National Register of Historic Places. The porch still has rocking chairs for passersby needing a restful moment.

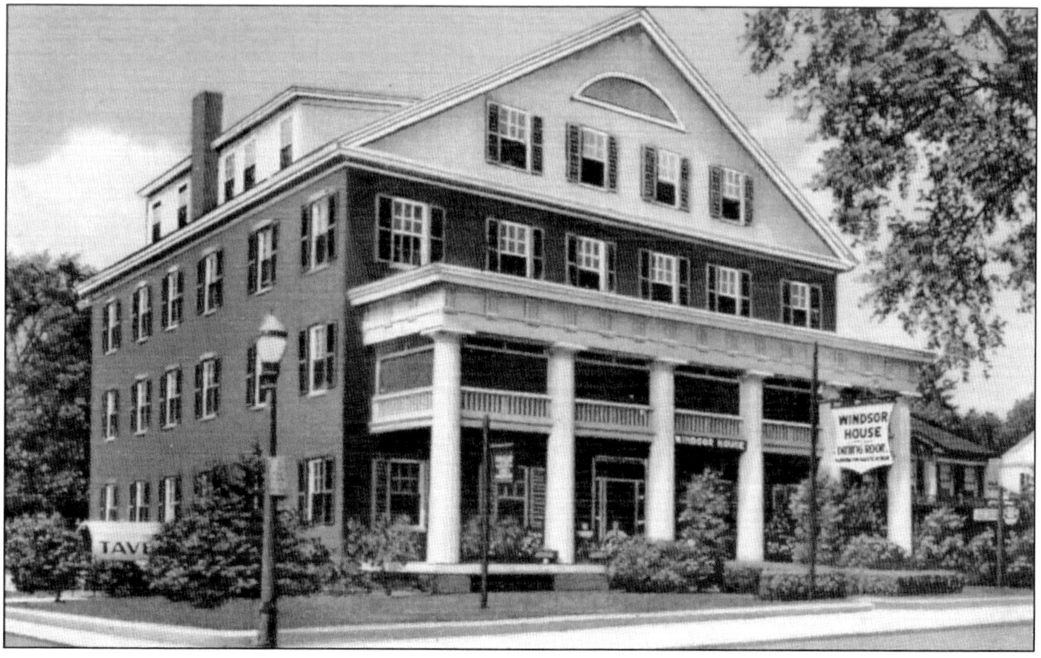

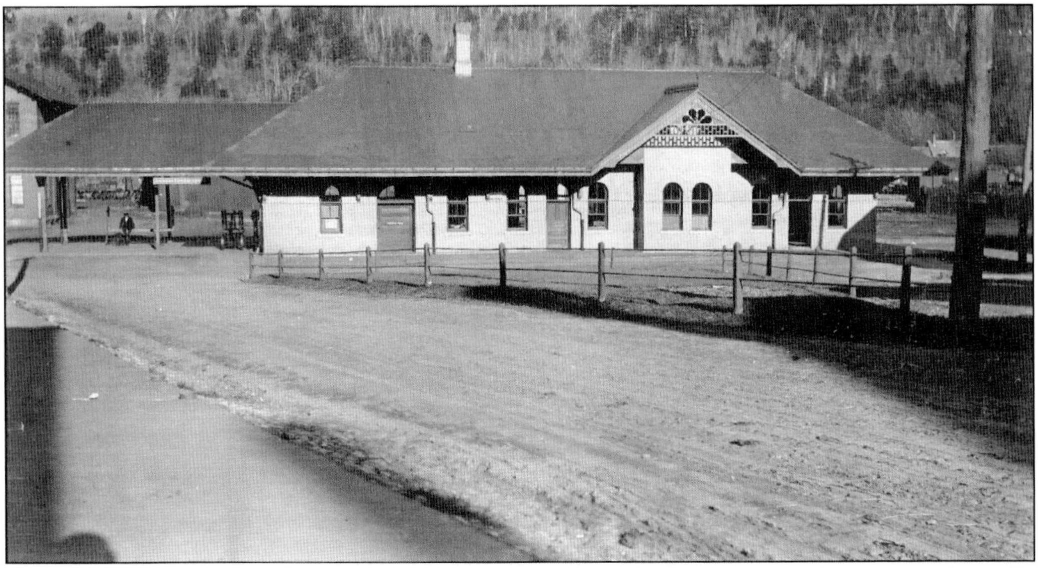

The first trains came through Windsor on January 31, 1849. Three passenger cars came from the north and eleven from the south. Sewell Belnap entertained over 400 guests at his home for dinner that evening, and the party continued through the night at the Windsor House. Six months later, Belnap died at the age of 37, penniless and in debt for over $89,000. Windsor remained a major junction for the railroad until 1895, when the main depot moved to White River Junction.

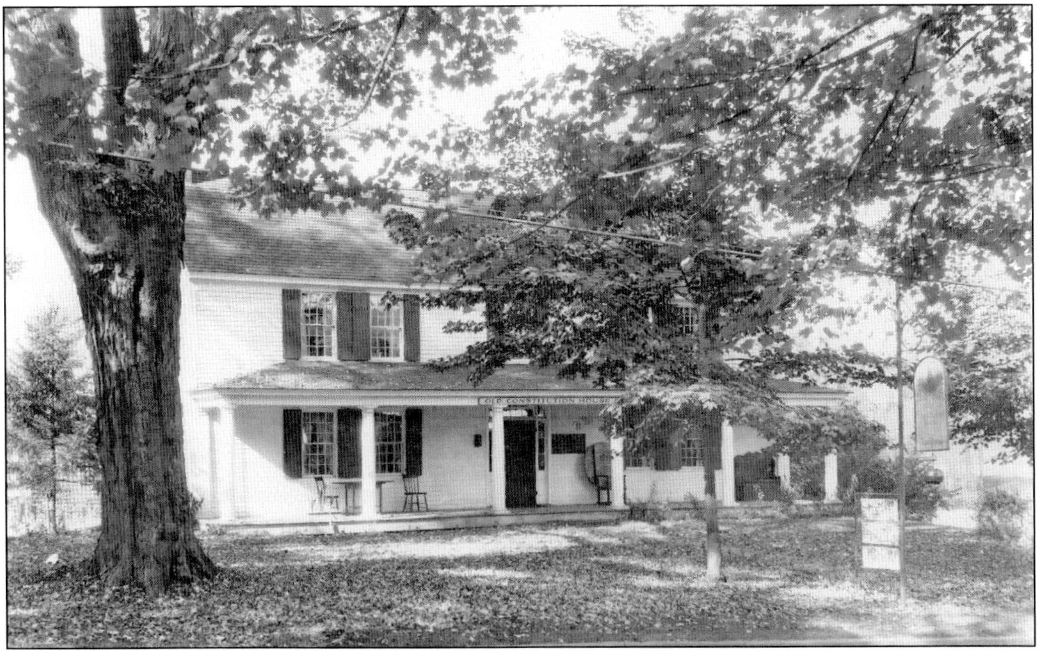

The Old Constitution House, which was founded as a tavern in 1774, was also where the *Vermont Journal* was published until 1829. It remained a tavern until 1848. It was moved once around 1870 to make way for construction of the brick Fay Block, and then again as it was saved from demolition. Before the state assumed ownership in 1961, it functioned as a museum and a tearoom. It is now a museum once again, with serene gardens along the shore of Lake Runnemede. It has been designated a Vermont Historic Site.

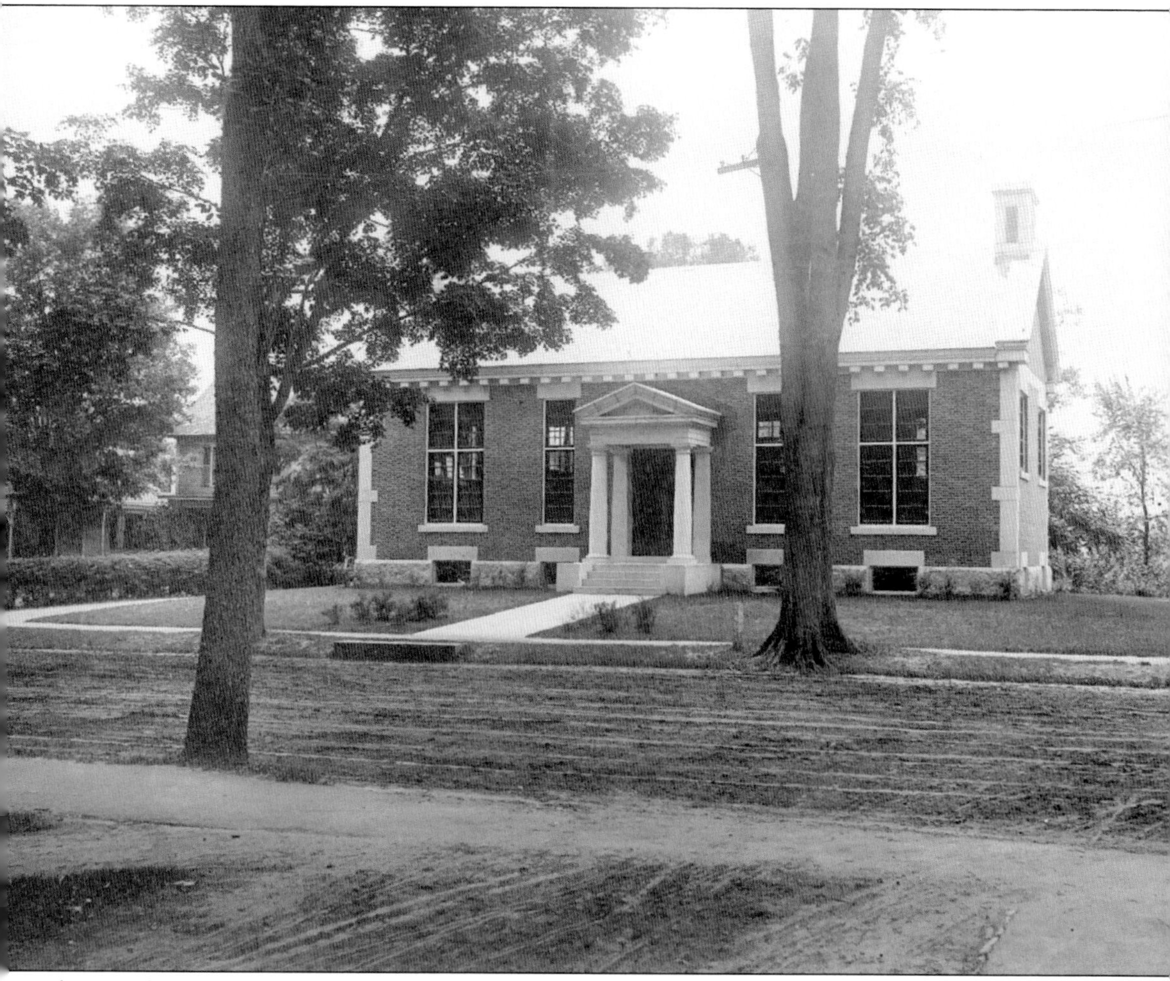

The Windsor Library on State Street was dedicated in September 1904. The architect chosen for the project was Henry Bacon, who had designed the Lincoln Memorial in Washington, DC. Prior to the building of the library, the collection had been housed in the Hiram Harlow house. The Hiram and Rachel Harlow Estate left their house, funds, and land as a bequest to the library.

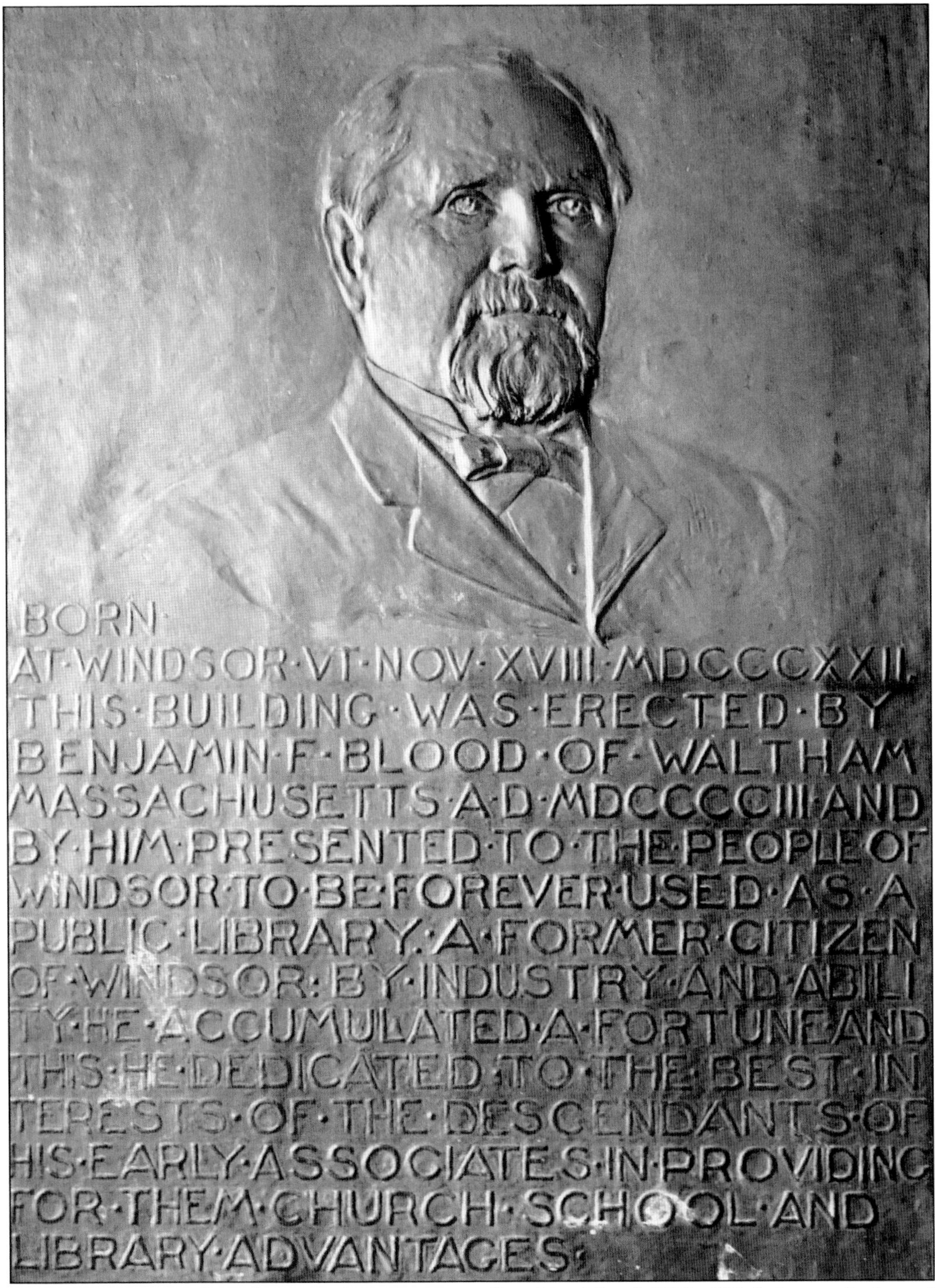

The library was a gift to the town from Benjamin Franklin Blood (1822–1904). It was the last of three libraries paid for and donated by Blood to towns in Vermont. Benjamin F. Blood is quoted, "It is my hope that this building will prove for all time an inspiration to noble deeds, honest industry, the love of choice reading, and to crown all, good citizenship." (Courtesy David Westby.)

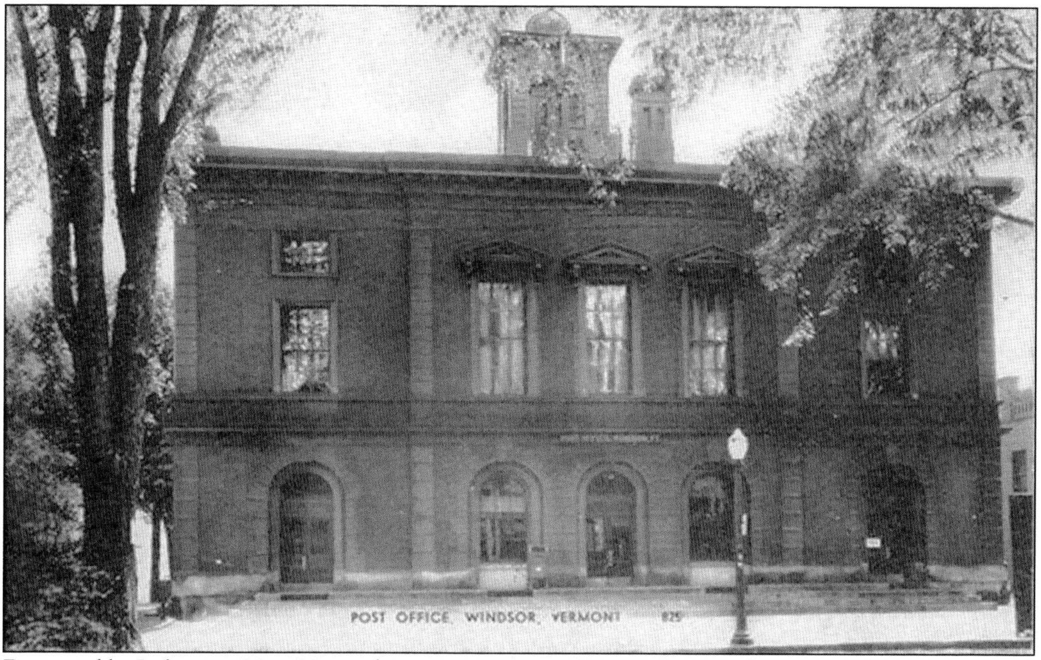

Designed by Lebanon, New Hampshire, native Amni Young, the Windsor Post Office was erected in 1859. Windsor was one of only five towns in Vermont designated in the young republic to have a post office. Young had been the supervising architect for the US Treasury Department and designed many significant government buildings throughout the country. Alden Spooner, the first postmaster, was also a printer and founder of *Spooner's Journal*, later renamed the *Vermont Journal*.

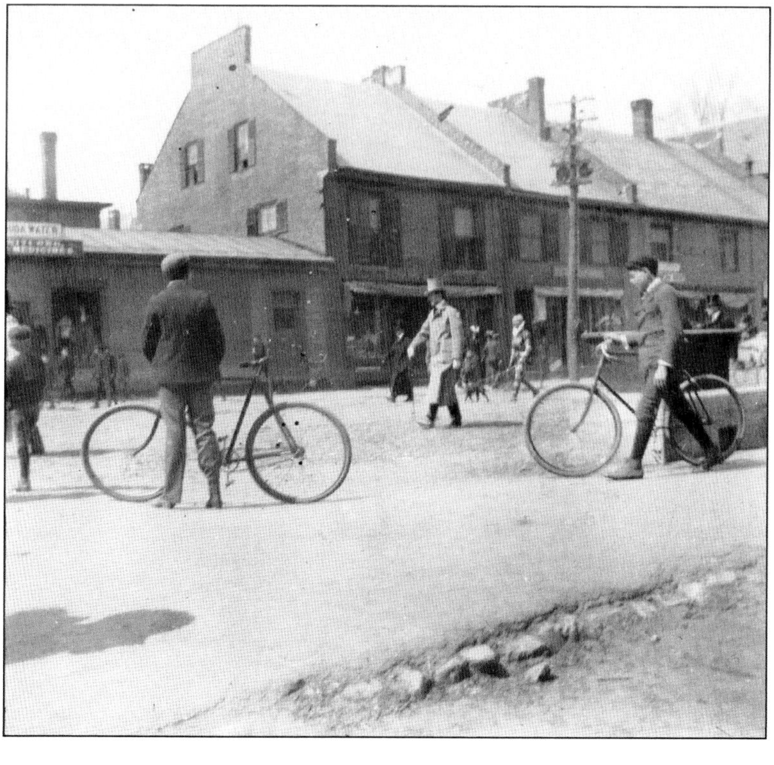

The Tontine Block was built in 1825 in the Federal style. One of several commercial blocks built on Main Street, today only the section on the left remains. The 1929 construction of a J.J. Newberry building replaced the central and right sections of the Tontine Block and employed new construction techniques and materials, such as large glass windows.

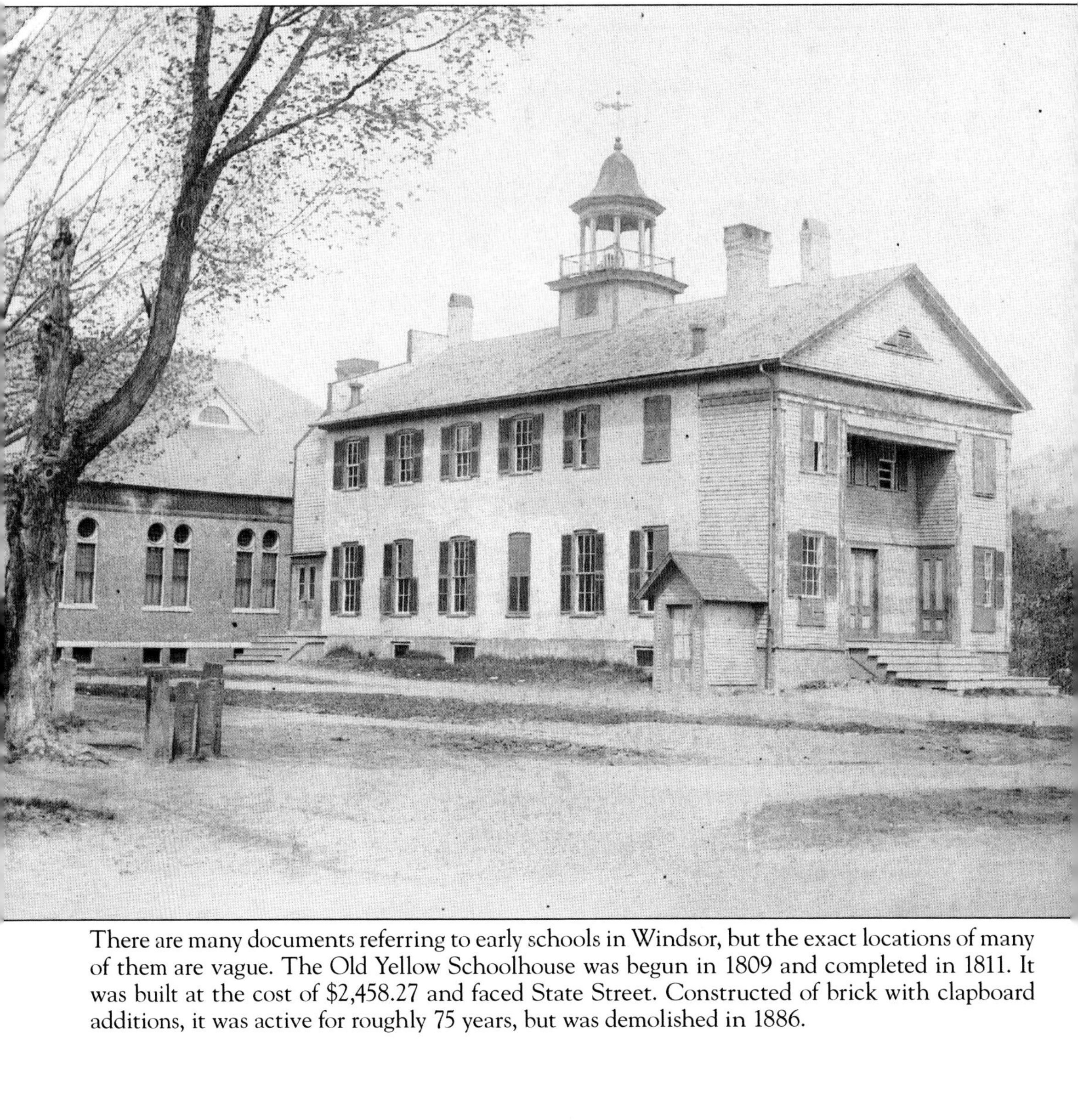

There are many documents referring to early schools in Windsor, but the exact locations of many of them are vague. The Old Yellow Schoolhouse was begun in 1809 and completed in 1811. It was built at the cost of $2,458.27 and faced State Street. Constructed of brick with clapboard additions, it was active for roughly 75 years, but was demolished in 1886.

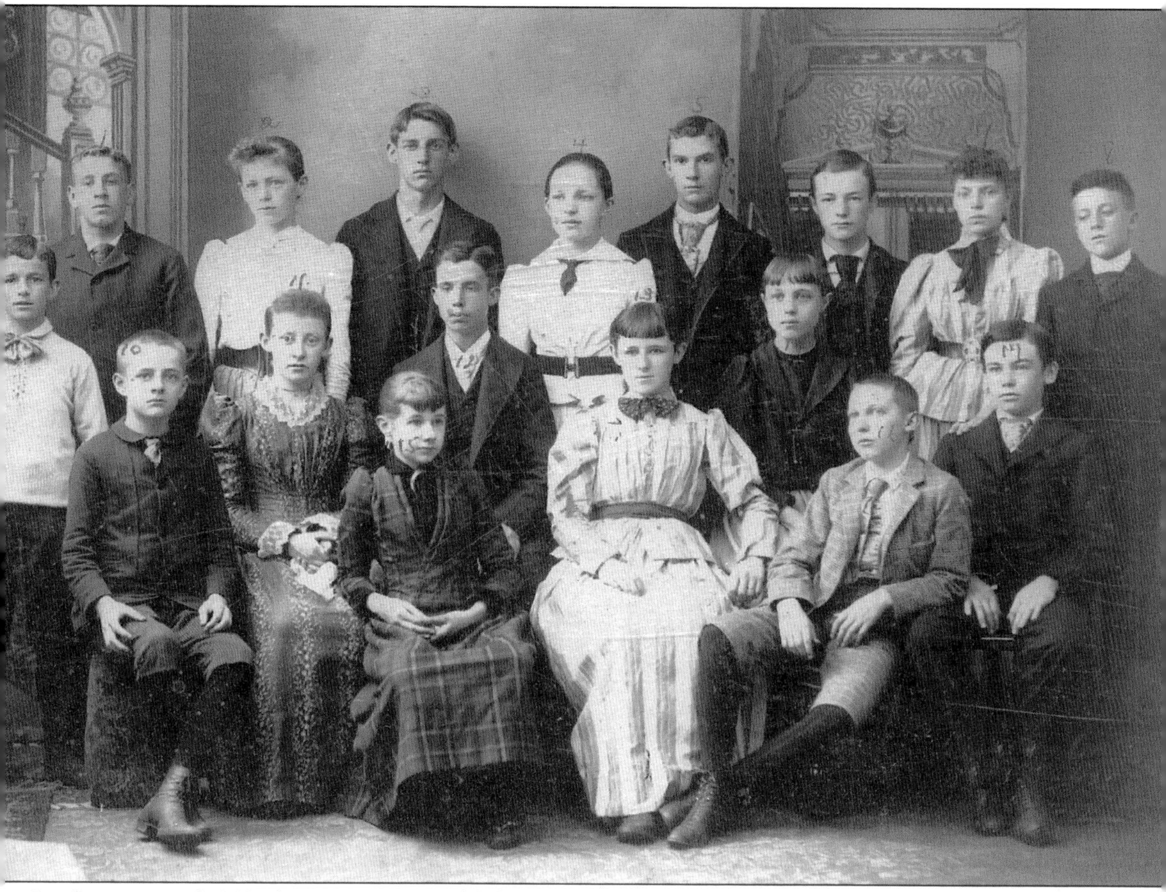

In the spring of 1809, this notice was published in the local paper: "Grammar School (Windsor). The Grammar School is this day opened for the spring term in this place. Tuition for those who study Latin, Greek, or Mathematics, 25 cents per week; for those who study English Grammar, write & c. 20 cents per week. Windsor." This graduating class of 1892 probably paid a bit more than the 1809 prices. Pictured from left to right are (first row) Belle Morgan, George Grieny, and George P. Cheney; (second row) Henry Weston, Sophronia Ruggles, Merton Robinson, Grace Crilly, and Florence Smith; (third row) George Enright, Martha Davis, Leonard Sherman, Lucy Mc Clary, Sidney Wellman, Edward Brown, Anna Wheeler, and Louis E. Williams.

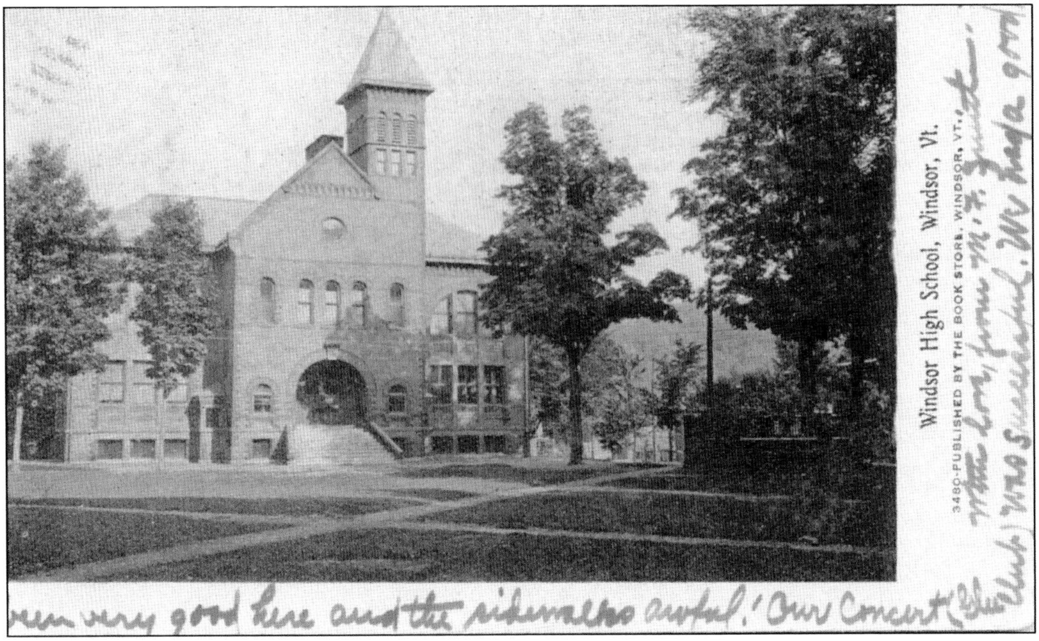

Windsor High School was built in 1887 on what was the site of the Old Yellow School House. It was added to in 1899, but closed in 1939. The writer of the postcard above, sent in 1909 from a visitor in Windsor to Oak Park, Illinois, complained of the poor sidewalks but said that their "glee club concert went very well!" The graduating class of 1889 sat in front of Old Windsor High School for their class photograph, which seems to have included all the students, not just those graduating.

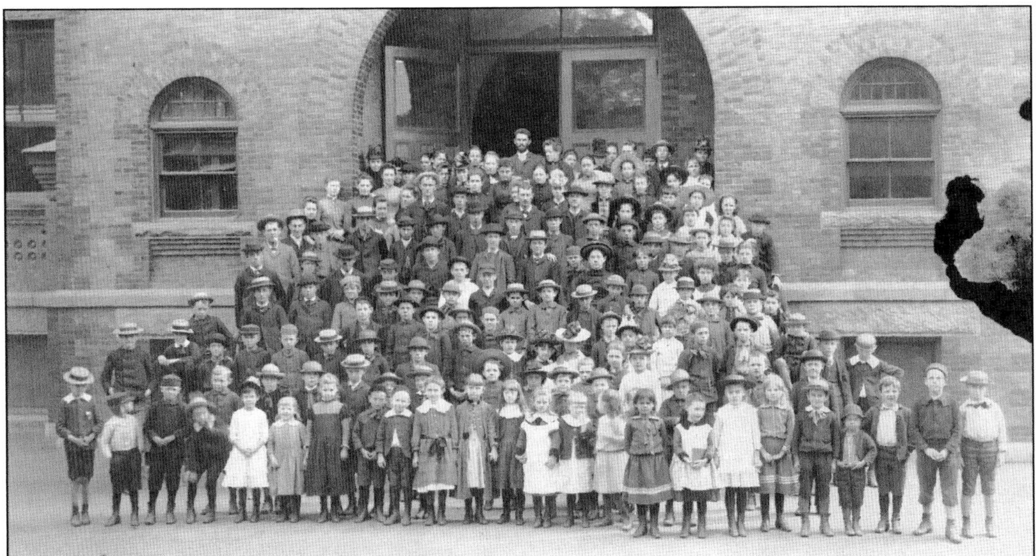

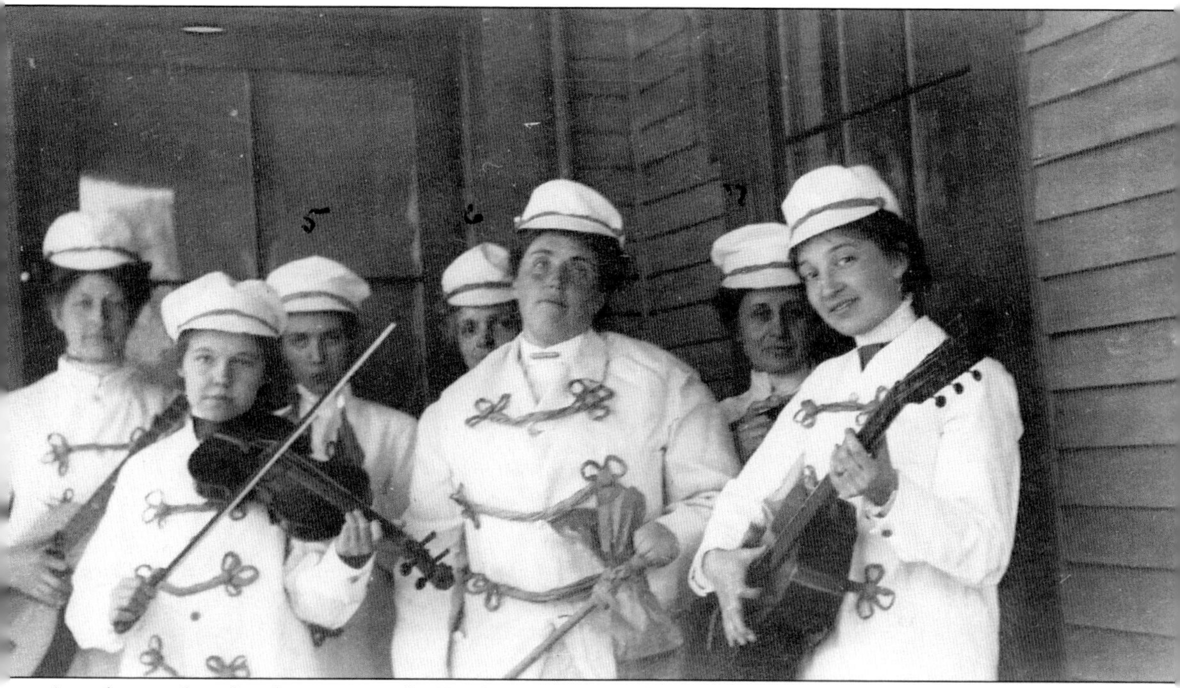

Another early school notice read, "Fowler, Rev. (Windsor). Mr. Fowler proposes to take a few scholars, this summer, at his own house, to instruct in any of the branches of Science, commonly taught in Schools and Academies. Those who may think proper to honor him with the care of their children may rely on having a careful attention paid to their manners and morals, as well as to their improvement to useful knowledge. Windsor 5 June 1809." Members of the high school orchestra, pictured quite a few years later, included, from left to right, Eva Jones, Addie Morgan, Helen Stowell, Florence Cabot, Claire Harlow, Gertrude Cole, and Hazel Clough.

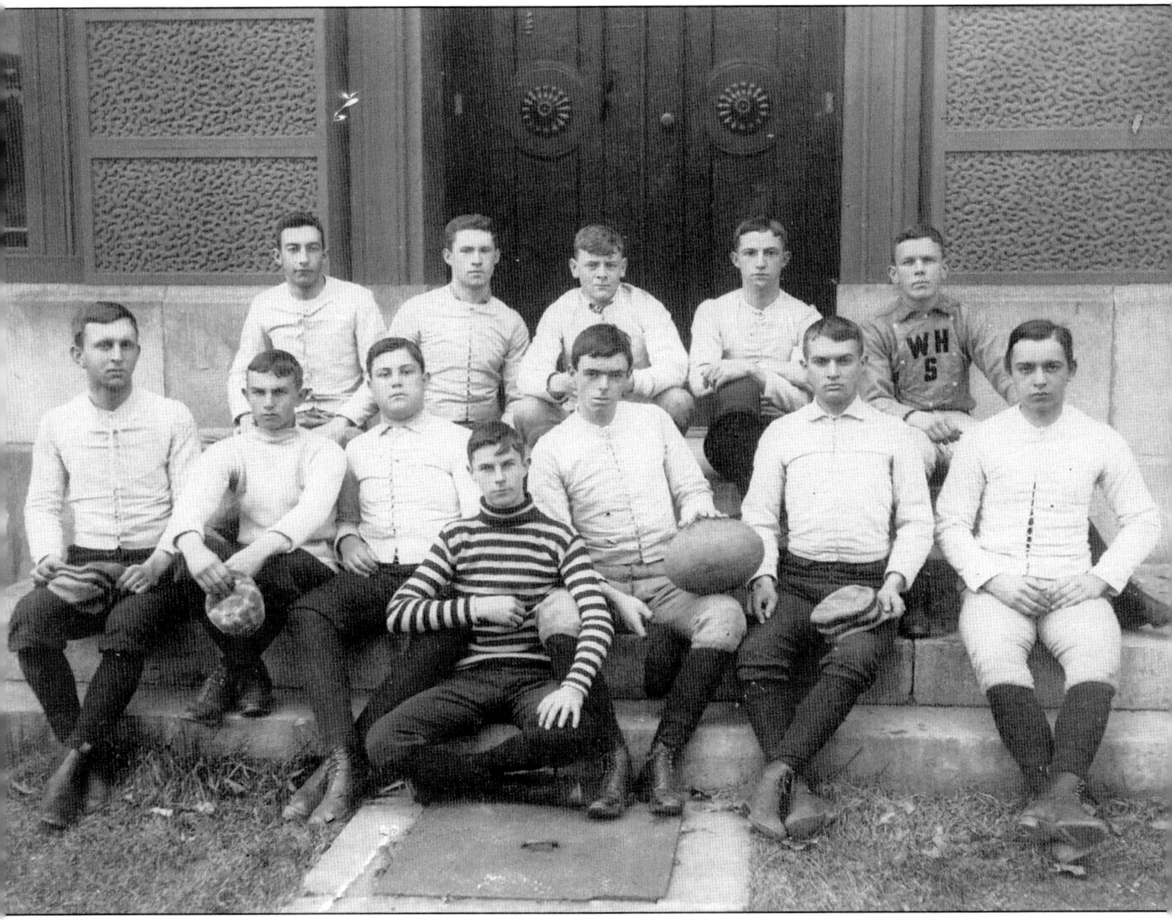

The Windsor High School football team is pictured in 1891 in front of the side entrance to the Windsor Post Office. The back of the photo reads, "Donated by Miss Dunn, who inherited Gay House, State Street, May 4, 1958." What is now the historic Stephen Jacob House had been known more recently as the Gay House. Second from left in the second row is William Gay, who played right halfback.

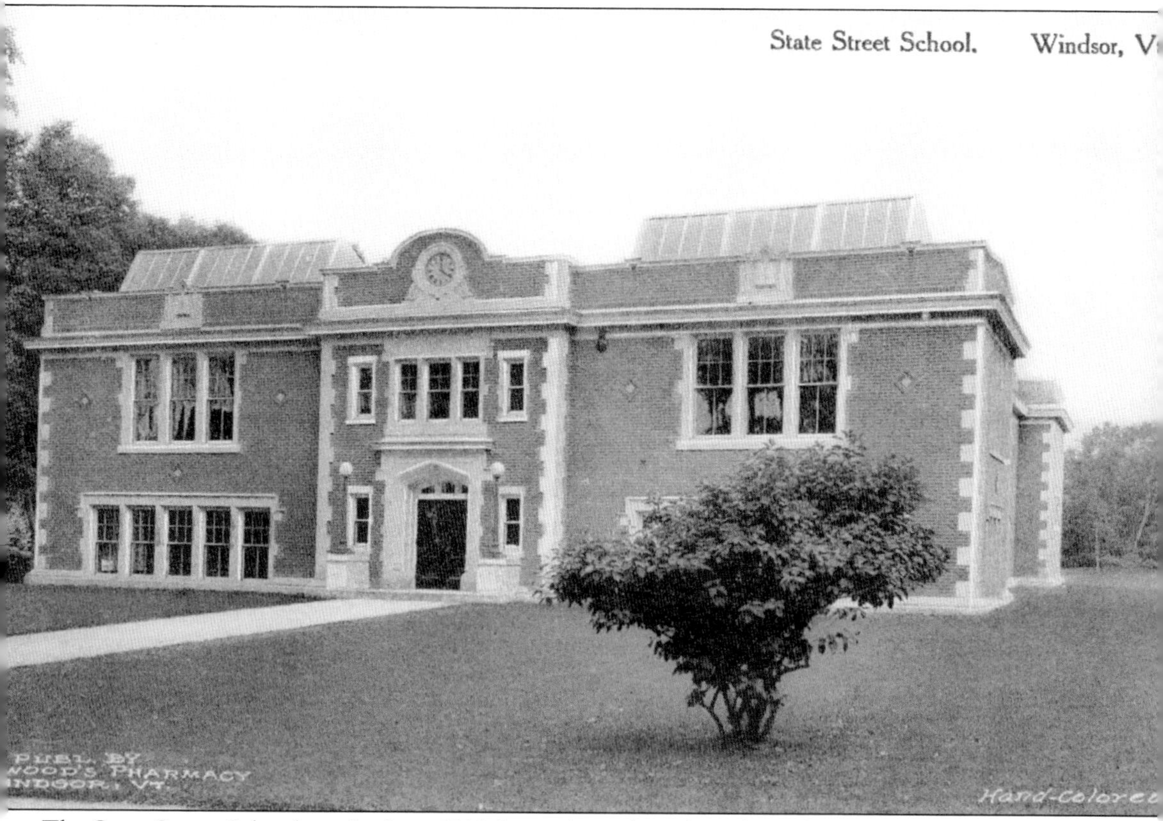

The State Street School was built in 1915 for students from first through eighth grades. A third floor was added in the mid-1930s to accommodate more students. The Rockwood Pharmacy on Main and State Streets published this postcard. Another elementary school, Union Street Elementary, was built in 1922 and was in use until 1939.

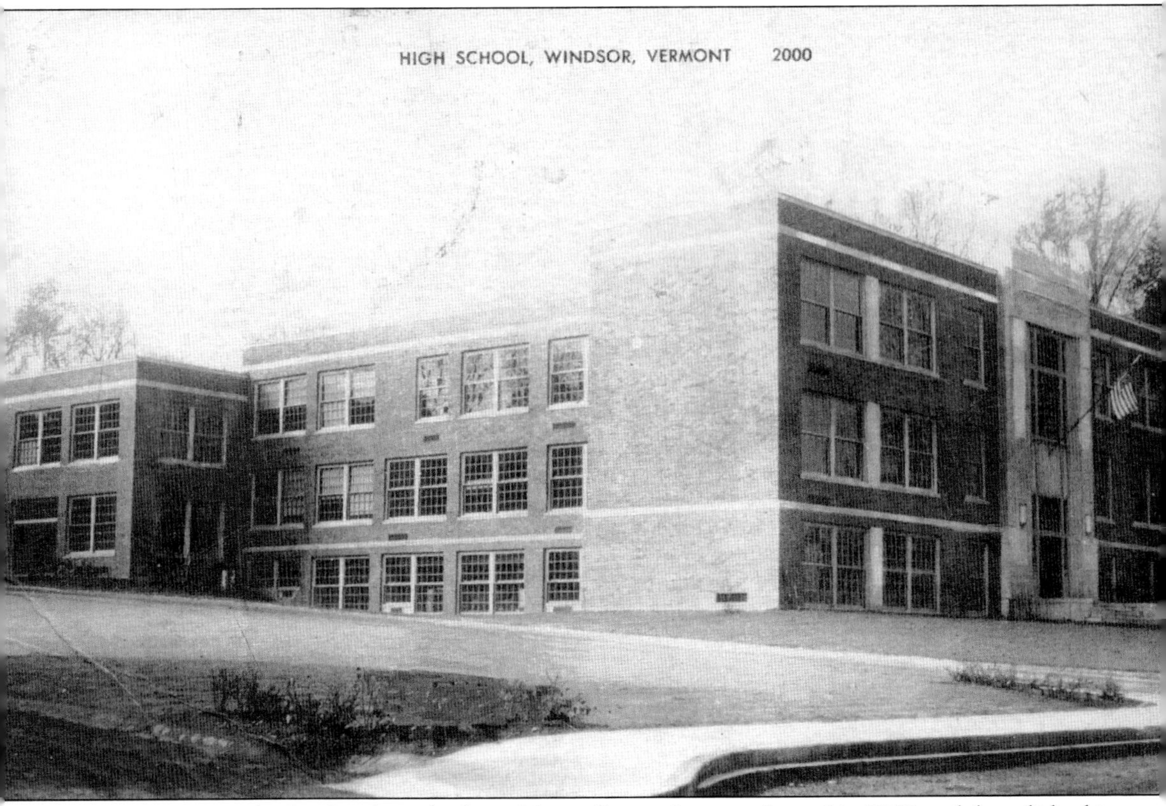

In 1939, a new high school was built on Union Street. It was enlarged in 1958 and demolished in the 1990s; however, the gymnasium was saved and is now part of the Windsor Municipal Complex, which includes the town offices and public recreational facilities. Writing to her cousin in Maine in 1949, this writer said, "the country up here is just beautiful!"

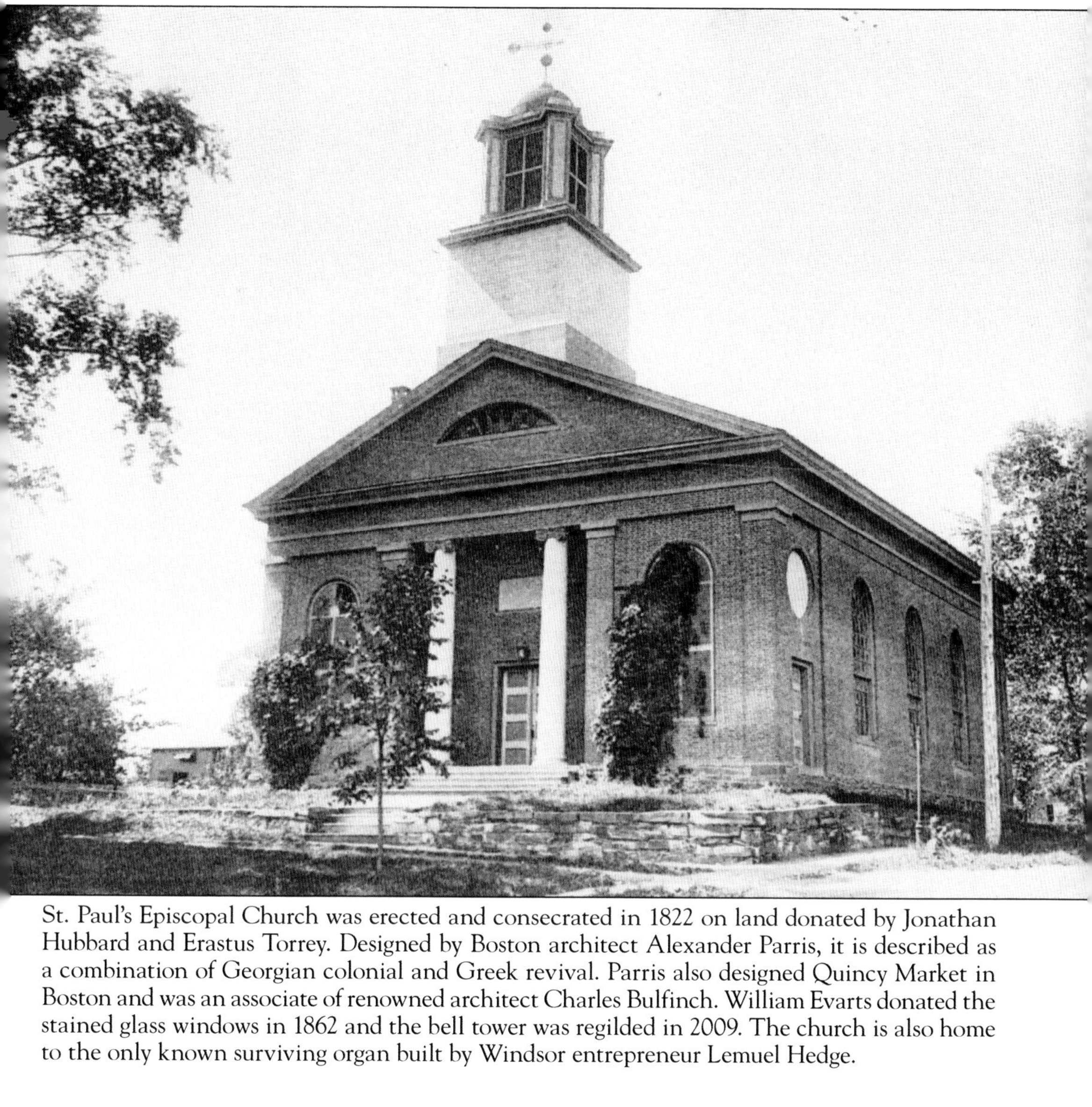

St. Paul's Episcopal Church was erected and consecrated in 1822 on land donated by Jonathan Hubbard and Erastus Torrey. Designed by Boston architect Alexander Parris, it is described as a combination of Georgian colonial and Greek revival. Parris also designed Quincy Market in Boston and was an associate of renowned architect Charles Bulfinch. William Evarts donated the stained glass windows in 1862 and the bell tower was regilded in 2009. The church is also home to the only known surviving organ built by Windsor entrepreneur Lemuel Hedge.

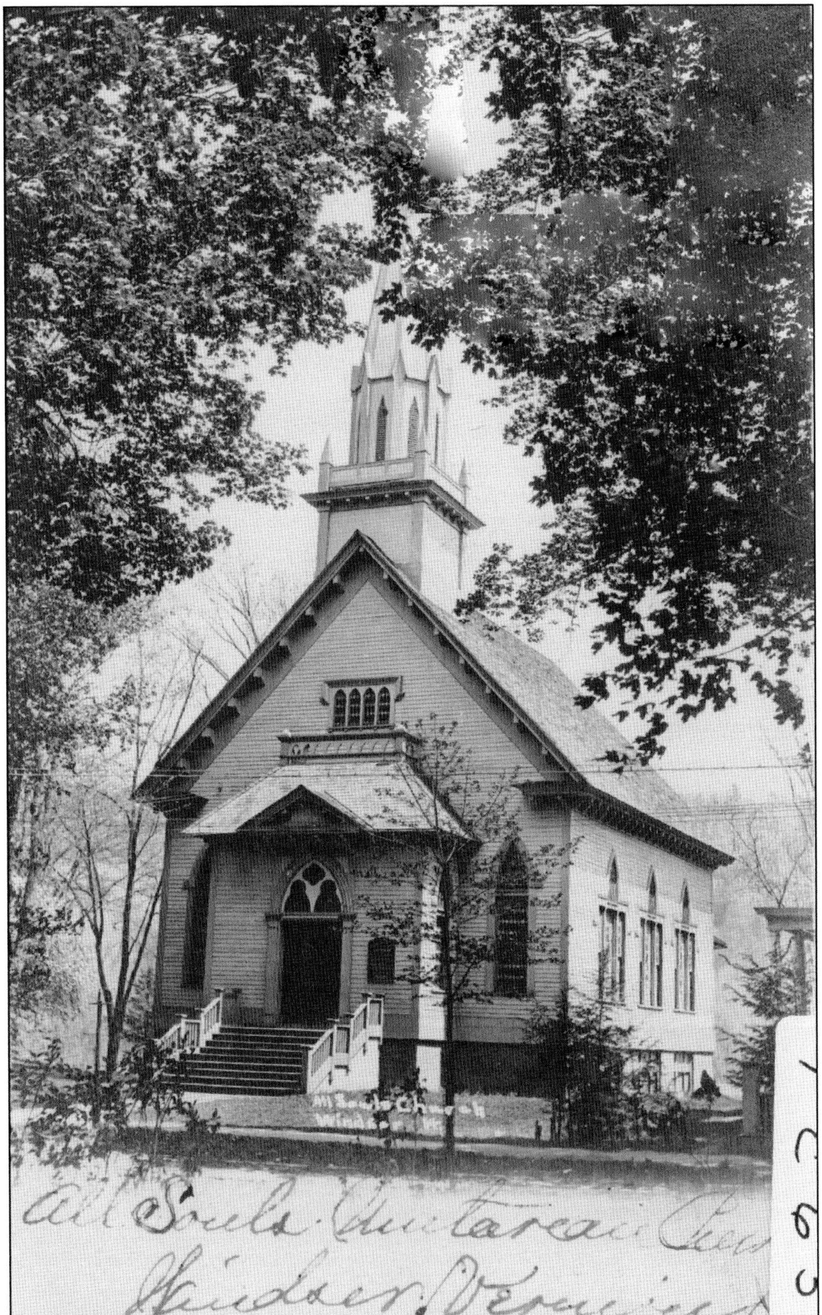

The First Unitarian Society of Windsor was formed in 1836 and held its meetings in the courthouse. In 1846, on land generously given by the Hubbard family, the All Souls Unitarian Church on Main Street was dedicated. Roughly 50 years later, the church was completely remodeled and set back 12 feet to allow for the building of a vestry. The remodel and associated stained glass windows were the gift of Frank and Charlotte Kennedy. The building was sold in 1973 when the congregation joined that of the Universalist Society in Claremont, New Hampshire. It is now a sculptor's studio.

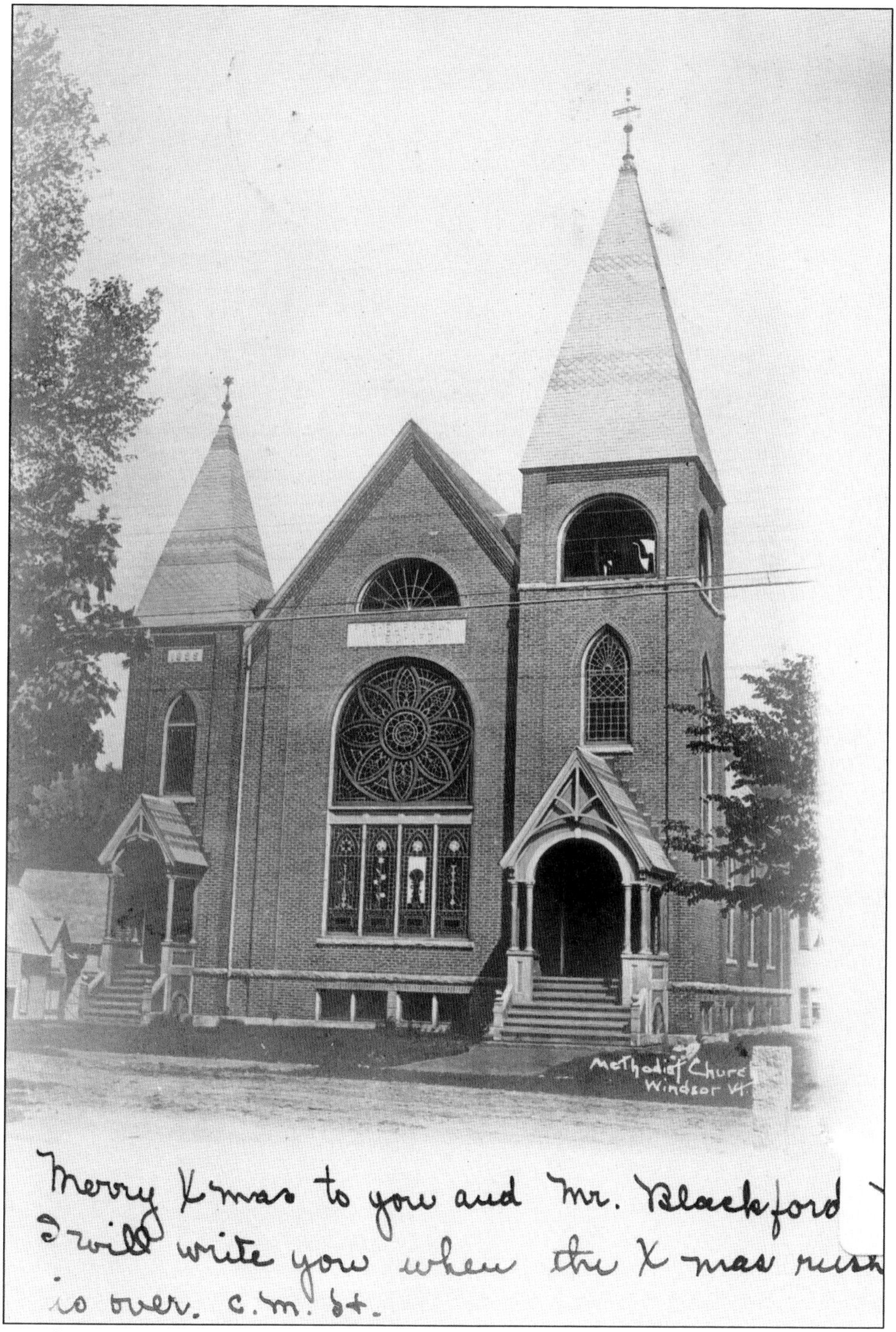

The Methodist Church was built in 1895 through the generous donation of Rachel S. Harlow. Located on the corner of Main and Durkee Streets, it was dedicated in February 1896. During a celebration of its anniversary 50 years later, an electric organ was dedicated through a bequest in the will of Lucy Hammond. A parsonage was built on land acquired in 1901.

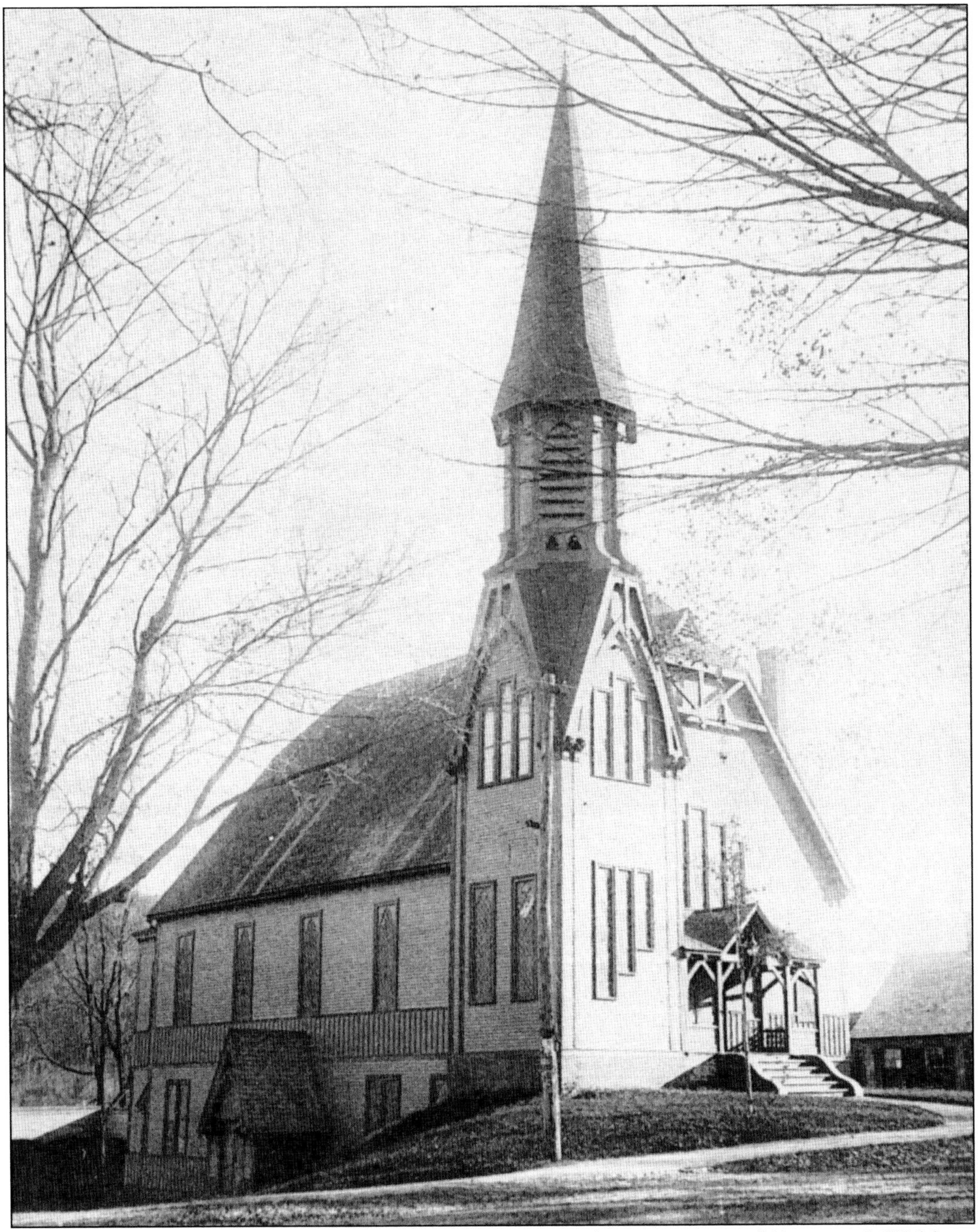

This Baptist Church was completed in 1874. In 1917, the controversial Reverend Waldron disregarded President Wilson's request that the "Star Spangled Banner" be sung and bells rung to kick off the first Liberty Bond drive. He resigned in November 1917 and was arrested in December of the same year. He was tried and convicted of sedition and sentenced to 15 years in prison in Atlanta. President Wilson pardoned him after one year. This was the same church that had its steeple torn off by the hurricane of 1938.

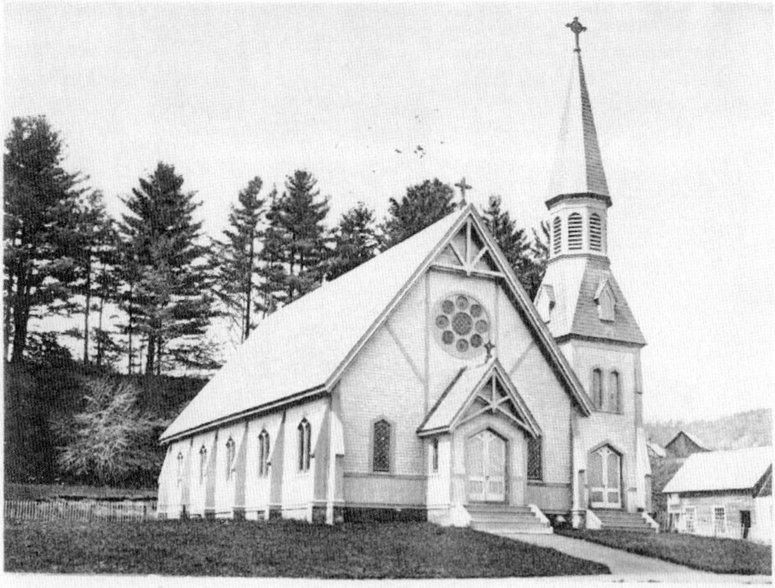

CATHOLIC CHURCH.

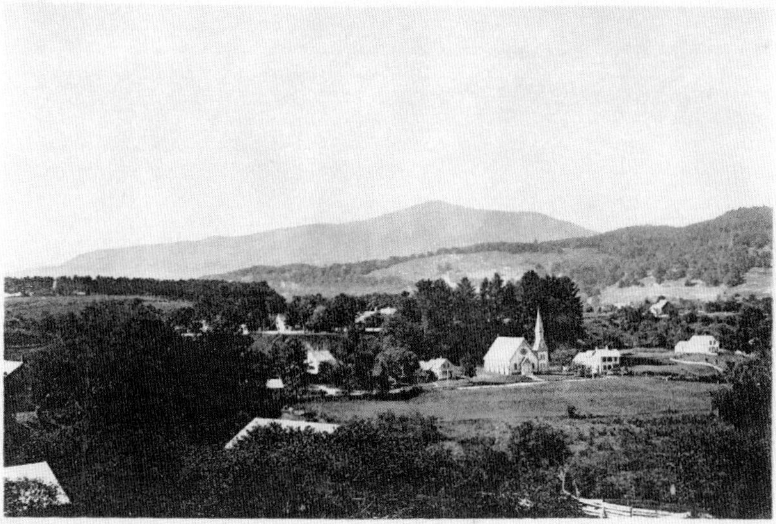

VIEW FROM "OLD SOUTH" CHURCH TOWER.

Missionaries first brought the teachings of the Catholic Church to Windsor in the early 1800s. Mass was celebrated twice a year in private homes, but an influx of railroad and cotton workers who came to the town created a need for a more permanent house of worship. In 1881, a parcel of land was purchased and ground was broken in October. W.P. Morse of White River Junction received the contract and the Hon. William M. Evarts donated the bell. The church was in use through 1953, when ground was broken for a new church. Dedicated in 1954, it burned to the ground in 1972, but was replaced by the current church, Saint Francis of Assissi. This church is home to a series of murals depicting the Seven Sacraments by celebrated artist George Tooker, who was presented with the National Medal of Arts in 2007.

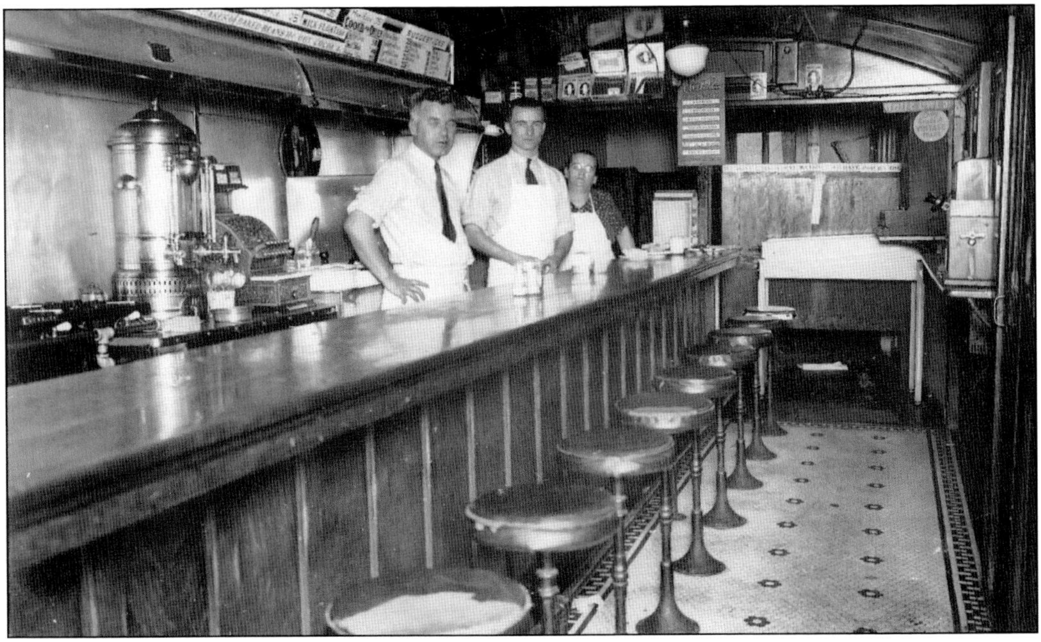

The Windsor Diner was one of the last diners manufactured by the Worcester Lunch Car Company in Worcester, Massachusetts. Operating between 1906 and 1957, the earliest lunch cars were built on wheels. In an effort to gain more respectability, the concept morphed into a dining car called by the nickname "diner." The diners were all given serial numbers during production. The one pictured is diner number 835. In the modern style, the diner has a streamlined profile and employs the classic "quilted look" stainless steel and red porcelain enamel siding. Above, standing behind the counter in 1934 from left to right are Bill Forbes, Leo De Bernardi, and Lora Richards. Below, two guests and two servers pose outside during some exterior painting in 1935.

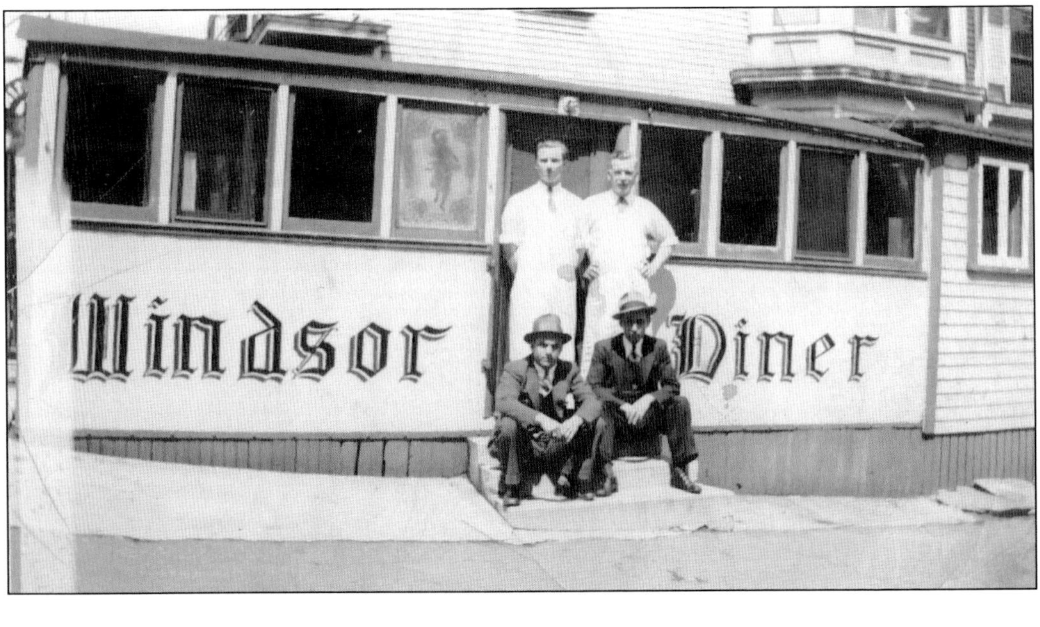

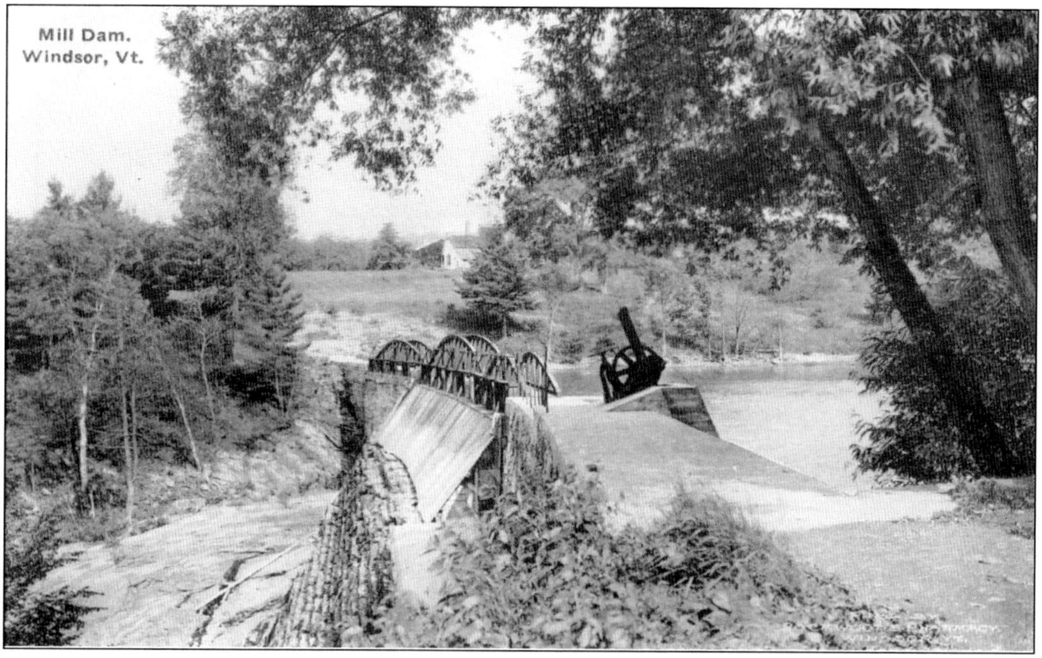

The Ascutney Mill Dam was built in 1834 and designated a National Civil Engineering Landmark in 1970. It has found no rivals to its claim of being the "oldest masonry dam of significant size as well as the oldest and possibly the first gravity-arch dam in the country." Constructed of locally quarried granite, the dam provided hydroelectric power to local sawmills and gristmills. It measures 120 feet long and 42 feet high. Pictured above is the dam as it looked when it had a walking bridge across the top. Below is the Mill Brook Dam sited to the right of the Precision Museum.

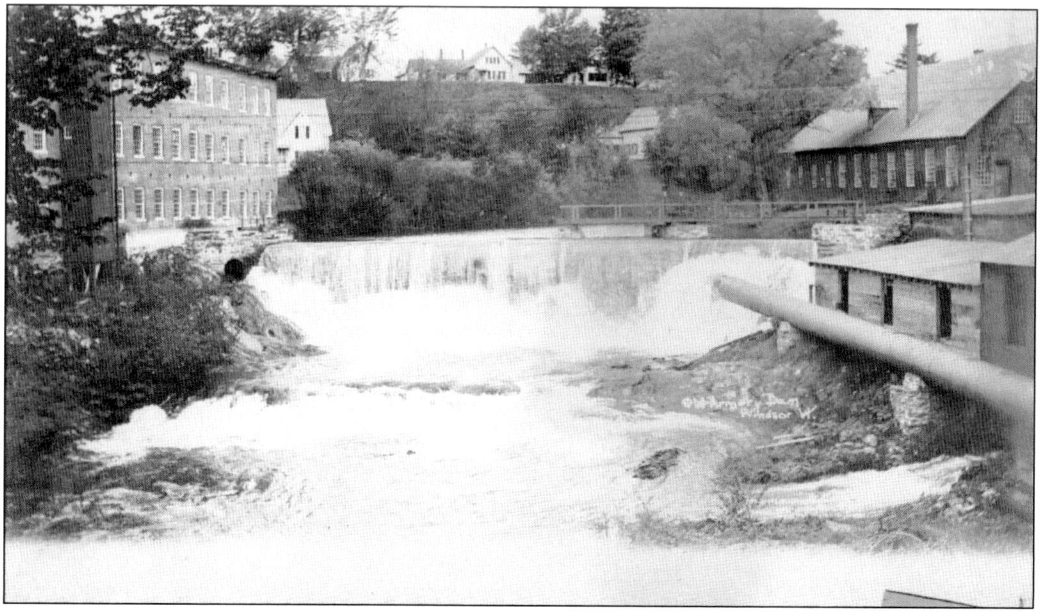

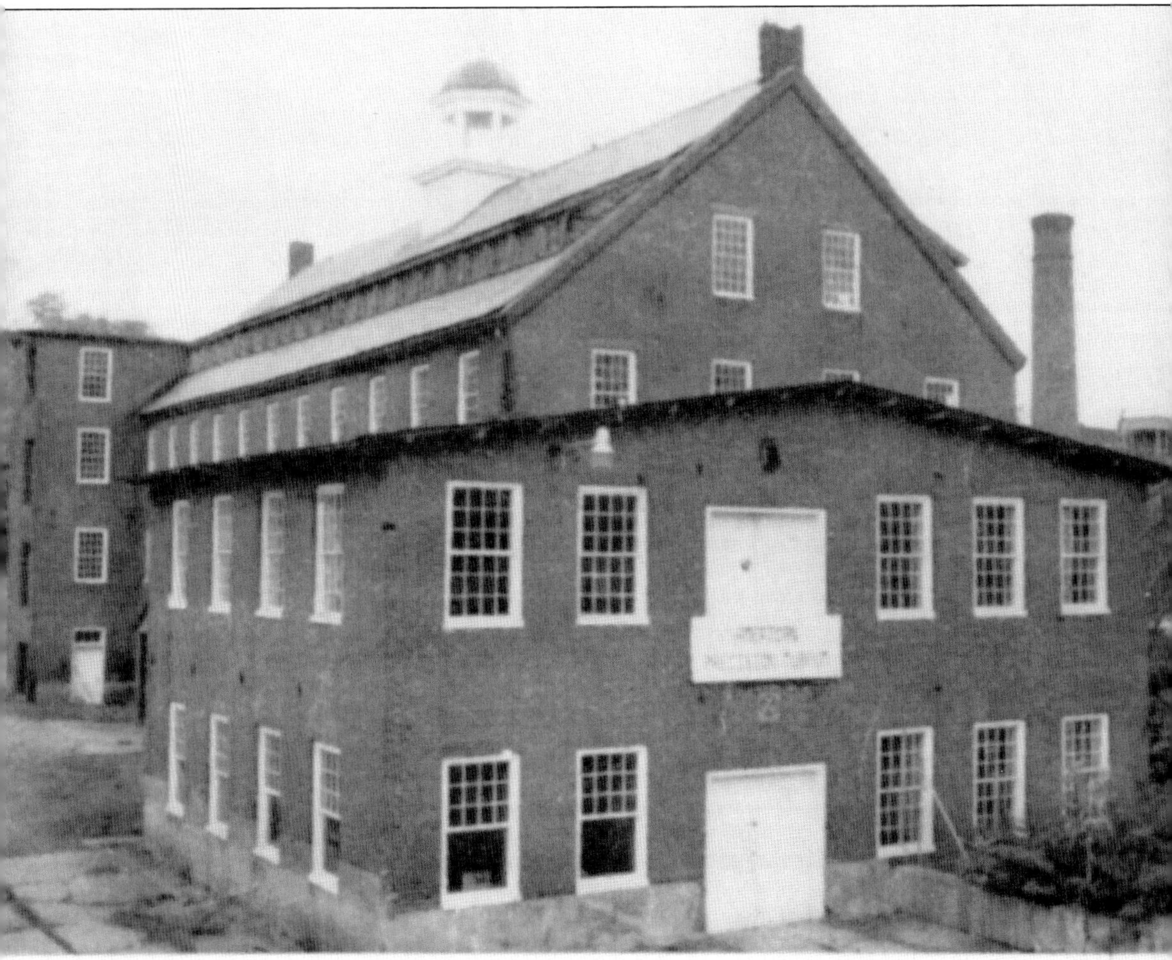

The American Precision Museum

Formerly the site of much of the industry that helped build Windsor, the brick building along Mill Brook and the Mill Brook dam now houses the American Precision Museum. Begun by collector Edwin Albert Battison in 1966, it features original machinery as well as working examples of many of the machines that were designed and employed in manufacturing in Windsor. The building was once powered by a 14-foot-wide and 18-foot-diameter waterwheel, the remains of which have been recently excavated. It housed the Windsor Manufacturing Company sewing machine factory from 1857 to 1870, followed by the Jones and Lamson Cotton Factory from 1870 to 1886. As Battison was acquainted with Maxfield Parrish, there is a stained glass window of his design in the upper wall of the newer section.

Nine

The Bridge

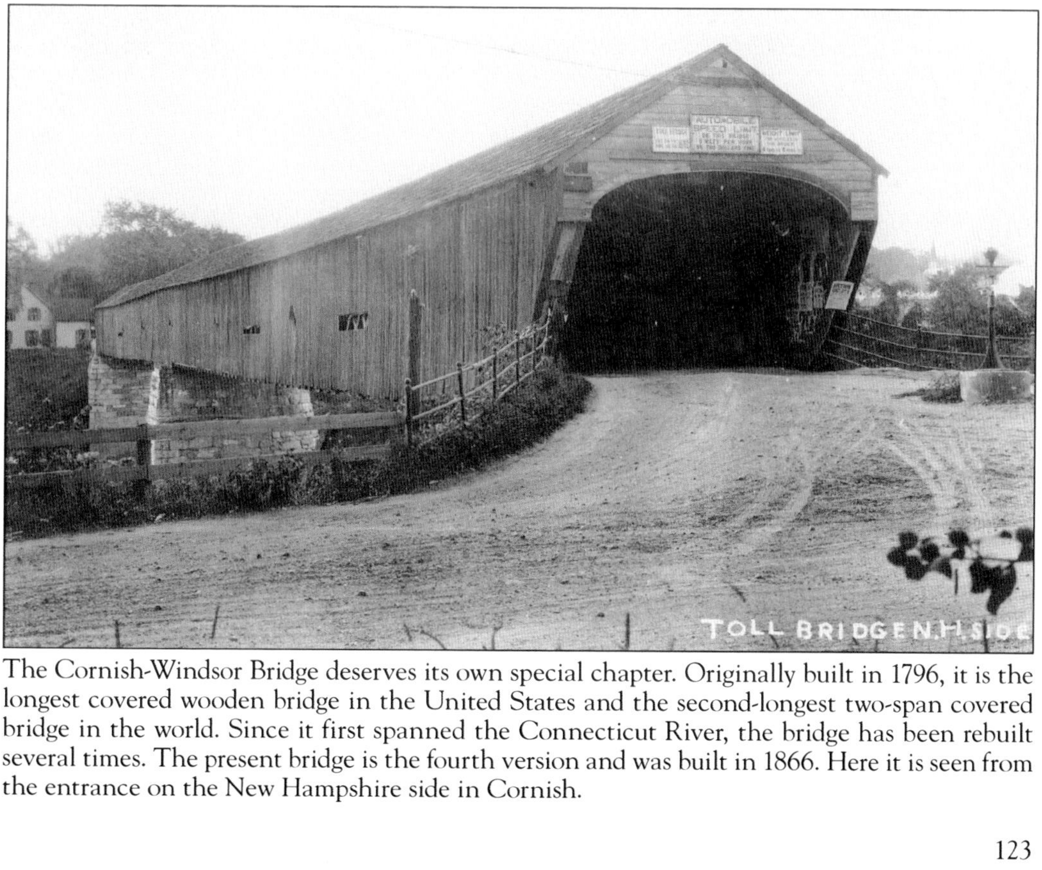

The Cornish-Windsor Bridge deserves its own special chapter. Originally built in 1796, it is the longest covered wooden bridge in the United States and the second-longest two-span covered bridge in the world. Since it first spanned the Connecticut River, the bridge has been rebuilt several times. The present bridge is the fourth version and was built in 1866. Here it is seen from the entrance on the New Hampshire side in Cornish.

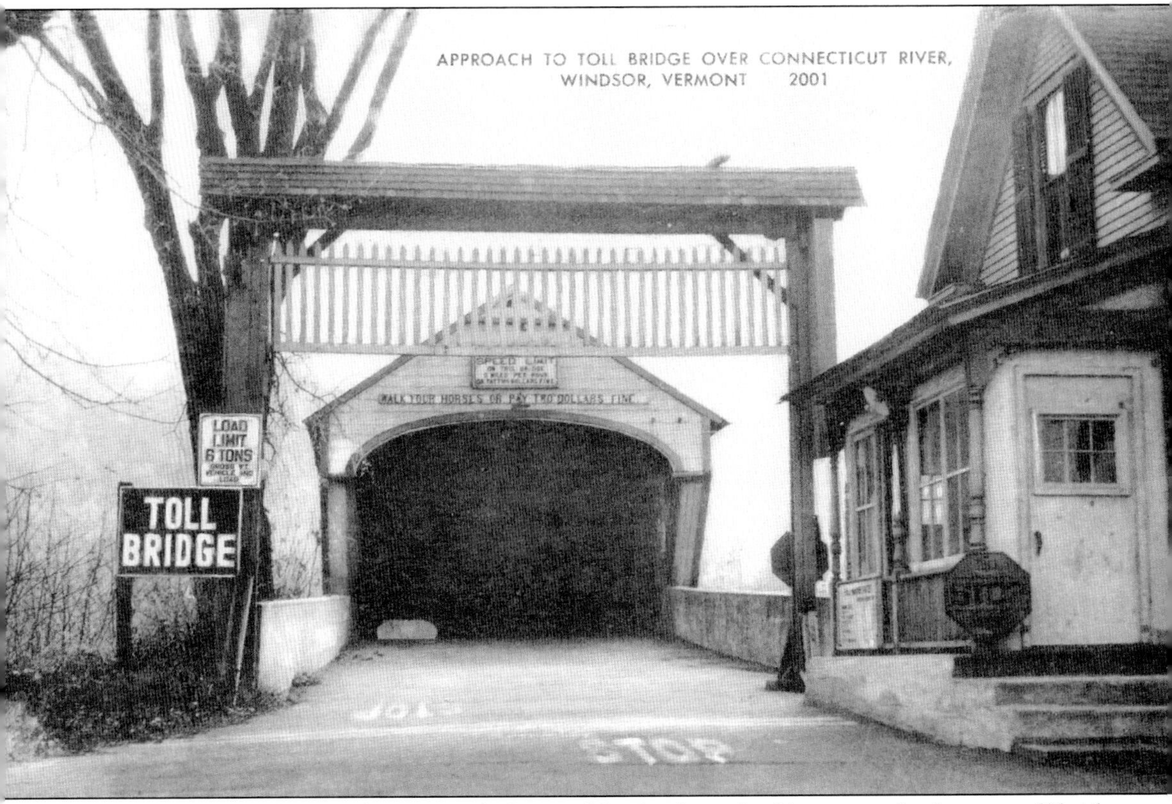

Pictured here is the Windsor-Cornish Covered Bridge from the Vermont side. It was a toll bridge until 1943, when the Windsor Select Board voted to end the toll. There had already been great strain put on the community due to the war, and this gesture acknowledged the sacrifices that had been made by the community. On the 100th anniversary of the bridge, there was a huge centennial celebration. Forces all came together to celebrate the town's past and its more recent accomplishments. The Cone Automatic Machine Company celebrated its 50th anniversary on the same day, with the company band in full regalia. The last addition to the festivities was the opening of the doors to the American Precision Museum for the first time.

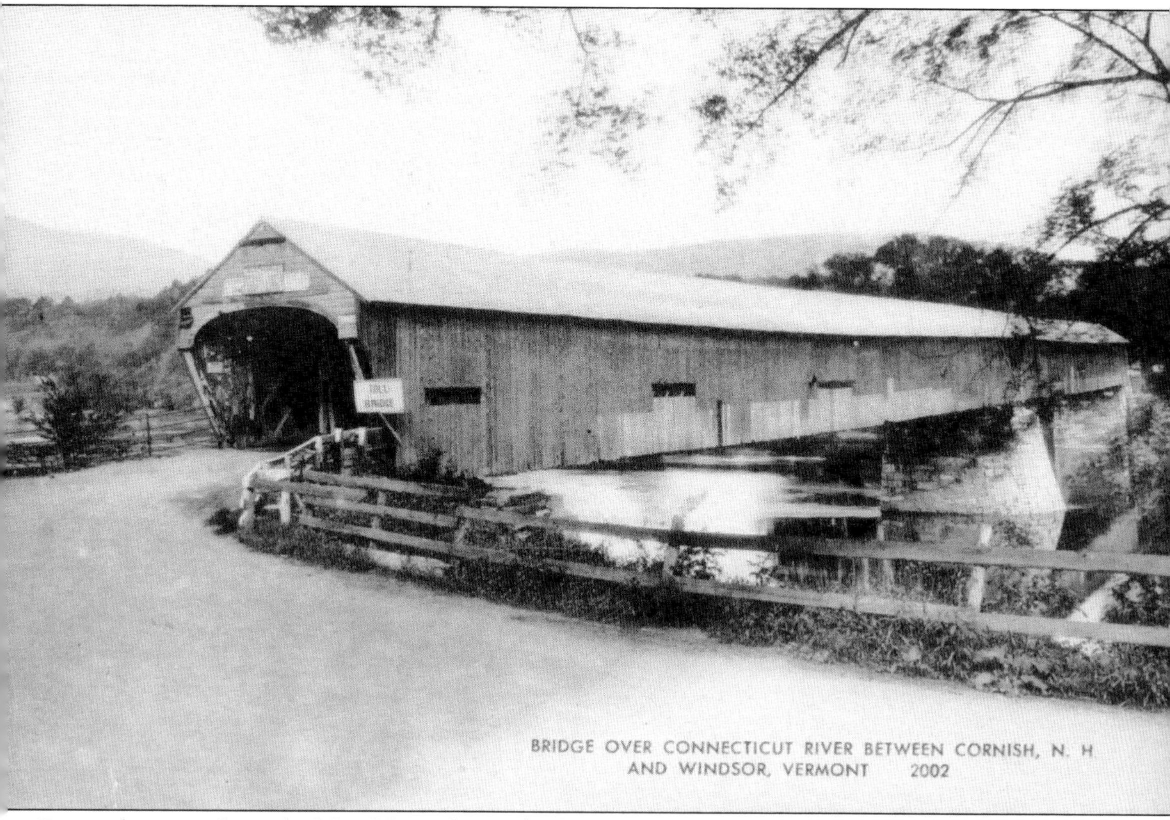

In another view from the New Hampshire side, the sign posting the speed limit replaced the one that warned a fine for not walking your horses across the bridge. This one promised a penalty of $2 for driving faster than five miles per hour. The weight limit was four tons or four wheels, with no mention of the horse.

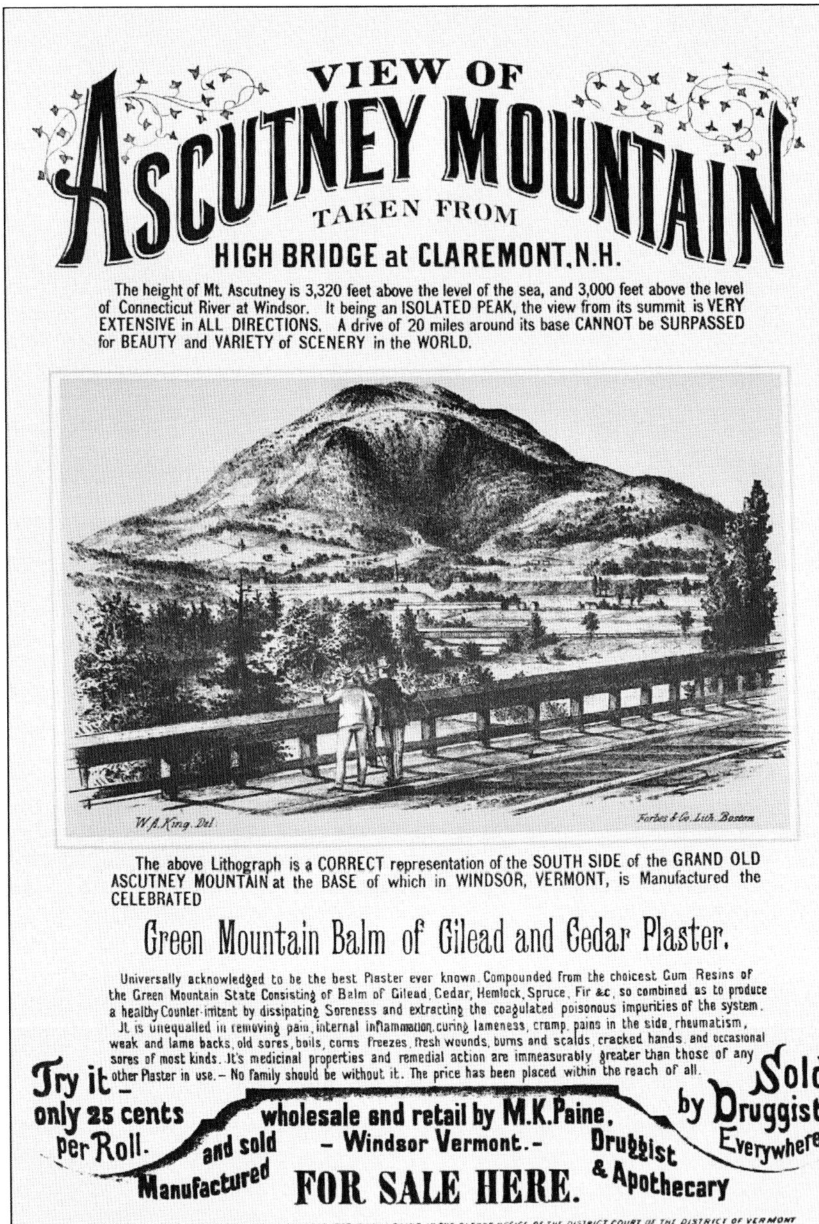

This ad for Green Mountain Balm of Gilead and Cedar Plaster by M.K. Paine celebrates Windsor and Mt. Ascutney, as seen from the New Hampshire side of the Connecticut River. Nearby is the Cornish-Windsor Covered Bridge. Former Vermont resident John Andrew Graham, when writing back to England on a visit to the state in 1797, said, "This bridge is universally allowed to be the best and most perfect in America, and is the first of the kind thrown across the Connecticut River." In the late 18th century, an ad was published in *Spooner's Vermont Journal* requesting "Fifteen Men! The subscriber wishes to hire fifteen good steady, active laboring men, to work at Cornish Bridge until November next; for which CASH will be given. The business will be principally digging, drawing, and boating stone. —Isaac Green." The bridge was designated a National Historic Civil Engineering landmark on October 7, 1970.

Bibliography

Bellamy, John Stark II. *Vintage Vermont Villainies, Tales of Murder and Mystery from the 19th & 20th Centuries.* Woodstock, Vermont: The Countryman Press, 2007.

Blaise, Suzanne Hebert. *Ain't That the Truth: A Hodgepodge of Windsor Memorabilia.* Hartland, Vermont: Marus Printing Company, 1991.

Conlin, Katherine. *Chronicles of Windsor.* Taftsville, Vermont: Countryman Press, 1977.

———. *Windsor Heritage, Birthplace of Vermont's Constitution and Industry.* Published for the Windsor Bicentennial Committee. Taftsville, Vermont: The Countryman Press, 1975.

Dryfhout, John H. *This Land of Pure Delight: Charles C. Beaman and Blowmedown Farm.* Cornish, New Hampshire: Augustus Saint-Gaudins Memorial, 2000.

Historic Windsor, Inc. *An Architectural and Historical Walking Tour of Windsor, Vermont.* Historic Windsor Inc., 2010.

McEnaney, Dorothy Dana. *Buena Vista Houses 1848–2008.* Taftsville, Vermont: the Countryman Press, 1977.

Spooner, Alden. *Spooner's Vermont Journal.* Windsor, Vermont: 1792–1818.

Wardner, Henry Steele. *The Constitution House and Its Neighbors.* Vermont Journal. 1921–1922.